G000161570

The German Constitution Turns 60

Abbrevs.:
"fns" means "footnotes"

Res Publica

ÖFFENTLICHES UND INTERNATIONALES RECHT

Herausgegeben von Udo Fink, Dieter Dörr
und Rolf Schwartmann

Band 13

PETER LANG

Frankfurt am Main · Berlin · Bern · Bruxelles · New York · Oxford · Wien

Jürgen Bröhmer (ed.)

The German Constitution Turns 60

Basic Law and Commonwealth Constitution

German and Australian Perspectives

PETER LANG

Internationaler Verlag der Wissenschaften

Bibliographic Information published by the Deutsche Nationalbibliothek
The Deutsche Nationalbibliothek lists this publication in the Deutsche Nationalbibliografie; detailed bibliographic data is available in the internet at http://dnb.d-nb.de.

ISSN 1614-838X
ISBN 978-3-631-60248-5
© Peter Lang GmbH
Internationaler Verlag der Wissenschaften
Frankfurt am Main 2011
All rights reserved.

All parts of this publication are protected by copyright. Any utilisation outside the strict limits of the copyright law, without the permission of the publisher, is forbidden and liable to prosecution. This applies in particular to reproductions, translations, microfilming, and storage and processing in electronic retrieval systems.

www.peterlang.de

Table of Contents

5

Preface

On 23 May 2009, the German Constitution, the *Grundgesetz*, turned 60. Not very old compared to Australia's Commonwealth Constitution or even the US-Constitution. It is perhaps an irony of history that old countries have young constitutions and young countries old ones. By any measure, 60 years of *Grundgesetz* has been and continues to be a success story. From post-war reconstruction, through the terror years of the seventies to the reunification of Germany after the demise of Communism in Eastern Europe, the *Grundgesetz* has weathered all challenges and found deep acceptance in the German populace at large.

The constitutional systems of Germany and Australia bear many differences but also some similarities. Fundamental rights and their protection figure prominently in the German *Grundgesetz* but not so much in the Australian constitutional context. Both countries are federations to name the most prominent similarity.

The anniversary of the *Grundgesetz* on 23 May 2009 was sufficient cause to assemble in Canberra at the ANU constitutional scholars from both countries to address some core issues from a German and Australian perspective respectively. This book contains the written versions of the presentations in the order in which they were presented.

The two-day conference on 22 and 23 May 2009 and the publication of this collection, perhaps the first in-depth comparative constitutional law study of the *Grundgesetz* and the Commonwealth Constitution, would not have been possible without the help of many people: Foremost I have to thank the authors of the essays contained in this book. They all followed my invitation without hesitation and they all helped in making the event a successful one. My Australian colleagues will forgive me when I extend my special thanks to the German colleagues who came to Canberra from the other side of the world to be part of this event. I am also grateful to the Australian National University and Dean *Michael Coper* from the College of Law for hosting this event and for their help in organizing it. Michael Coper and and His Excellency Dr. Michael Witter, Ambassador of the Federal Republic of Germany to Australia opened the conference. Thanks are in order for the keynote speakers for their opening words on both days of the conference, the Honorable Justice *Chris Maxwell*, President of the Court of Appeal in Victoria and the Honorable *Jon Stanhope*, MLA, Chief Minister of the Australian Capital Territory. The conference could not have taken place without the immense help of *Thomas John* in his role as Co-convenor of the European Focus Group of the International Law Section of the Law Council of Australia and of *Hendryk Flaegel*, also of the Law Council of Australia. The German Embassy provided a festive environment by organizing a memorable reception which brought together conference attendees and many others.

Jürgen Bröhmer
Armidale, August 2010

Biographies of Participating Authors

Nicholas Aroney

Nicholas Aroney is a Professor of Constitutional Law and a Fellow of the Centre for Public, International and Comparative Law at the TC Beirne School of Law, University of Queensland. He teaches constitutional law, comparative constitutional law and legal theory, and has published widely in these fields, with particular emphasis on free speech and federalism. He is the recent author of *The Constitution of a Federal Commonwealth: The Making and Meaning of the Australian Constitution* (Cambridge UP) and editor of *Restraining Elective Dictatorship: The Upper House Solution?* (University of Western Australia Press). He is also currently writing *The Jurisprudence of a Federal Commonwealth* (Cambridge UP) and editing *Shari'a in the West* (Oxford UP).

Jürgen Bröhmer

Jürgen Bröhmer came to the University of New England in 2006 and has been the Head of the Law School since 2007. He received his law degree from Mannheim University in Germany and his doctorate and post-doctoral habilitation from Saarland University in Saarbrücken, Germany and worked at the Europa-Institute of Saarland University before coming to Australia. His areas of expertise are German Constitutional, European Union and Public International Law. Jürgen has authored two and co-authored one monograph, edited a number of other books (the latest, 60 Years German Basic Law: The German Constitution and its Court – Landmark Decisions of the Federal Constitutional Court of Germany in the Area of Fundamental Rights was published in late 2010), and published numerous articles and book chapters.

Simon Bronitt

Simon Bronitt is Director of the Centre of Excellence in Policing and Security (CEPS) and based at Griffith University in Queensland. He was previously a Professor of Law in the ANU College of Law and Associate Director of the Australian Centre for Military Law and Justice, ANU. Between 2006-9 he served as the Director of the ANU Centre of European Studies in the Research School of Humanities. Drawing on comparative and interdisciplinary perspectives, Simon has published widely on criminal justice issues, including counter terrorism law and human rights, covert policing, telecommunications interception and international criminal law. His publications include Principles of Criminal Law (3rd ed, Thomson Reuters 2010) and Law in Context (3rd ed, Federation Press, 2006). He was the lead Chief Investigator of ARC-funded Discovery Project on counter-terrorism law (2005-2008), which culminated in the publication of Miriam Gani & Penelope Mathew (editors), Fresh Perspectives on the "War on Terror" (2008).

Craig Collins

Craig Collins is a lecturer with the College of Law at the Australian National University. He worked for 12 years as a litigation lawyer, including as a partner with Gadens Lawyers Melbourne, where he developed a specialist interest in defamation law. In practise, Craig represented and advised a range of clients, including a State Premier, State Attorney General, a former Prime Minister and the Olympian Ron Clarke - who obtained a record jury award for defamation damages of over $1 million. Craig moved into academia 6 years ago at UNE, where he is pursuing PhD research on the legal history topic, 'Defamation, Law and Public Opinion in the Australian Colonies, 1824-1874'.

Dieter Dörr

Dieter Dörr is Professor for Constitutional Law, International and European Union Law and Media Law at the Johannes-Gutenberg University in Mainz, Germany and Director of the Mainz Media Institute. Previously he has served as in-house counsel for one of the state broadcasting networks. He is a member and former chairman of the German Commission for the Determination of Concentration in the Media Sector and serves as ad-hoc judge at the Superior Provincial Court (Court of Appeal, Oberlandesgericht) Koblenz.

Katharine Gelber

Katharine Gelber is an Associate Professor in Public Policy at the School of Political Science & International Studies at the University of Queensland. She completed her undergraduate degree at the University of Tasmania, an Honours (I) degree at the University of Sydney and her PhD at the University of Sydney. She worked at the University of New South Wales for nine years, before commencing an appointment at UQ. Her research interests are in human rights policy, with a particular emphasis on freedom of speech and the regulation of hate speech. Katharine is the recipient of several ARC grants, including the current ARC DP 'The Impact of Hate Speech Laws on Public Discourse in Australia' (2010-2012) with co-CI Professor Luke McNamara (University of Wollongong), as a co-CI on the ARC Linkage 'Democratic Dialogue and Capabilities: New Opportunities in Post-Reconciliation Era Australia' with Prof Pat Dodson and A/Prof Sarah Maddison (UNSW), and the now-completed ARC DP 'Securing Freedom: Freedom of Political Speech in Australia'. She is the President of the Australian Political Studies Association, a member of the human rights research streams of the International Political Science Assocation, the International Studies Association and the American Political Science Association. Her recent books include Vromen, Gelber & Gauja *Powerscape: Contemporary Australian Politics* (Allen & Unwin, Sydney, 2009); Gelber & Stone (eds), *Hate Speech and Freedom of Speech in Australia* (Federation Press, Sydney, 2007) and Gelber, *Speaking Back: the free speech versus hate speech debate* (John Benjamins Ltd, 2002). She has recently published articles in *Review of International Studies*, the *Australian Journal of Human Rights*, the *Australian Journal of Political Science* and *Melbourne University Law Review*.

Saskia Hufnagel

Saskia Hufnagel is a Research Fellow at the ARC Centre of Excellence in Policing and Security (CEPS). She completed her PhD studies at the Australian National University (ANU) on the topic 'Comparison of EU and Australian cross-border law enforcement strategies' in 2010. Saskia worked as an Assistant Professor at the University of Canberra (Faculty of Law) between 2009 and 2011 and taught and convened a range of courses at the ANU College of Law and the ANU Centre for European Studies since 2007. Her current research interests are comparative criminal and constitutional law, regulation of police cooperation techniques and emergency law. Her publications include 'German perspectives on the right to life and human dignity in the "war on terror"' (2008) 32 Crim LJ 1000 and "'The Fear of Insignificance': New Perspectives on Harmonising Police Cooperation in Europe and Australia" (2010) 6(2) JCER 165. Saskia is a qualified German legal practitioner and accredited specialist in criminal law.

Thomas John

Thomas John is the Co-convenor of the European Focus Group of the International Law Section of the Law Council of Australia. Holding law degrees from the University of Konstanz, Germany, and the University of Queensland, Thomas John is admitted to practice as a barrister at the High Court of Australia as well as the Supreme Courts of Queensland and the ACT. His previous and current roles at the Attorney-General's Department, the Australian Government Solicitor, the Federal Parliament's Research Services and Queensland's Crown Law equipped Thomas with a particular expertise in constitutional law. He co-authored 'Australian Constitutional Law: Commentary and Cases' published in 2007 by Oxford University Press.

Cornelia Koch

Cornelia Koch is a Senior Lecturer in the Adelaide Law School at the University of Adelaide. Before coming to Australia in 1998, Cornelia lived in Germany where she obtained her undergraduate law degree. Her postgraduate qualifications, a Master of Comparative Law and a Juris Doctor degree, are from the University of Queensland. Her primary research interests are constitutional law, comparative law and European Union law. Her research has been published in leading international journals and she is a co-author of Australian Constitutional Law: Commentary and Cases (Oxford University Press).

Andrew Lynch

Andrew Lynch is the Director of the Gilbert + Tobin Centre of Public Law and an Associate Professor in the UNSW Faculty of Law. Andrew's research in recent years has concentrated on the topics of judicial dissent in the constitutional law decisions of the High Court of Australia, federal reform and the intersection of public law and legal responses to terrorism. He is an author of Equity and Trusts (2001 and 2005), What Price Security? Taking Stock of Australia's Anti-Terror Laws (2006) and a co-editor of Law and Liberty in the War on Terror (2007), as well as journal articles, conference and seminar papers in these and other areas. Additionally Andrew has frequently been called before parliamentary and non-government inquiries to speak to submissions on matters of public law and Australia's counter-terrorism legislative scheme. He writes regularly on public law issues in the media. He teaches Public Law and Federal Constitutional Law.

Rolf Schwartmann

Rolf Schwartmann is a German law professor at the Cologne University of Applied Sciences where he holds the Chair in Public Law and International Business Law. He is also Head of the *Kölner Forschungsstelle für Medienrecht*, an institute and research center for Media Law which is concerned with latest developments in media law and policy and just established a master degree program in Media Law and Media Management. Prof. Schwartmann has edited numerous publications in International Law, European Law, Environmental Law and Media Law and is also co-writer of the well-established and probably most comprehensive commentary of the Basic Constitutional Law of the Federal Republic of Germany, the *Bonner Kommentar zum Grundgesetz.*

Torsten Stein

Torsten Stein is Professor of International, European Union and Comparative Constitutional Law and Director of the Institute of European Studies (Law Department) since 1991. Before, he spent many years as Senior Research Fellow at the Max-Planck-Institute of Comparative Public and Public International Law, Heidelberg (Germany), and as Professor at Heidelberg University's Law Faculty. After serving in the German Air Force (today Colonel in the Air Force Reserve), he received his legal education at the Universities of Berlin and Heidelberg, and obtained his Doctorate in Law and post-doctoral habilitation from the Law Faculty in Heidelberg. Torsten Stein is President of the German Branch of the International Law Association (ILA), Honorary Treasurer of the ILA and member of its Executive Council and has repeatedly been Rapporteur and Chairman of different international committees of the ILA. He is a frequent guest lecturer at foreign universities and consultant for governments and NGOs. He has published several books and numerous articles in his fields of law and is the editor of a European Law Journal and of a series of monographs on European Union and Public International Law.

George Williams

George Williams is the Anthony Mason Professor of law and Foundation Director of the Gilbert + Tobin Centre of Public Law at the Faculty of Law, University of New South Wales. He has held visiting positions at Osgoode Hall Law School in Toronto, Columbia University Law School in New York and University College London, and has written and edited books such as A Charter of Rights for Australia, Australian Constitutional Law and Theory and The Oxford Companion to the High Court of Australia.

Jürgen Bröhmer

The Federal Element of the German Republic Issues and Developments

I. Introduction

1. Historical Development

The entity that today forms the Federal Republic of Germany has historically always been a federation. That is to say that present day Germany's federal structure is not a result of recent history. Rather, Germany has evolved over the centuries from a collection of smaller and larger dispersed monarchical entities into a nation of now 16 states (*Länder*), of which three are city states[1], and the other 13 are states comprising of many municipalities and the surrounding territory.[2]

Some of today's 16 *Länder* are, however, rather artificial constructs put together by the victorious powers after World War II. Other states incorporate historical entities, such as Bavaria, which has existed as a kingdom for many centuries, or the city-states (*Stadtstaaten*), such as Bremen and Hamburg, who owe their status as a *Land* largely to history, when these cities belonged to the medieval trading block of the *Hanse*.

The artificially created states, often recognizable by their somewhat awkward composite names and often comprising of rivaling neighboring regions, have, perhaps surprisingly, become remarkably resilient. The states of Rhineland-Palatinate, Baden-Württemberg or North Rhine-Westphalia are examples for this. As inconceivable as it might have been not too long ago that people from Baden and the Swabians around Stuttgart might be organized in a common entity as inconceivable is it only 60 years later that they would dissolve their "union" and organize in different states. Conversely, an attempt in 1996 to amalgamate Berlin and the surrounding Brandenburg failed in the separate referenda required for such endeavors in all participating entities under Article 29 Basic Law (*Grundgesetz*, GG).

---

1   Berlin, Hamburg, and Bremen.
2   Baden-Württemberg, Bavaria, Brandenburg, Hesse, Lower Saxony, Mecklenburg-Western Pomerania, North Rhine-Westphalia, Rhineland-Palatinate, Saarland, Saxony, Saxony-Anhalt, Schleswig-Holstein and Thuringia.

2. The Status Quo of the German Federation

The various *Länder* are quite diverse. They range in population from over 16 million in North Rhine-Westphalia to just 1 million in the Saarland and from roughly 3.5 million in the city-state of Berlin to just over 600.000 in the city-state of Bremen. One of the larger states, Baden-Württemberg, covers an area of 35.752 square kilometers, has a population of 10.7 million and a GDP of approximately AUD 600 million. New South Wales, in comparison, covers 809.444 square kilometers and is thus more than 20 times the size of Baden-Württemberg. It has, however, only 7 million inhabitants, almost 4 million less than Baden-Württemberg and with a GDP of 320 billion, commands an economy of approximately half the size of Baden-Württemberg.

The larger *Länder* are sub-divided into governmental districts (*Regierungsbezirke*), with supervisory functions for local governments and other administrative authorities. The various municipalities within the *Länder* are a further sub-division with constitutional relevance as these municipalities, the cities and towns, enjoy a constitutionally guaranteed right of effective self-administration (Article 28 GG).

II. Principle Elements of German Federalism

1. Introductory Remarks

Before proceeding to some of the core issues of German Federalism and especially German fiscal federalism, one of the most striking differences between the Australian and German constitutions should be pointed out. The German constitution can be amended relatively easily. All that is required under Article 79.2 GG is a two-thirds majority in both houses of parliament. The Commonwealth Constitution, by contrast, is much more difficult to amend, requiring absolute majorities in both houses of parliament and majorities in referenda to be held in all states and territories.[3]

---

3   Article 128 Commonwealth Constitution:
     "This Constitution shall not be altered except in the following manner:
     The proposed law for the alteration thereof must be passed by an absolute majority of each House of the Parliament, and not less than two nor more than six months after its passage through both Houses the proposed law shall be submitted in each State and Territory to the electors qualified to vote for the election of members of the House of Representatives. [...]

Hence, the German constitution is in that sense, a 'living instrument', a fluid document open for developments, subject to getting longer, not necessarily always better, and much more subject to become the focus of political interest groups, as is illustrated, for example, by the addition of environmental and animal protection as official state objectives in Article 20a GG. As always, openness to change facilitates corrections or adaptation to new circumstances, but of course it also invites change of a nature that perhaps should better not have been undertaken.

2. The Allocation of Powers

The German constitution operates on the principle that all power lies with the states, the *Länder*, rather than the federal level (Article 30 GG). The federal level has only those powers that are explicitly attributed to it by the Basic Law (principle of enumerated powers, Articles 30, 70.1 and 83 GG).

The Basic Law distinguishes between legislative powers and administrative powers. The administrative powers do not necessarily follow the legislative powers. It is common that the legislative power will lie with the federal level, whereas the administrative power, that is the power to administer, implement and execute that legislation, lies with the states.

As far as legislative powers are concerned, the Basic Law distinguishes between exclusive competences (Articles 71, 73 GG) and concurring or parallel competences (Articles 72, 74 GG). The concurring or parallel powers are coupled with an exhaustion principle, with the result that these concurring powers fall to the federal level once and in so far as the federal legislator has acted on them and passed relevant legislation. In essence, concurring powers are powers that become federal powers once the federal parliament has acted and it has legislated in these fields. As part of the federal reform package 1 Article 72 GG was amended and a new section 3 authorizes the *Länder* to pass deviating "variance" legislation in certain subject-matter areas, effectively creating 'opting-out' rights for the *Länder*.

Examples for matters of exclusive federal jurisdiction, that is matters where legislative powers lie exclusively with the federal houses of parliament (*Bundestag* and *Bundesrat*), are foreign affairs and defense, citizenship, free movement and passports, currency, international trade, national cultural assets,

---

And if in a majority of the States a majority of the electors voting approve the proposed law, and if a majority of all the electors voting also approve the proposed law, it shall be presented to the Governor-General for the Queen's assent. [...]".

air transport and railroads.[4] Examples for matters of concurring jurisdiction are the civil, that is the private and commercial law, criminal law including criminal procedure, the law of association, the laws dealing with the residence of foreigners and refugees, public welfare, economic matters, labor law, research promotion, expropriation or the abuse of economic power.[5]

From the perspective of the number and weight of the various subject matters enumerated in Articles 73 and 74 one can only conclude that there is a strong bias towards the centre. That is quite obvious for the matters that are exclusively powers of the centre, but it also is true for matters that fall under concurrent jurisdiction. That is the case not only because the federal parliament has legislated in many of these fields in the past 60 years, it is also true because the original safeguard contained in the old Article 72.2 GG to protect the *Länder* against the assumption of federal concurring powers was largely unsuccessful because the Federal Constitutional Court had given broad discretion to the federal legislator to determine whether the necessity requirements for federal legislation stipulated there originally had been met or not.[6]

In essence, the *Länder* of the German Federation are left with legislative powers for only four subject matters:

I.   The police power, i.e. legislation in all matters that have to do with the police and its preventive function. This legislative power does not extend to the repressive police function, i.e. criminal prosecution, which is part of the catalogue of concurring federal powers;

II.   Primary, secondary and tertiary education (schools and Universities). The federal level has retained some funding powers for capital infrastructure of universities;

III. Culture and the arts, i.e. all matters to do with theatres, music, or anything else that, in the broad sense of the word, falls under the heading of art and culture;

IV.   Broadcasting and the regulation of broadcasting, i.e. radio, television and all other electronic media including new technologies such as the internet.

It is interesting to note that most notably in two of these areas, in education and in broadcasting, a quasi federal centralization has taken place, in that practically all important decisions in these fields are reached by the *Länder* through

---

4   For more details see Article 73 GG.
5   For more details see Article 74 GG.
6   The old version of the Article 72.2 GG required the determination of a "need" for federal legislation and the Court had consistently held that it would not interfere with the determination of such a need by the legislator. See for example BVerfGE 78, 249 (270), http://www.servat.unibe.ch/fallrecht/bv078249.html.

compacts concluded between them and implemented by law internally. The various *Länder* have in essence created a third level of federal cooperation, beyond the federation as such and the individual *Länder*, where decisions are reached without participation of the Federal Government or Parliament.

At this point, we can conclude that the *Länder* in the German Federation have a very limited subject matter portfolio, but have retained substantial powers with regard to the implementation, the administration and the execution of federal legislation.

3. Participation of the Länder on the Federal Level

However, what appears to be a deficit in genuine subject-matter legislative powers is compensated by the fact that the German states have extensive participation rights in the legislative process on the federal level through the second chamber of parliament, the *Bundesrat* (Federal Council). The representation of the *Länder*, in the *Bundesrat*, is not by way of elected representatives. Rather, members of their respective executive branches represent the *Länder* in that body.[7] This is in stark contrast to the federal systems, for example, of the United States of America[8] or of the Commonwealth of Australia[9], where the second chamber is not or not anymore a chamber genuinely representing the states on an institutional level, but a chamber in which a different type of delegate, elected by the people within the state, represent their state on the federal level but without institutional links to the state as an institution and to the political decision-making process within state institutions.

---

7   Article 51 GG: "(1) The Bundesrat shall consist of members of the *Land* governments, which appoint and recall them. Other members of those governments may serve as alternates. (2) Each *Land* shall have at least three votes; *Länder* with more than two million inhabitants shall have four, *Länder* with more than six million inhabitants five, and *Länder* with more than seven million inhabitants six votes. (3) Each *Land* may appoint as many members as it has votes. The votes of each *Land* may be cast only as a unit and only by Members present or their alternates."

8   Amendment XVII passed by Congress 13 May 1912, ratified 8 April 1913, amending Article I section 3 of the US Constitution, see http://www.archives.gov/exhibits/charters/constitution_amendments_11-27.html.

9   Section 7.1 Commonwealth of Australia Constitution Act: "The Senate shall be composed of senators for each State, directly chosen by the people of the State, voting, until the Parliament otherwise provides, as one electorate." See http://www.austlii.edu.au/au/legis/cth/consol_act/coaca430/xx7.html.

All legislation passed on the federal level must also pass the *Bundesrat*. However, there are two different types of legislation. The first type requires the positive assent of the *Bundesrat*. That means that a majority of the executive representatives must vote in favor of such legislation for it to become law and due to the block-voting requirement that means in essence a majority of the *Länder*. The second type of legislation allows the *Bundesrat* to object to it, but that objection is subject to being overturned by the lower house, the *Bundestag*, by absolute majority vote. This 'objection legislation' raises the procedural bar in the *Bundestag*, but does not make the passage of legislation impossible. The Basic Law enumerates all cases of assent-legislation. Between 1949 and 2005 more than 50% of all legislation was assent legislation and that number continued to increase.[10]

The direct influence of the *Länder* in the legislative process on the federal level has and is of political consequence. "Blockade-politics" describes a constellation whereby the political majority carrying the federal government in the *Bundestag*, does not possess a corresponding majority among the *Länder* governments assembled in the *Bundesrat*. Such constellations, which have been the rule in Germany for much of the past 30 years, can have the effect of largely blocking any reform agenda a federal government might have. This has been perceived as a disadvantage. On the other hand it does give the *Länder* immense power to influence and shape political decision-making on the federal level.

However, diverging majorities on the federal level in the *Bundestag* and *Bundesrat* have certainly led to a blurring of governmental responsibilities. It is often not transparent who actually is responsible for not delivering on election promises. Hence such constellations favor obstructionism and disillusionment in the electorate.

Another significant effect of this relationship between *Bundestag* and *Bundesrat* is the immense importance of the Mediation (Conference) Committee.[11] The Mediation Committee, composed of 16 representatives of

---

10   Until the Federalism Reform I package with the amendment, inter alia, of Article 84.1 GG, almost 60% of the legislation required the assent of the *Bundesrat*. After the reform this number decreased to approx. 44%, see BT Drs. 16/8688, 2.4.2008, p. 2, 3 and Annex 2, available at http://dip21.bundestag.de/dip21/btd/16/086/1608688.pdf.

11   The Mediation Committee is similar to the Conference Committee of the US-Congress. Article 77.2 GG states: "(2) Within three weeks after receiving an adopted bill, the Bundesrat may demand that a committee for joint consideration of bills, composed of Members of the Bundestag and of the Bundesrat, be convened. The composition and proceedings of this committee shall be regulated by rules of procedure adopted by the Bundestag and requiring the consent of the Bundesrat. The members of the Bundesrat on this committee shall not be bound by instructions. When the consent of the Bundesrat is required for a bill to become law, the Bundestag and the Federal Government may likewise demand that such a committee be

Bundestag and *Bundestag* respectively[12], gains enormous power and influence in constellations of diverging majorities and becomes a kind of "secret" government of the day as it is this committee which will have to bring the diverging positions together and find a compromise and it conducts its business by necessity largely outside public view.[13]

4. Federalism Reform Package I (2006) and II (2009/2010)

The German federal system has recently undergone major reform, which is made possible by the fact that the German Basic Law can – not only theoretically but actually – be amended. The Federalism Reform Package I of 2006 brought with it a number of amendments of the Basic Law.[14] One important amendment seeks to reduce the instances of assent legislation. The resulting loss of participatory powers of the *Länder* was compensated by reducing the subject-matter areas under federal jurisdiction and thus re-allocating these areas to the legislative authority of the *Länder*. Changes were also made to the concurring legislative powers, where the *Länder* were given the power to pass diverging legislation (Article 72.3 GG), effectively giving the *Länder* an opting-out right under certain circumstances. In addition, a special type of legislative power concerning the so called joint tasks in article 91a and 91a GG were reformulated to better protect the interests of the *Länder* and finally a new provision was introduced to the Basic Law dealing with a new option for financial assistance from the federal level to the *Länder* for certain investments (Article 104b GG).

The federalism reform package II was passed in the second half of 2009[15] and will be applied for the first time to the 2011 federal budget. The main focus of this reform is on new constitutional rules concerning limits on *Länder* and federal deficits. The previously practiced investment expenditures limit rule of Article 115.1 GG has been replaced. Under the old rule, federal deficits were limited in size to that share of the overall budget that was characterized as

---

convened. Should the committee propose any amendment to the adopted bill, the Bundestag shall vote on it a second time." For the role of the Mediation Committee see BVerfGE 120, 56 (73–6), http://www.servat.unibe.ch/dfr/bv120056.html. A summarizing press release in English is available at http://www.bverfg.de/pressemitteilungen/bvg08-026en.html. See also BVerfGE 112, 118 (137–40), http://www.servat.unibe.ch/dfr/bv112118.html.

12 § 1 of the Rules of the Conference Committee, http://www.bundesrat.de/nn_8962/DE/br-dbt/va/go/go.html (2.7.2010).

13 For a critical assessment of the intransparency connected to the work of the Mediation Committee see Bröhmer, Jürgen, Transparenz als Verfassungsprinzip, 2004, p. 111–113.

14 52nd Amendment of the Basic Law, 28.8.2006, Official Gazette (BGBl. I), p. 2034 (2006).

15 57th Amendment of the Basic Law, 29.7.2009, Official Gazette (BGBl. I), p. 2248 (2009).

investment spending. This rule has never really achieved its goal of avoiding excessive budget deficits. The new Article 115 moves away from this approach and attempts to limit deficit spending by restricting it to 0.35% of GDP in "normal" years and instituting stricter rules of deficit reduction in better economic times.[16]

The principle of balanced budgets is in conflict with other objectives of government such as high employment and economic growth. The "global financial crises" of 2008 with the resulting general economic downturn and the ensuing European debt crises illustrate the difficulties in this area.[17] To be operable exceptions are required and provided for to cover times of economic downturn and natural catastrophes. Whether the defined consequences and processes for the deficits still incurred will be better able to control deficit spending remains to be seen.

5. The European Union as a Third Layer in the Federal Structure

There is and has been for some time strong concern among the *Länder* in the German federation that the exercise of power by the European Union weakens

---

16 The new Article 115 is an impressive example of the constitutionalization of John Meynard Keynes and his anti-cyclic theories by reminding government that Keynes not only spoke of deficit spending in times of economic downturn but also of deficit reduction in times of economic growth, the latter having been seemingly forgotten in many countries.

17 The official Declaration of the G-20 Summit in Toronto, Canda on June 26–27, 2010, http://g20.gc.ca/toronto-summit/summit-documents/the-g-20-toronto-summit-declaration/, summarizes the conflict in an illustrating manner: "10. We are committed to taking concerted actions to sustain the recovery, create jobs and to achieve stronger, more sustainable and more balanced growth. These will be differentiated and tailored to national circumstances. We agreed today on: Following through on fiscal stimulus and communicating *"growth friendly" fiscal consolidation* plans in advanced countries that will be implemented going forward. Sound fiscal finances are essential to sustain recovery, provide flexibility to respond to new shocks, ensure the capacity to meet the challenges of aging populations, and avoid leaving future generations with a legacy of deficits and debt. The path of adjustment must be carefully calibrated to sustain the recovery in private demand. *There is a risk that synchronized fiscal adjustment across several major economies could adversely impact the recovery. There is also a risk that the failure to implement consolidation where necessary would undermine confidence and hamper growth.* Reflecting this balance, advanced economies have committed to fiscal plans that will at least halve deficits by 2013 and stabilize or reduce government debt-to-GDP ratios by 2016. [...] *Fiscal consolidation plans will be credible, clearly communicated, differentiated to national circumstances, and focused on measures to foster economic growth."* [emphasis added]

their influence and power internally. This may seem odd at first sight, not only because of the limited subject-matter powers of the *Länder* within the German federation but also because these subject matters are by and large not part of the enumerated powers of the European Union. The European Union does not legislate in the field of preventive police work, it does not legislate in the area of schools and universities[18], it does not legislate in the area of the arts and culture and it has only very limited legislative powers in the area of broadcasting.[19]

However, the concerns of the *Länder* have less to do with the loss of their own exclusive subject-matter powers to the European Union, they have more to do with the loss of federal legislative powers to the European Union and the corresponding loss of their participation powers through the *Bundesrat* in the domestic legislative process. Whenever a subject matter that used to be regulated by the member states of the European Union moves away from the member states to the European Union, it means that in Germany the *Länder* are losing their legislative participation powers in the *Bundesrat* as well. A constitutional amendment of Article 23 in the early 1990's tried to find a solution by formulating a complicated balance of power between the federal and state level with

regard to representation of the Federal Republic in the decision making process of the European Union.[20] In some cases, that can lead to Germany being represented on the European Union level not by a member of the federal government, but rather by a member of the *Bundesrat* named by the *Bundesrat*.

6. Conclusion

The direct participation of members of the *Länder* governments in the federal legislative process through the *Bundesrat* gives the *Länder* a very strong

---

18 With some exceptions in the area, for example, of student and academic exchange, such as the Erasmus/Socrates programs to name a well-known example. The Bologna process, which has led to almost revolutionary changes in the European higher education sector, is not a European Union process. The Bologna Process is the process of creating the European Higher Education Area (EHEA) and is based on cooperation between ministries, higher education institutions, students and staff from 47 countries, with the participation of international organizations, see http://www.ond.vlaanderen.be/hogeronderwijs/bologna/.

19 See Directive 2007/65/EC of 11 December 2007 amending Council Directive 89/552/EEC on the coordination of certain provisions laid down by law, regulation or administrative action in Member States concerning the pursuit of television broadcasting activities, OJ L 332/27 (2007), http://eur-lex.europa.eu/LexUriServ/LexUriServ.do?uri=OJ:L:2007:332:0027:01: EN:HTML.

20 38th Amendment of the Basic Law, 21.12.1992, Official Gazette (BGBl. I), p. 2086 (1992).

position. The *Länder* are represented institutionally, rather than territorially and hence the political will of the each *Land* can directly translate into the decision-making process on the federal level. One practical consequence is that in German political reality, *Länder* politicians and especially *Länder* prime ministers play a much more prominent role on the federal political stage than state premiers in Australia or governors in the United States of America. Whereas German *Länder* have only limited subject-matter powers, less than their Australian or US counterparts, they have a much stronger institutional role in the federation in the sense of participatory federalism.

III. Germany's System of Fiscal Federalism – Complex Interdependence

1. Basic Principles – Income

Article 105 GG distributes legislative powers for taxation between the federal level and the *Länder*. There are some exclusive federal powers (Article 105.1) and some exclusive state powers (Article 105.2a). The powers for the bulk of and especially for the important taxes, i.e. the power to legislate for taxes that generate significant revenue, mainly the income tax and the value-added tax (VAT)[21], are construed as concurring powers. Concurring means that the power lies with the *Länder* until and in so far as the federal level takes on its legislative role. Rather unsurprisingly this has happened in the area of the two most relevant revenue taxes.

The Basic Law then regulates the distribution of that tax revenue in a separate step. The income of some taxes goes exclusively to the *Länder*, the income from other taxes goes exclusively to the federal government. However, the revenue of the taxes generating the most income, the income tax and the VAT, is shared between the federal level and the *Länder* and that distribution is governed by constitutional provisions concerning the horizontal and vertical tax revenue distribution in Article 106, 107 GG.

Under the vertical tax revenue distribution scheme the revenue earned by these taxes is distributed between the federal government and the *Länder* as a

---

21   The official name of the VAT is "turnover tax" (*Umsatzsteuer*) but it is commonly referred to as VAT which takes into account that turnover achieved at every stage of a production process is only taxable to the degree that value was added to the product. See also Council Directive 2006/112/EC of 28 November 2006 on the common system of value added tax, OJ L 347/1 (2006).

whole (Article 106 GG). After that exercise the horizontal tax income distribution sets in, distributing the *Länder* portion of the money between the several *Länder* under complicated constitutional provisions (Article 107 GG), complemented by a constitutionally mandated statutory framework[22] and under strict supervision by the Constitutional Court[23] to ensure the fiscal equalization objectives set by the Basic Law.[24]

2. Special Fiscal Levies

The question arose whether the federal level is limited in its revenue quest to the taxation powers stipulated in the relevant provisions of the Basic Law concerning taxation or whether it can use other subject matter powers attributed to it to also legislate revenue relevant aspects. The constitutional court has consistently ruled that this is not possible unless some very narrowly defined criteria are met.[25] The Court reasoned that allowing the federal level to legislate income relevant legislation on the basis of generic subject-matter titles found in the Basic Law, such as public welfare, economic matters, research promotion, public health and so on, would undermine the principal structure of fiscal federalism in the Federal Republic, because it would lead to an erosion of the revenue earning capability of the income and value added and other taxes and that would have to diminish the amount of money available for distribution between the federal level and the *Länder*.

3. Basic Principles – Expenses, Article 104a GG

The foundation for expenses is laid by Article 104a. 1 which stipulates that

"the federation and the *Länder* shall separately finance the expenditures resulting from the discharge of their respective responsibilities insofar as this Basic Law does not otherwise provide."

---

22 The Fiscal Equalization Statute (*Finanzausgleichsgesetz*), http://www.gesetze-im-internet.de/finausglg_2005/BJNR395600001.html and the "constitutional distribution criteria statute" (*Maßstäbegesetz*), http://www.gesetze-im-internet.de/ma_stg/BJNR230200001.html.

23 See BVerfGE 1, 117 (http://www.servat.unibe.ch/dfr/bv001117.html); 72, 330 (http://www.servat.unibe.ch/dfr/bv072330.html); 86, 148 (http://www.servat.unibe.ch/dfr/bv086148.html); 101, 158 (http://www.servat.unibe.ch/dfr/bv101158.html).

24 See infra Financial Solidarity (Fiscal Equalization – Article 107 GG) (p. 25).

25 See BVerfGE 108, 186 (216–18) with references to earlier decisions, http://www.servat.unibe.ch/dfr/bv108186.html.

This provision is one of the principal foundations of German fiscal federalism. It was integrated into the *Grundgesetz* during the 1969 constitutional reform to counter tendencies that the federal level would put the states under psychological and political pressure by offering financing in subject matter areas where only the states had jurisdiction to prescribe. It was (and is) the very purpose of this constitutional provision to counter the risk of financial usurpation by the federal level and preserve the *Länder* – and the federal level as well – as genuine political and legal entities and independent constituent parts of the federation.

Article 104a.1 stands in stark contrast, for example, to section 92 of the Commonwealth Constitution and the grants power introduced there. The grants power has shaped the Australian fiscal reality and allowed the federal level to intrude into the sphere of the states by providing fiscal incentives tied to political conditions for subject matters it otherwise would not have the power to regulate. The German provision, by contrast, specifically prohibits the federal level from using its financial prowess in this manner even if the states were to consent.

4. Piercing Financial Political Independence of the *Länder*?

There are two limited instruments by which the federal level can gain at least some indirect influence on the *Länder* by financial means. The first such instrument are the so-called joint tasks governed by Article 91a and 91b GG. Article 91a deals with the improvement of regional economic structures including agriculture and coastal preservation. Article 91b deals with research cooperation and projects both in universities and other institutions and investment in capital infrastructure in this area. Projects under these joint tasks are co-financed between the federal level and the *Länder* and the consent of the *Bundesrat* or prior agreements with all the states are necessary prerequisites before such joint task can be undertaken. Nonetheless the offering of co-financing incentives by the federal level can be used to achieve some political leverage, although this is counterweighed by a high level of institutional participation of the *Länder* through the *Bundesrat*.[26]

The new instrument of financial investment assistance (Article 104b) is limited to areas where the federal level actually does have legislative power and cannot be used for projects falling within state subject matter areas. Grants given under the financial investment assistance instrument must also be regressive and a federal law requiring the assent of the *Bundesrat* must regulate the details.

---

26 The Federalism Reform Package II added a similar third provision, Article 91c, addressing information technology systems.

5. Financial Solidarity (Fiscal Equalization – Article 107 GG)

The distribution of tax revenue between the federal level and the *Länder* as a whole, the so-called vertical tax income distribution (Article 106 GG) has already been mentioned. The vertical tax income distribution is followed by a horizontal tax income distribution, that is the distribution of the relevant tax revenue among the several *Länder* (Article 107 GG).

The total *Länder* share of income tax revenue is distributed to the individual *Länder* on the basis of territorial tax earnings, i.e. on the basis of the taxes paid to the revenue administration within the various *Länder*. Special corrective measures are put in place for the city states, especially Bremen and Hamburg, where many work while living and paying income tax in a neighboring *Land*, causing a structural shortfall for these city states. The total share of value added tax is distributed among the *Länder* on a per capita basis.

This first step of horizontal tax income distribution is followed by a second step of fiscal equalization.[27] This means the application of a correctional formula to put the *Länder* on a comparable, some would say much too equal, financial footing. Fiscal equalization is the practical application of the principle of *Länder* solidarity as expressed in Article 107.2 GG. The 'rich' *Länder* must share their financial resources with their 'poorer' brethren. The details are regulated in a statute required and governed by Article 107.2 GG. The statute elaborates on the calculations, that determine who will be the 'givers' and the 'takers' according to certain standards and benchmarks. The statute requires the assent of the Bundesrat.[28]

The final element of fiscal equalization are additional grants from the federal level for especially 'needy' states under Article 107.2.3 GG. The federal level might be required to allocate such funds for a number of reasons, for example in case of special financial hardships encountered by a *Land* because of structural imbalances in welfare expenses or simply for debt relief for highly indebted *Länder* (such as Berlin, Bremen, and the Saarland). Proceedings on the alleged entitlement of the city-state of Bremen and the Saarland to such additional federal grants are currently pending in the Constitutional Court.[29] In an earlier

---

27 See   http://www.bundesfinanzministerium.de/nn_4480/DE/BMF__Startseite/Service/Down
    loads/Abt__V/The_20Federal_20Financial_20Equalisation_20System_20in_20Germany,
    templateId=raw,property=publicationFile.pdf (29.6.2010).
28 See supra fn. 22.
29 The Court has, however, addressed the issue for Berlin, which is not only the capital city but
    also a *Land* and whose finances are in dire straights. The Court came to the conclusion that
    Berlin is not entitled under the Basic Law to receive such additional federal aid. See BVerfGE
    116, 327, http://www.servat.unibe.ch/dfr/bv116327.html. It is unlikely that the Court will

judgment the Constitutional Court ruled that fiscal equalization measures must not lead to financial equality. The financially poorer *Land* must remain the poorer *Land* even after the equalization measures. The gap may only be narrowed, but it must not be closed.[30]

6. Conclusion

The fiscal federalism model of Germany could be characterized as a unitarian federalism model with competitive elements, where the latter are on the rise but which is nonetheless firmly rooted in the concept of comparable equality across the federation, i.e. in achieving very similar living conditions in all states. The revenue mechanisms of the Basic Law are strongly unitarian and complemented by a fiscal equalization regime which does not allow the states to develop competitive advantages into significant fiscal advantages. The visible advantage is that living conditions by and large do not depend on where you live in Germany in so far as these living conditions are a function of the fiscal capabilities of the respective *Land*. That is not to say that there are no visible economic differences, for example between the western and eastern or some northern and southern *Länder*. But the differences are not linked to mechanisms of fiscal federalism, e.g. a significantly higher comparative revenue base in one state versus another. The disadvantage of this lies in the fact that it is not easy to see how comparative advantages that some *Länder* have over others are linked to the political efficiency of their respective governments. The overall fiscal position of, for example, Bavaria and the Saarland or Bremen is dramatically different. Their respective debt levels are dramatically different. But from the point of view of federalism it is not easy to attribute this to the performance of the respective *Länder* governments or to determine that policy changes on the *Länder* level could alleviate the situation. Effective government on the level of the *Länder* is by and large limited to more subtle means of policy making, such as good administration and governance over the long term, clever industrial policies, attractive educational and cultural offerings etc. The crude instruments of increasing tax revenue and spending in comparison to other *Länder* are not really available. One consequence of this is a comparatively lower voter turnout

---

come to a different conclusion in the case of the city state of Bremen and the Saarland despite the fact that much could be said in favor of the claims made by these states. See expert opinion by Georg Ress and Jürgen Bröhmer of 22.2.2006, available at http://www.finanzen.bremen.de/sixcms/media.php/13/Gutachen_Ress_Broemer.pdf.

30   BVerfGE 101, 158 (221–2), http://www.servat.unibe.ch/dfr/bv101158.html.

at *Länder* elections and a tendency to punish *Länder* governments for discontent with federal politics. In other words the federal objective of bringing political decisions and political accountability closer to the citizen is not fully reached. However, it is not possible to pursue comparative equality of living conditions across the federation and competitive federalism at the same time without conflict. In Germany comparable standards of living have always been regarded as more important than allowing for more competition between the various states, with the perceived danger of a race to the bottom.

IV. Results

Germany's federal system empowers the constitutive entities, the Länder, in three main ways:

First, rather than attributing to the *Länder* broad areas of subject-matter jurisdiction, the *Länder* are given a strong institutional participatory role on the federal level through the Federal Chamber, the *Bundesrat*.

Second, the *Länder* retain a very important exclusive role in administering many federal laws within the confines of the rule of law.

Third, the *Länder* have retained more financial independence in the sense that the federal level is much less able to effectively usurp subject matter jurisdiction from the *Länder* by extending funds to them and tie these funds to political conditions. However, the strong participatory rights of the *Länder* have not been sufficient to fully defend against the passage to legislation on the federal level without adequate financial resourcing to cover the expenses. This has been especially problematic with a view to the local government tier (municipalities). Complex fiscal equalization has been successful in creating a comparative equality in living conditions across the federation but has come under pressure from those favoring a more competitive approach to federalism.

Nicholas Aroney[*]

Bund, Bundesstaat and *Staatenbund*: The German Element in Australian Federalism

Introduction

The philosophical origins of the Australian constitution[1] are usually, and rightly, attributed to predominantly British and North American sources.[2] As British settlements the several Australia colonies inherited the English common law as the foundation of their legal systems, and as they progressively secured rights of local self-government through the course of the nineteenth century their constitutions were modelled upon the British system of parliamentary responsible government. When, in the late nineteenth century the colonies considered the possibility of establishing a system of government for the entire Australian continent, they naturally looked to the American and Canadian federal systems as constitutional models. Consistent with this general preference for the British, American and Canadian political systems, the framers of the Australian constitution looked primarily to writers from those countries on matters such as constitutionalism, federalism and parliamentary government.[3]

Much of this is reasonably well-known. What is not well-known or understood is that the Australians also looked carefully at other constitutional models, especially the Swiss and the German. Indeed, the Australians adopted the Swiss referendum as the mechanism for the amendment of the constitution[4]

[*] Professor of Constitutional Law, Centre for Public, International and Constitutional Law, TC Beirne School of Law, The University of Queensland. This chapter draws on material published in Nicholas Aroney, 'The Influence of German State-Theory on the Design of the Australian Constitution' (2010) 59 *International and Comparative Law Quarterly* 669. The author wishes to thank the participants at the *60 Years Deutsches Grundgesetz* conference held at the Australian National University, 22–23 May 2009, and especially Dieter Dörr, Rolf Schwartmann, Torsten Stein and Jürgen Bröhmer, for their comments, as well as James Farr, Ian Hunter, Donald Kommers and Stanley Paulson.
[1] The Constitution of the Commonwealth of Australia is to this day contained within a British statute, the *Commonwealth of Australia Constitution Act 1900* (UK).
[2] R.D. Lumb, *Australian Constitutionalism* (Sydney: Butterworths, 1983).
[3] Nicholas Aroney, *The Constitution of a Federal Commonwealth: The Making and Meaning of the Australian Constitution* (Cambridge: Cambridge University Press, 2009) chs 3–4.
[4] Australian Constitution, s 128.

but also for its ratification,[5] and they came remarkably close to instituting a federal executive council along the lines of the Swiss model aswell.[6] Further, while the German Imperial Constitution of 1871 was generally thought to be so dominated by Prussia that it was irrelevant to Australian circumstances and aspirations,[7] German state-theory had a significant though largely overlooked influence on the debate over the kind of federation that would be established in Australia.

This transmission of the ideas of the German *Allgemeine Staatslehre* tradition to Australian shores is especially remarkable when the significant differences between the two countries is considered. One was located in the middle of Europe, surrounded by often hostile powers, and embedded in a long and tumultuous history; the other was a British colony established in the Antipodean New World. One was part of the Continental civil law tradition; the other had inherited the English common law and was subject to British imperial authority. And yet, there were important similarities. The German states, formerly constituent elements of the Holy Roman Empire, had long taken a very different path to the consolidated nation-states of France, Spain and the United Kingdom.[8] Although the unification of the German states in 1871 was decisively shaped by Prussian economic and military power, the constitution of the German Empire was in the form of an international treaty, agreed to by the constituent states.[9] Likewise, the Australian colonies, though sharing a common allegiance to the British Crown, believed themselves to be mutually independent, self-governing political communities possessing the right to determine for themselves whether and, if so, on what terms they would enter into a federal union.[10]

Two very important figures in late nineteenth and early twentieth century German legal scholarship, Johann Caspar Bluntschli (1808–1881) and Georg Jellinek (1851–1911), wrote treatises about constitutional law and political theory that influenced the Australians very deeply. The better educated and intellectually influential among the Australians were familiar with Jellinek and

---

5   Enabling Acts passed in each of the Australian colonies provided that a proposed federal constitution would be drafted at a federal convention and then submitted for approval to the voters in each colony before being sent to London for enactment by the British Parliament.

6   Aroney, *Constitution of a Federal Commonwealth*, 113–4, 174, 201–2, 210–12.

7   See, eg, John Quick, *A Digest of Federal Constitutions* (Bendigo: J.B. Young, 1896), 60–77; Richard Baker, *Executive in a Federation* (Adelaide: C.E. Bristow, Government Printer, 1897), 5–8.

8   David Blackbourn, *History of Germany, 1780–1918: The Long Nineteenth Century* (2nd ed, Wiley-Blackwell, 2003), 10–20.

9   *Verfassung des Deutschen Reiches* (1871), Preamble.

10   Aroney, *Constitution of a Federal Commonwealth*, ch 5.

Bluntschli – they read about their ideas through various Anglo-American translations and interpretations, and they debated the implications of their theories for the design of the Australian federal system.[11] In particular, two Anglophone scholars, Edward Freeman (1823–1892) and John W. Burgess (1844–1931), relied heavily on Bluntschli and Jellinek when formulating theories of federalism, and the Australians who read Burgess and Freeman drew on them to defend their own conceptions of the kind of federation that they thought Australia should become. Indeed, Bluntschli and Freeman on one hand, and Jellinek and Burgess on the other, were taken by the Australians to embody the two basic, contending theories of the nature of federalism that lay at the heart of the debate over the design of the Australian Constitution.

This essay seeks to summarise the influence of German state-theory on the making of the Australian Constitution, especially in its federal aspects. The objective is to survey the approaches to state-theory advanced respectively by Bluntschli and Jellinek and to show how their ideas were used in the Australian debate. To do this the discussion will focus in particular on Bluntschli and Jellinek's accounts of *Bundesstaat* ('federation') and *Staatenbund* ('confederation'), placing special emphasis on what they considered to be the distinguishing features of the two kinds of constitutional arrangement. The chapter will also sketch the way in which Freeman, Burgess and the Australians appropriated the ideas of Bluntschli and Jellinek, constructing their own accounts of the nature of a genuinely 'federal' government, appropriate to Australian conditions and consistent with their own aspirations. While the Australians were generally limited in their capacity to read in languages other than English, it will be shown that many of the underlying ideas used by the Australians had their genesis in the German *Staatslehre* tradition, especially in the writings of Bluntschli and Jellinek.

II. German State-Theory

German state-theory had long been confronted with unique problems of national identity and state-form. Down to the time of its formal dissolution in 1806, the Holy Roman Empire of the German Nation was a complex patchwork of multi-layered jurisdictions which presented perplexing questions of analysis and categorisation, and many varied and conflicting accounts of its nature were

---

11   See Aroney, *Constitution of a Federal Commonwealth*, ch 4.

advanced.[12] Later incarnations of German nationhood – the Confederation of the Rhine of 1806, the *Deutsche Bund* of 1815, the North German Confederation of 1866 and the German Empire of 1871 – though less complex than the old Empire, continued to present difficult problems of classification.[13] As Michael Stolleis has argued, two of the most pressing questions concerned whether the structure of government under the Imperial Constitution of 1871 was to be understood as a federal-state or as a union of states, and whether ultimate sovereignty was located in the member states or the empire as a whole.[14]

These two questions, among many others, were addressed by Bluntschli and Jellinek, and their answers to these questions were later adopted by Freeman and Burgess, only to be taken up in turn by the framers of the Australian Constitution. For the Australians, designing a federal system in the absence of a long-standing set of institutional practices and expectations of the kind represented by the German experience, three things would be particularly relevant. First, what was the institutional design of the German Empire? Second, what conceptual system was appropriate to the classification and explication of such a system of government? Third, what normative principles should be inferred from the German system as a constitutional model and from its classification as a particular kind of system of government? The Australians looked to Bluntschli and Jellinek, among others, for answers to questions such as these.

---

12   See Heinz Eulau, 'Theories of Federalism under the Holy Roman Empire' (1941) 35(4) *American Political Science Review* 643; Patrick Riley, 'Three 17th Century German Theorists of Federalism: Althusius, Hugo and Leibniz' (1976) 6(3) *Publius: The Journal of Federalism* 7, 21–25; Peter Schröder, 'The Constitution of the Holy Roman Empire after 1648: Samuel Pufundorf's Assessment in His Monzambano' (1999) 42(2) *The Historical Journal* 961, 962; Peter H. Wilson, 'Still a Monstrosity? Some Reflections on Early Modern German Statehood' (2006) 49(2) *The Historical Journal* 565; Robert von Friedeburg and Michael J. Seidler, 'The Holy Roman Empire of the German Nation' in H. A. Lloyd, G. Burgess and S. Hodson (eds), *European Political Thought 1450–1700: Religion, Law and Philosophy* (New Haven: Yale University Press, 2008) 102.

13   See Hans Boldt, 'Federalism as an Issue in the German Constitutions of 1849 and 1871' in Herman Wellenreuther (ed), *German and American Constitutional Thought: Contexts, Interaction, and Historical Realities* (New York: Berg, 1990) 259, 260–78, 260–78; Christopher Clark, 'Germany 1815–1848: Restoration or Pre-March?' in John Breuilly (ed), *Nineteenth-Century Germany: Politics, Culture and Society 1780–1918* (London: Arnold, 2001) 40, 41–6.

14   Michael Stolleis, *Public Law in Germany, 1800–1914* (New York: Berghahn Books, 2001), 341–45. See also Abigail Green, 'The Federal Alternative? A New View of Modern German History' (2003) 46(1) *The Historical Journal* 187.

A. Johann Bluntschli

Johann Bluntschli was born in Zurich, educated in Berlin and Bonn, and appointed Professor of Constitutional Law, first at Munich University and later at Heidelberg. During his illustrious career he wrote several very important treatises in public, private and international law. Two of them were especially influential in Australia: his *Geschichte des schweizerischen Bundesrechtes* (1875) and his *Lehre vom modernen Staat* (1875–1876), itself consisting of three volumes under the titles *Allgemeine Staatslehre*, *Allgemeines Staatsrecht* and *Politiks*.[15] An English translation of the *Allgemeine Staatslehre* (published in 1885)[16] was read and cited by several of the Australians. His *Geschichte des schweizerischen Bundesrechtes* was similarly relied upon by Edward Freeman, who was himself cited frequently by several Australians.[17]

Bluntschli understood states to arise when distinct peoples, possessing a common language, culture and history, form themselves into separate nations (*Völker*) and as nations become conscious of their political unity and legal personality.[18] He accordingly defined a state as large body of persons, connected to a particular territory, conscious of its identity as a nation (*Volk*) and in possession of sovereignty (*Souveränität*).[19] However, 'people', 'nation' and 'state' were not necessarily coterminous. While the unity of the state was one of its essential features, Bluntschli recognised that a state could be composed of several constituent states.[20] While distinct peoples often form themselves into their own separate states, a single people might, for various reasons, separate into several states, or several peoples might be united into one state.[21] In the latter case, Bluntschli observed three possible tendencies over time: the several distinct peoples might eventually be assimilated into one people; the peoples might separate from one another to form distinct states; or the combination of several peoples in one state might be maintained, either by raw military force or else through a federal union of self-governing republics, as in his native Switzerland.[22] Bluntschli thus saw it as quite legitimate for a state to be

---

15   *Geschichte des schweizerischen Bundesrechtes von den ersten ewigen Bünden bis auf die Gegenwart*, 2 vols (Stuttgart: Meyer & Zeller, 1875); *Lehre vom modernen Staat* (Stuttgart: J.G. Cotta, 1875–1876).

16   Johann K. Bluntschli, *The Theory of the State*, D.G. Ritchie, P.E. Matheson and R. Lodge (trans.) (Oxford: Clarendon Press, 1885; 2nd ed, 1892; 3rd ed, 1895).

17   See section 3 below.

18   *Theory of the State* (3rd ed), 86–92.

19   *Theory of the State*, 15–17.

20   *Theory of the State*, 17.

21   *Theory of the State*, 98–100.

22   *Theory of the State*, 100–103.

composed of more than one people, and he considered that the ideal form in which such an arrangement could be preserved was through some kind of federal constitution.

Within this context Bluntschli considered federal arrangements, not as more or less static systems of government in which functions are definitively divided between federal and state organs of government, but principally in terms of their origins, understood in the context of a broad discussion of the formation of states generally.[23] According to Bluntschli, a state may historically come into being in three fundamentally different ways: first, as the political expression of a particular people where no state or states already exist; second, as an emanation of a particular people in a context that is dependent upon an existing state or states; and, third, as arising through the action of an existing state external to the people of the newly created state.[24] Bluntschli held that the original emergence of a state out of a pre-existing people does not, as a matter of history, come about as the result of the consent of all of the individuals composing the society, but rather as a result of the people of a particular place becoming conscious of their identity as a nation and resolving to form themselves into a state as an exercise of the common will of the nation as a whole.[25]

Bluntschli in turn distinguished two ways in which a state may emerge as an emanation of a particular people in a way that is dependent upon an existing state or states: those that involve the integration of several states into one state and those that involve the disintegration of one state into several states. The former of these, the union of several states into one, typically occurs, he said, when several states wish to join together for the purpose of common defence or to attain a sense of national identity. As Bluntschli explained, such unions of states come into being on the basis of a contract between states, resulting in what he called a *Bund*. Such arrangements, he argued, could in turn be distinguished into two basic kinds, which he respectively called *Staatenbund* (confederation) and *Bundesstaat* (federal-state or federation). Bluntschli conceived both categories of *Bund* as 'composite' political bodies. The basic difference between the two, he said, was that a federal-state exists where the sense of national unity is relatively greater and the fundamental law of the system is conceived more as constitutional law than as a contract between states.[26]

The precise nature of the distinction between federations and confederations was of course the critical question, and Bluntschli's treatment of the issue was

23   *Theory of the State*, 259–75.
24   *Theory of the State*, 260.
25   *Theory of the State*, 264.
26   *Theory of the State*, 268–70.

36

complex. As noted, he suggested that although a confederation is and remains based upon a contract or treaty between the constituent states, a federal-state is somehow to be conceived as being founded upon a single nation and a common state, under a constitution. However, he classified even the federal-state as something initially formed by contract (*Bund*) and he described the transition from confederation to federal-state as occurring, historically, when a subjective feeling of unity becomes stronger than the countervailing feeling for diversity.[27] Most importantly in this connection, Bluntschli made no mention of the location of sovereignty; at most he conceived the constitution of a federal-state to be derived from the singular will of a single nation and common state.[28] Rather, the key institutional difference between confederation and federal-state concerned the nature and reach of the centralised organs of government within the *Bund*. According to Bluntschli, a confederation lacks a centralised state apparatus; the administration of a confederation is left either to one of the constituent states as the presiding state or to an assembly of delegates of all the states. By contrast, he said, a federal-state has independently organised federal organs of government, legislative and executive, which operate directly upon individuals.[29]

Bluntschli thus presented the federal-state as somehow grounded conceptually upon a constitution and distinguished from a confederation on account of the nature and reach of its centralised organs of government. Later expanding upon the institutional differences between a federal-state and a confederation, he observed that except for very limited purposes a confederation has no legal personality and lacks any governmental organs of its own, whereas in a federal-state both the collective state (*Gesamtstaat*) and the particular states (*Einzelstaaten*) have a complete set of organs of government which operate independently of each other and as effectively as if each were simple states. There is also a kind of joint citizenship in a federal-state, he said, in the sense that both the federation and the particular states possess an organic unity and identity, so that we can speak of Americans, and yet also of Pennsylvanians and Virginians, and of the Swiss nation as well as of the Bernese and Genevese. In turn, Bluntschli explained, the existence of two kinds of states within the same territory is made possible through a precise demarcation of the powers of each and by keeping the governments and representative bodies of the two as separate and independent as possible.[30]

---

27   *Theory of the State*, 268.
28   *Theory of the State*, 269.
29   *Theory of the State*, 269.
30   *Theory of the State*, 487–9.

It was only after all this that Bluntschli turned in his book to a detailed analysis of the nature of sovereignty.[31] For Bluntschli, sovereignty (*Souveränität*) was indeed an essential principle of the state, inhering not in the people or the nation (*Volk*), but in the state itself, understood as a kind of corporate entity possessing legal personality.[32] Bluntschli defined sovereignty in its 'positive side' as the complete and sole power of the state over its territory to enforce its laws and execute its decrees over all persons, land and things within its jurisdiction, as well as in its 'negative side' as the right to exclude every other state and external power from interference within its territory.[33] However, he was emphatic that sovereignty must not be conceived of as a kind of absolute power, for in its external aspect a state is always subject to international law and in its internal aspect it is limited by its own nature and by the rights of its members.[34] Thus, while Bluntschli added (almost in passing) that sovereignty must be unitary in nature (for a division of sovereignty 'paralyses and dissolves' a state[35]) he nonetheless affirmed that not every subjection of a state destroys its sovereignty, for in composite states such as confederations and federations the particular states, though in certain respects subordinate to the whole, yet retain a relative sovereignty, 'limited in extent but not in content'.[36]

Bluntschli's account of the nature of sovereignty and its relationship to his account of federal-states and confederations was thus capable of alternative interpretations. His insistence on the essential sovereignty of the state could lead to the conclusion that a federal-state is distinguished from a confederation because it is based on a constitution that derives from the people of the nation as a whole and not from a contract between the constituent states. However, he did not assert that the distinction between the two forms lay in the location of sovereignty per se, and he wrote as if the key institutional difference lay in the proposition that a federal-state has at its disposal a full and independent set of governing institutions operating directly on the individual citizens of the federation as a whole.

As such, the Australians who read Bluntschli understood him to be saying that federations and confederations both arise through a kind of federative covenant or *Bund*, and that the critical difference between the two is that in the former the central government directly executes federal laws against individuals, whereas in the latter centralised decisions can only be executed by the governing organs of

---

31 *Theory of the State*, 493–6.
32 *Theory of the State*, 497–502 .
33 *Theory of the State*, 244, 495, 501, 506–7.
34 *Theory of the State*, 495.
35 *Theory of the State*, 495.
36 *Theory of the State*, 506.

the states. Such an account of the distinction between the two preserved the idea that a federation, though in some sense based on a constitution, is nonetheless best conceived of as a kind of federative arrangement founded upon its constituent states, and not as a system of government owing its existence to the putatively sovereign people of the nation as a whole. This left it fully open for Bluntschli's Australian readers to conclude that it was by no means essential that a federal constitution give effect to the sovereignty of the people of the nation as a whole, for example in its representative institutions and amendment clauses. Indeed, several highly influential Australians argued that it was entirely appropriate for the proposed Australian Parliament, following the American and Swiss examples, to be partly representative of the peoples of the constituent states and partly representative of the people of the nation as a whole, as well as for the people of the constituent states to have a distinct voice in deliberations concerning any proposed amendments to the constitution.

B. Georg Jellinek

Georg Jellinek was born in Leipzig, educated in Leipzig and Vienna, and held appointments at the Universities of Vienna, Basel and Heidelberg.[37] In 1882 he published *Die Lehre von den Staatenverbindungen* and in 1895 he published *The Declaration of the Rights of Man and the Citizen*.[38] His most ambitious work, *Allgemeine Staatslehre*, was first published in 1900, went through several editions, and was profoundly influential.[39] However, this latter work was published too late to be of any influence on the Australians. Rather it was his *Die Lehre von den Staatenverbindungen* that had an important though indirect impact. The influence was indirect because Jellinek's work was not translated into English. However, another key writer of the time, the American political scientist and constitutional lawyer, John W. Burgess, was influenced very substantially by Jellinek and was the key route through which Jellinek's ideas

---

37 Stanley L. Paulson, 'Jellinek, Georg (1851–1911)', in *Encyclopedia of Law & Society: American and Global Perspectives* (SAGE Publications, 2007). On Jellinek's influence, see Stolleis, *Public Law in Germany, 1800–1914*, 440–44.

38 *Die Lehre von den Staatenverbindungen* (Vienna: Alfred Holder, 1882); *The Declaration of the Rights of Man and the Citizen: A Contribution to Modern Constitutional History*, trans. Max Farrand (New York: Henry Holt and Co, 1901). See Duncan Kelly, 'Revisiting the Rights of Man: Georg Jellinek on Rights and the State' (2004) 22(3) *Law and History Review* 493.

39 Georg Jellinek, *Allgemeine Staatslehre* (Berlin: O. Härting, 1900; Hermann Gentner Verlag, Bad Homburg Vor Der Höhe, 1960).

would migrate to Australian shores. Burgess was an important influence on a small but significant group of Australians, particularly in relation to his theory of the nature of the sovereign state, and the way in which he distinguished between a federation and a confederation.

In *Die Lehre von den Staatenverbindungen* Jellinek argued that the ordinarily essential characteristic of a state is its sovereignty (*Souveränität*).[40] A state arises historically, he said, when a particular people, conscious of their organic unity, establish themselves as a collective juridical personality, with fully constituted organs of government which are recognised by the people as giving effect to the will of the nation. For Jellinek, the sovereignty of a state involves a relationship of domination by the state over all individuals and groups within its territorial jurisdiction, as well as a condition of independence from the will of any other state. Each state, on this view, is in principle equally free and independent in the possession and exercise of its sovereignty. And yet, Jellinek's conception of sovereignty did not entail an absolute plenitude of power in terms of the old Roman definition, *summum imperium, summa potestas*. Sovereignty, for Jellinek, was 'the quality of the state by virtue of which it can only be legally bound by its own will.'[41] Thus, constitutional limits on the power of the organs of a state, as well as binding juridical relationships between states, could certainly exist, but they had to originate in an exercise of sovereign will by the state or states concerned.

According to Jellinek, the internal organisation and external relationships of a state could take many forms, and these forms could be classified into many kinds. Jellinek distinguished fundamentally between what he called 'non-organised' and 'organised' connections between states (*Staatenverbindungen*), as well between relations that were merely historical-political in character and those that were legal or juridical.[42] Relations among states that were primarily historical and political included for him cases of 'subject' territories or colonies, the historical incorporation or annexation of states into a single state and situations where the personal holder of sovereignty happened to be common to

---

40 *Die Lehre von den Staatenverbindungen*, 16–36. I rely here on the summaries of Jellinek's argument in Sobei Mogi, *The Problem of Federalism: A Study in the History of Political Theory* (London: Allen & Unwin, 1931) and Peter Stirk, 'The Westphalian Model, Sovereignty and Law in Fin-De-Siècle German International Theory' (2005) 19(2) *International Relations* 153.

41 *Die Lehre von den Staatenverbindungen*, 34 (translation in Stirk, 'The Westphalian Model', 159).

42 *Die Lehre von den Staatenverbindungen*, 58–60.

40

more than one state.[43] Among 'non-organised' relations between states, Jellinek also distinguished various kinds of treaty relationship involving for example the administrations of territories, alliances and protectorates, as well as what he called *Staatenstaat*, the loose kind of 'state of states' exemplified in the structure of the Holy Roman Empire.[44] All of these kinds of connections between states lacked, however, a common organ created by, or expressive of, the union between the states. Arrangements in which such an organ did exist Jellinek classified separately into four separate sub-categories, which he respectively called administrative unions (*Internationale Verwaltungsvereine*), confederations (*Staatenbund*), real unions (*Realunion*) and federal-states (*Bundesstaat*).[45]

For Jellinek – unlike Bluntschli – the key difference between a confederation and a federal-state lay in the location of sovereignty. According to him, a confederation is formed when several independent states agree by treaty to form a permanent set of central institutions calculated to secure certain political objectives, such as uniformity of laws and administration or mutual protection and defence, but in which each constituent state retains its sovereignty. The central institutions of government of a confederation may be organised in diverse ways and various decision-making rules may be adopted, but what is essential to the existence of a confederation is its formation through a treaty between states, and the maintenance of the sovereignty of those states under the confederation, with the consequence that each state retains the right to exercise its own judgment about the scope of the powers of the central organs of government and a capacity to deem central laws and acts of administration null and void, and if necessary to secede at will from the confederation as a whole.[46]

Jellinek taught that in contrast to a confederation, a federal-state is in essence a single state which happens to be organised on the basis of a permanent distribution of powers between central and regional organs of government. On this view, the constituent states of a federal-state do not possess sovereignty. Even though the federal-state may have come into being through a process that involved several previously independent states agreeing to the formation of a federal union, the legal foundation of a such an arrangement could *not* be conceived as a treaty between several states exercising their sovereign powers. Rather, the essential foundation of the federal-state had to be the existence of a newly-formed constitution which comes into being when a particular people become conscious of their organic unity as a nation and form themselves into a

---

43   *Die Lehre von den Staatenverbindungen*, 63–88.
44   *Die Lehre von den Staatenverbindungen*, 91–157.
45   *Die Lehre von den Staatenverbindungen*, 158–314.
46   *Die Lehre von den Staatenverbindungen*, 172–97.

collective juridical personality, with a set of fully constituted organs of government that are recognised by the people as giving effect to the will of the nation. On such a conception, a federal-state derives its existence from the nation (*Volk*), and the powers distributed to the national and state governments derive from this act of national self-constitution. The original states may continue to be called 'states', but by definition they remain non-sovereign political communities. As such, they are merely public-legal corporations to which powers of legislation and administration are permanently conferred under the constitution.[47]

On Jellinek's account, a confederation typically involves a central governing assembly which is in reality a congress of envoys from the constituent states, equally represented, voting on instructions and reserving to themselves the sole power to enforce or execute laws of the confederation. The compact between states upon which a confederation is founded also typically requires, he said, that the terms of the compact can only be altered by unanimous vote. Moreover, and importantly, Jellinek denied the possibility of an intermediate form between confederations and federal-states, such as a system in which sovereignty is somehow either 'divided' or 'shared' between the federation and the states, as promoted for example in the theory of Georg Waitz.[48] For the same reason, Jellinek also rejected the interpretation of the United States Constitution advanced by Max von Seydel[49] and John C. Calhoun, which on Jellinek's analysis presented the United States as a kind of confederation, with sovereignty reserved to the states, but in which the federal government directly executed federal laws against individuals, rather than having to rely upon the states to execute the law.[50] For Jellinek, such an interpretation was both illogical (because inconsistent with the principle that sovereignty must rest either in the whole or in the parts) and had been overtaken by historical events (namely the outcome of the American civil war, in which the military force of the Union overcame the secessionist states, eliminating their claimed rights to nullify federal laws and secede from the federation). Rather, for Jellinek, the United States was constituted as a fully formed federal-state, the essential characteristic of which was a unitary locus of sovereign power vested in the nation as a whole, together with a constitutional division of powers between the federal and state organs of government. Such a system may have been formed historically out of a union of

---

47   *Die Lehre von den Staatenverbindungen*, 253–314.
48   Georg Waitz, *Grundzüge der Politik* (Kiel: Verlag von Ernst Homann, 1862), 164–6.
49   Max von Seydel, *Commentar zur Verfassungs-Urkunde für das Deutsche Reich* (1st ed, Würzburg, 1873; 2nd ed; Freiburg: J.C.B. Mohr, 1897).
50   *Die Lehre von den Staatenverbindungen*, 187–97.

previously independent states (as in the United States), but it could also be formed by the decentralisation of a previously unitary state (as in the then proposed Austrian federation). In turn, because a federal-state owes its existence logically to the nation and not to the states, it was to be expected that such a system of government would involve a direct relationship between the federal-state and the people of the nation, secured through the proportional representation of citizens in the federal legislature and the execution of federal laws directly against individuals. However, there was no necessity that the states in a federal-state be represented as such in the national legislature or have a direct say in the amendment of the constitution. It was only because a sovereign state has the capacity to bind itself by an act of its own will that Jellinek considered the terms of a federal constitution to be fixed and binding on the federal-state, guaranteeing to the constituent states the distribution of powers and other institutional structures and decision-making processes laid down in the constitution.

Unlike Bluntschli, therefore, Jellinek insisted that there is a radical difference between federations and confederations, based on the location of sovereignty in each kind of political system. For those Australians who wished to see a relatively nationalistic system of government established by the Australian Constitution, Jellinek offered an account which gave them reason to think that a true federation, in contrast to a confederation, will be conceptually grounded upon the sovereignty of the people of the entire federation. From this premise, those of relatively nationalistic temper argued that both houses of the federal legislature should be representative, not of the peoples of the states, but of the people of the nation as a whole. Drawing on Burgess's application of Jellinek's theory to the American experience, they argued that federal-states are distinguished from unitary states solely by the existence of a constitutional division of competencies between the central and regional governments, enforced by the courts. The 'compromise' reached at Philadelphia in 1787, in which the American States were represented in proportion to population in the House of Representatives while being equally represented in the Senate, was seen by the followers of Jellinek to be fundamentally inconsistent with the basic idea of a federal-state. However, proponents of this view had to contend with the fact that, as Bluntschli had emphasised and others like Edward Freeman would repeat, federations, just like confederations, typically arise through a kind of federative covenant or *Bund*, and this historical origin of the system, both as a matter of juristic logic and political negotiation, implied the need for both the peoples of the constituent states and the people of the federal-state as a whole to be separately represented in the federal legislature, as well as to have a say in the amendment of the constitution as the binding expression of that agreement.

III. The Reception of German State-Theory

Through the latter half of the nineteenth century, there was a significant cross-fertilisation of American, English and German constitutional ideas. The American Revolution was a source of fascination for German writers.[51] *The Federalist* and James Madison's *Notes on Ancient and Modern Confederacies* had discussed the Holy Roman Empire[52] and *The Federalist* was in turn widely read on the European continent.[53] Robert von Mohl published an appreciative compendium of American constitutional law in 1824.[54] Alexis de Tocqueville's *De la démocratie en Amerique* (1835, 1840) also did much to publicise the American model and enlarge its influence upon German and Swiss federal developments.[55] In 1854, Leopold von Ranke declared the American Revolution to 'exceed in importance all earlier revolutions' and to constitute 'a complete turnover in principle'.[56] Ignaz Troxler proposed that the Swiss federal system be revised along American lines,[57] an argument that fundamentally influenced the shape of the revised Swiss Constitution of 1848.[58] The failed German Constitution of 1849 as well as the successful Constitution of 1871 were to an extent also influenced by the American example.[59] Further, as has been noted, Georg Waitz in 1862 proposed a theory of the federal state that drew heavily on

---

51   See Horst Dippel, *Germany and the American Revolution, 1770–1800*, trans. Bernhard A. Uhlendorf (Chapel Hill: University of North Carolina Press, 1977).

52   Alexander Hamilton, James Madison and John Jay, *The Federalist Papers* (1787–8), Clinton Rossiter (ed.) (New York: New American Library, 1961), Nos. 12, 14, 19, 21, 42, 43, 80; James Madison, *Notes on Ancient and Modern Confederacies* in Robert A. Rutland and William M. E. Rachal (eds), *The Papers of James Madison*, Vol IX (Chicago: University of Chicago Press, 1975).

53   Willi Paul Adams, 'German Translations of the American Declaration of Independence' (1999) 85(4) *The Journal of American History* 1325, 1327, 1336–7.

54   Robert von Mohl, *Das Bundes-Staatsrecht der Vereinigten Staaten von Nord-Amerika* (Stuttgart, 1824).

55   Alexis de Tocqueville, *De la Démocratie en Amerique* (Paris: Charles Gosselin, 1835, 1840).

56   Leopold von Ranke, *Über die Epochen der neuren Geschichte* (1854), cited in Dippel, *Germany and the American Revolution*, xv.

57   Ignaz Paul Vital Troxler, *Die Verfassung der Vereinigten Staaten Nordamerikas als Musterbild der schweizerischen Bundesreform* (Schaffhausen: Brodtmann, 1848).

58   See James H. Hutson, *The Sister Republics: Switzerland and the United States from 1776 to the Present* (Washington: Library of Congress, 1991).

59   Compare Boldt, 'German Constitutions of 1848 and 1871', 260–74, 280–89, and Michael Dreyer, 'American Federalism – Blueprint for Nineteen-Century Germany?' in Herman Wellenreuther (ed), *German and American Constitutional Thought: Contexts, Interaction, and Historical Realities* (New York: Berg, 1990) 328.

Alexander Hamilton and Tocqueville,[60] while in 1873 Max von Seydel proposed an interpretation which followed that of John C. Calhoun.[61]

In this context, the German *Staatslehre* tradition represented by Bluntschli, Jellinek and many other German scholars was remarkably well received in the United States and the United Kingdom, especially through the course of the second half of the nineteenth century. And, as has been noted, two Anglophone writers, one American and the other English, were particularly important conduits of German state-theory: John W. Burgess, Professor of History, Political Science and International Law at Columbia University, drew very extensively on Jellinek's account of the sovereign state, while Edward Freeman, Regius Professor of Modern History at Oxford University, drew more specifically from Bluntschli.

John Burgess, a protégé of the German émigré, Francis Lieber,[62] studied under several leading German scholars at the Universities of Göttingen, Leibzig and Berlin, and brought their ideas back to the United States upon his appointment at Columbia in 1876.[63] In particular, Burgess's most important book, *Political Science and Comparative Constitutional Law* (1890),[64] was deeply influenced by Jellinek's theory of the nature of the state. At the foundation of Burgess's political philosophy was the idea of the 'nation', which he defined as a 'population of an ethnic unity, inhabiting a territory of a geographic unity'.[65] Burgess maintained that the state is an all-comprehensive, exclusive and sovereign organisation. It embraces 'all persons, natural or legal, and all associations of persons' and possesses 'original, absolute, unlimited, universal power' over all individuals and associations within its territory. In its highest form, he said, the democratic state is 'the people in political organization', the 'citizens in sovereign organization', democratically embodied in 'the sovereignty of the majority'. The state creates its government through a

---

60   Waitz, *Grundzüge der Politik*, 164–6.

61   Max von Seydel, *Commentar zur Verfassungs-Urkunde für das Deutsche Reich*, discussed in Peter C. Caldwell, *Popular Sovereignty and the Crisis of German Constitutional Law: The Theory and Practice of Weimar Constitutionalism* (Durham: Duke University Press, 1997), 28–9 and Mogi, *Problem of Federalism*, 414–7.

62   See Bernard Edward Brown, *American Conservatives: The Political Thought of Francis Lieber and John W. Burgess* (New York: Columbia University Press, 1951).

63   Dorothy Ross, *The Origins of American Social Science* (Cambridge University Press, 1991), 71.

64   Burgess's 'The Ideal American Commonwealth' (1895) 10 *Political Science Quarterly* 404 was also read and quoted by the Australians. However, his *Recent Changes in American Constitutional Theory* (New York: Columbia University Press, 1923), which protested against the expansion of federal government authority, came too late to influence them.

65   *Political Science*, I, 1–2, 21, 38–9.

constitution, but Burgess insisted that the state is not itself subject to that constitution, for the state is necessarily sovereign in essence and unitary in form. Accordingly, a state may 'constitute two or more governments', but there cannot be two organisations of the state within the same territory. Accordingly, Burgess thought that a confederation is in essence a union of sovereign states created by treaty, whereas a federation is a 'dual system of government under a common sovereignty'. A federation may previously have been 'divided into several independent states' which now agree to form a kind of unified state. However, the process by which federations come into being – as distinct from confederations – inevitably involves a revolutionary transfer of sovereignty from many states to a single unitary state. Consequently, while the new sovereign state may allow a residue of powers to remain with the old governments, it will necessarily retain the capacity to make further alterations in that distribution of power.[66]

Burgess was especially cited by those Australians who wished to see a strongly centralised federal government established in their country.[67] More explicitly than even Jellinek before him, Burgess advanced a highly nationalistic account of the American federal system which was used by a certain segment of the Australians to support the idea that sovereignty ought to be vested in the people of Australia as a whole and that the design of the Constitution ought to reflect that idea. However, these views were met by those who pointed out that a federation of the Australian colonies would have to secure the support of each of the colonies, and that the peoples and representatives of those colonies would legitimately expect to be represented within the decision-making institutions of the federal government.

This latter approach to the formation and nature of the federal-state received theoretical support from several of Edward Freeman's works,[68] most importantly

---

66   *Political Science*, I, 51–5, 57–8, 72–6, 79–80 (criticising Bluntschli), 88, 101; II, 4–9, 184.
67   See, eg, *Official Report of the National Australasian Convention Debates, Adelaide* (Adelaide: Government Printer, 1897), 181, 698, 1022 (Isaacs); *Official Record of the National Australasian Convention Debates, Sydney* (Sydney: Government Printer, 1897), 306–9, 426, (Isaacs), 433 (O'Connor's reply), 862 (Isaacs), 913 (Glynn's reply); H.B. Higgins, *Essays and Addresses on the Australian Commonwealth Bill* (Melbourne: Atlas Press, 1900), 73; John Quick and Robert Randolph Garran, *The Annotated Constitution of the Australian Commonwealth* (Sydney: Angus and Robertson, 1901), 325, 333–4; W. Harrison Moore, *The Constitution of the Commonwealth of Australia* (2nd ed, 1910), 68, 598.
68   On Freeman, see John Fiske, 'Edward Augustus Freeman' (1893) 71(423) *The Atlantic Monthly* 99; William Clarke, 'Edward Augustus Freeman' (1892) 12(5) *The New England Magazine* 607; H.A. Cronne, 'Edward Augustus Freeman, 1823–1892' (1943) 28 *History* 78.

his *History of Federal Government in Greece and Italy*.[69] As an historian situated firmly within the British empirical tradition, Freeman adopted an approach to the conceptualisation of federalism that was significantly more pragmatic and historical than that of Burgess and others deeply influenced by German *Staatslehre*. However, Freeman was also a enthusiast for the comparative method,[70] and drew occasionally upon German scholarship, in particular Bluntschli's *Geschichte des schweizerischen Bundesrechtes*.[71] Although the Australians of the late nineteenth century had direct access to Bluntschli's ideas through the English translation of his *Allgemeines Staatsrecht*, Freeman offered an additional and important conduit for the dissemination of Bluntschli's thought. Freeman in turn had a profound influence on a significant number of the framers of the Australian Constitution.[72]

Freeman's working definition of 'federal government', like Bluntschli's category of the *Bund*, was considerably broader than the definitions of Jellinek and Burgess.[73] For Freeman, federalism is a 'compromise between two opposite political systems' or 'two widely distant extremes'; it is a 'union of component members', more than an alliance, less than a consolidated state. In its 'perfect form', the component 'members' will be 'wholly independent' or 'sovereign' in the 'sphere' which concerns them alone, but 'subject to a common power in those matters which concern the whole body of members collectively'. And 'this complete division of sovereignty [is] essential', Freeman said, 'to the absolute perfection of the Federal ideal.'[74] Freeman considered that if a federal system was 'to be of any value' it a must arise out of the union of independent states, rather than the division of a united territory.[75] While he thus accepted that 'federal government' will involve a 'division of powers' between the federation and the States, the idea that a genuinely federal system comes into being through an agreement among constituent states remained central to his account.

Citing Bluntschli on this point, Freeman accordingly subdivided the different kinds of federal system in terms of their treatment of federal executive power,

---

69 Edward A. Freeman, *History of Federal Government in Greece and Italy* (2nd ed., London: Macmillan, 1893).

70 Stefan Collini, Donald Winch and John Burrow, *That Noble Science of Politics: A Study in Nineteenth-Century Intellectual History* (Cambridge: Cambridge University Press, 1983), ch. 7.

71 *History of Federal Government in Greece and Italy*, 8 (note 2).

72 For a fuller account, see Aroney, *Constitution of a Federal Commonwealth*, 87–92.

73 Cf Kenneth C. Wheare, *Federal Government* (4th ed; New York: Oxford University Press, 1967), 16–7.

74 *Federal Government*, 1–3, 7–8.

75 *Federal Government*, 70.

rather than in terms of the location of sovereignty.[76] In a 'system of confederated states', he explained, the 'federal power' represents and applies only to the governments of the member states, whereas in a 'composite state' or 'supreme federal government', the government of the federation both represents and acts directly upon individual citizens. According to Freeman, the United States under the Articles of Confederation had been a system of confederated states (*Staatenbund*); under the Constitution, it became a composite state (*Bundes-staat*); yet under both it possessed a 'real federal government'.[77] Freeman's definition of 'federal government', like Bluntschli's theory of the *Bund*, thus did not exclude 'confederation' – unlike the more extreme nationalist interpretations expounded by Jellinek and Burgess.

Freeman's historical research on the nature and development of the federal idea was highly influential in Australia for several reasons. First, he reinforced a belief in the 'federal ideal'.[78] He described federal government as 'a delicate and artificial structure' and 'a late growth of a very high state of political culture', and his influential expression of that 'ideal' stimulated the Australian captivation with the notion of an ideal federal government, which they thought exemplified in the United States and Switzerland. Under Freeman's influence, the Australian framers were concerned to construct a constitution in which an appropriate 'balance' between central and state power was achieved, avoiding the 'less perfect' embodiment of that ideal in Canada, Germany and the Netherlands.

Second, federalism was for Freeman a way in which the modern imperative of national statehood could be reconciled with the ancient ideal of local self-government.[79] Freeman's ideals were the city-states of Ancient Greece and the Free Cities of the Holy Roman Empire, and, in true Whiggish style, he found living relics of these same institutions in the *Landesgemeinden* of Uri and Appenzel, the parish vestries of the English shires and the town governments of New England.[80] Freeman's nostalgia for small-scale participatory democracy was combined nonetheless with his recognition of the 'necessities' of the

---

76 *Federal Government*, 8 (note 2), citing Johann Bluntschli, *Geschichte des schweizerischen Bundesrechtes*, I: 554.

77 *Federal Government*, 8–13, 69, 77–8, 156. Cf. Bluntschli, *Theory of the State*, 252–3.

78 *Federal Government*, 1–3, 7–8.

79 *Federal Government*, 34, 64, 69.

80 See Edward Freeman, 'The Landesgemeinden of Uri and Appenzel' (1864) 17 *Saturday Review* 623; Edward Freeman, *The Growth of the English Constitution from Earliest Times* (3rd ed., London: Macmillan, 1898), 9–10, 37, 60, 66. Freeman was cited on this point by Edmund Barton: *Convention Debates, Adelaide* (1897), 388.

modern nation-state.[81] All of this reinforced in his Antipodean readers a determination to create a federal system that would allow the people of each Australian colony to continue to participate in their own self-government, while enabling the Australian people as a whole to govern themselves on a continental scale without having to rely upon the intervention of the British colonial office.

Third, Freeman drew the attention of his readers to many diverse examples of federalism, as well as to older understandings of the idea. Freeman's wider genus of 'federal government' included 'confederal' arrangements, such as the ancient Achaean League, the more recent United Provinces of the Dutch Republic, the U.S. Articles of Confederation and the secessionist Confederate States of America, as well as the strictly 'federal' arrangements represented by the American and Swiss Constitutions.[82] By thus expanding the genus ('federal government') and identifying two separate species ('confederation' and 'federation'), he underscored the continuities between federation and confederation, continuities which make it much easier to think of a federation as something which, like a confederation, comes about through an agreement among states, rather than through a revolutionary assertion of national sovereignty, as Jellinek and Burgess had argued.

As such, the theories of Jellinek and Burgess on one hand, and of Bluntschli and Freeman on the other, presented very different accounts of the nature of the federal-state, and were used to this effect by their Australian readers. Henry Bournes Higgins, for example, drew on the views of Jellinek, Burgess and A.V. Dicey[83] to argue that in every political society there must be a particular institution in which 'ultimate sovereignty' is located, and that in Australia sovereignty in its 'practical' expression ought to be located in the Australian people as a whole.[84] Adopting a similar view, and citing Burgess to this effect, Isaac Isaacs argued that Australian Constitution ought to be conceived as emanating from the Australian people, and that the only respect in which the Constitution should be 'federal' is that it ought to provide for a division of powers or competencies between the federal and state governments.[85] Accordingly, both Higgins and Isaacs maintained that the people of the nation, lying behind the Constitution, should be fully represented in the national

81 See *Federal Government*, 29, 38, 40, 49, discussed in Collini *et al*, *Noble Science of Politics*, 222.
82 See *Federal Government*, 211.
83 See Aroney, *Constitution of a Federal Commonwealth*, 130–33.
84 Higgins, *Essays and Addresses*, 9, 11, 13.
85 *Official Report of the National Australasian Convention Debates* (Sydney: Acting Government Printer, 1891), 308–9 (Isaacs), citing Burgess, 'Ideal American Commonwealth'. See also *Convention Debates*, *Adelaide* (1897), 171–8, 660 (Isaacs).

institutions of government, and if there were to be two houses of the federal legislature, both ought to be representative of the people of the nation as a whole.[86] Alternatively, if it had to be conceded that the Senate was to be somehow representative of the states,[87] then the powers of the Senate should be strictly limited so as to enable the House of Representatives, as agent of the entire nation, to have a final determinative say in case of any disagreement between the houses.[88] Relatedly, Isaacs and Higgins vigorously advocated the adoption of a system of parliamentary responsible government along traditional Westminster lines because this would make the House of Representatives the chamber in which governments would be formed; and in order to ensure that this was the case, they argued that Senate power over financial bills ought be highly restricted if not eliminated altogether.[89] Finally, and again citing Burgess to this effect, they thought that any procedure for the future amendment of the Constitution ought to place final determinative control in the hands of the people of the nation as a whole, whether directly by a national plebiscite, or indirectly through a national convention or a special procedure within the national Parliament.[90]

This picture of what the Australian Commonwealth might become was contradicted, however, by two simple facts. The first was that, contrary to the theory advanced by Jellinek and Burgess, the Australian Constitution was being formed through a process in which each of the constituent colony-states entered the federation negotiations as an equal, each sending its own delegates to the federal conventions, and in which the Constitution was finally approved by the voters of each colony, such that no colony was forced to enter the federation without its consent. This fact of inter-colonial negotiation and agreement belied the abstract theory that the federation might be conceived as emanating from the

---

86   *Convention Debates, Adelaide* (1897), 101–2 (Higgins), 171–8 (Isaacs), 641–9 (Higgins); *Convention Debates, Sydney* (1897), 303–313 (Isaacs), 259–65, 345–51 (Higgins); Higgins, *Essays and Addresses*, 8–16.

87   Isaacs and Higgins regarded the American model of the House of Representatives as representative of the nation and the Senate as representative of the States to be a mere 'compromise' rather than as a 'principle' of federation. See, e.g., *Convention Debates, Adelaide* (1897), 171–3 (Isaacs). However, acknowledging that their case was hopeless, Isaacs eventually voted with the inevitable majority.

88   Cf Higgins, *Essays and Addresses*, 16–17.

89   *Convention Debates, Adelaide* (1897), 96–7 (Higgins).

90   Higgins, *Essays and Addresses*, 6–8; 52, 73, 85, 104, 111, 115; *Convention Debates, Adelaide* (1897), 181–2, 1022 (Isaacs, citing Burgess); *Official Record of the Debates of the National Australasian Convention: Melbourne* (Melbourne: Government Printer, 1898), 716, 718–722 (Isaacs, citing Burgess).

people of the nation as a whole.[91] It was true that the federal agreement was not simply negotiated by the executive governments of each colony and was therefore in this respect unlike an ordinary international treaty. However, the initiative towards federation still had to be taken by the executive governments of each colony, and those governments and their respective legislatures agreed to a federating process which involved the elements just mentioned.

The second important fact was that among those who drafted the Constitution very few wanted to create a nationalistic federal system along the lines advanced by Isaacs and Higgins, sustained as it was by the theories of Jellinek, Burgess and others. By far the majority of the Australians saw themselves as representing the interests of their respective colonies and were committed to the view that the federation ought to be based on the consent of the people of the several colonies. Accordingly, they argued that the drafting of the Constitution should properly take into account the rights and interests of both the separate peoples of each State, as well as the rights and interests of the people of the entire federation that they hoped might come into being as a result of their labours.[92] On this view, their common objective was to create a 'federal commonwealth' or a 'commonwealth of commonwealths',[93] by which they meant a federal-state originally constructed out of a plurality of states, as well as a federal-state composed of several constituent states in an ongoing sense. On this view, following Bluntschli and Freeman, the distance between a federation and confederation was not so great, and it followed that the structure of the federal system of government should reflect many of the kinds of features that federations and confederations have in common.

Thus adapting the American and Swiss models to their own purposes, a majority of the Australian framers believed that the peoples of the states should be equally represented in the Senate, that the people of the entire nation should be represented in the House of Representatives and that the two houses should possess virtually equal powers.[94] For them, the difference between a federation

---

91   See, e.g., *Convention Debates, Sydney* (1897), 259–60 (Wise).

92   For this set of general attitudes, see, eg, *Official Record of the Proceedings and Debates of the Australasian Federation Conference, Melbourne* (Melbourne: Government Printer, 1890), 8 (Griffith); *Convention Debates, Adelaide* (1897), 105–110 (Wise), 303 (Clarke), 650 (Deakin), 656 (Quick), 665 (Higgins, responding to Barton); *Convention Debates, Sydney* (1897), 340 (Barton).

93   James Bryce, *The American Commonwealth* (2nd ed., London: Macmillan, 1889), Vol. I, 12–15, 332.

94   See, e.g., Richard Baker, *Federation* (Adelaide: Scrymgour and Sons, 1897), 3–5, 10, 19; *Convention Debates, Adelaide* (1897), 443–4 (Barton); *Convention Debates, Sydney* (1897), 340, 620, 622–3 (Barton). For a detailed account, see Aroney, *Constitution of a Federal Commonwealth*, chs 7–8.

and a confederation lay in the nature and scope of the centralised institutions of government in each system. Virtually all of the framers wished to create a 'federal government' in what they understood to be the fullest sense of the word.[95] Citing Bluntschli and Freeman on this point, highly influential figures such as Samuel Griffith and Richard Baker considered that this was one in which the central organs of government, though in part composed of representatives of the constituent states, would have independent powers of legislation, administration and adjudication directly applied to the population without needing to rely on the states to enforce federal law and policy.[96] However, because they did not understand the federation to be grounded upon the people of the nation as a whole, the Australians agreed to a amendment procedure in which a majority of voters in the nation as well as a majority of voters in a majority of States would have to agree to any proposed constitutional alteration. Inspired by the American and Swiss examples, they even provided that the boundaries of each State, as well as its representation within the federal parliament, could not be altered without the consent of the people of that State.[97]

In these respects, fundamental to the Constitution, the vast majority of the Australians settled upon the creation of a 'federal commonwealth' very much in the image in which Bluntschli and Freeman had envisaged it. The only major sticking point concerned the composition of the executive government and, in particular, the precise shape that would be given to the system of parliamentary responsible government provided for in the Constitution. Parliamentary responsible government very substantially depends on the powers over financial bills formally possessed by the parliament, as the control over government finance is the constitutional foundation of parliamentary control over the executive. In this respect, since a majority of the framers expressed the desire to see a system of responsible government develop at a federal level, they decided, after long debate, to give the House of Representatives sole control over the initiation and amendment of financial bills – that is, control over the formation of government policies and priorities as reflected in the annual budget. But they deliberately reserved to the Senate the power to refuse to pass financial bills,

---

95   See Aroney, *Constitution of a Federal Commonwealth*, 116–7, 146–8, 193–4.

96   See, e.g., Richard Baker, *A Manual of Reference to Authorities for the use of the Members of the National Australasian Convention* (Adelaide: E.A. Petherick and Co, 1891), 31; *Conference Debates, Melbourne* (1890), 8–9 (Griffith); Samuel Griffith, *Notes on Australian Federation: Its Nature and Probable Effects* (Brisbane: Government Printer, 1896), 5; Samuel Griffith, *Australian Federation and the Draft Commonwealth Bill: A Paper Read before the Members of the Queensland Federation League* (Brisbane: Government Printer, 1899), 8.

97   See, e.g., *Convention Debates, Sydney* (1891), 884–5 (Gillies), 893–4 (Cockburn, Griffith); *Convention Debates, Melbourne* (1898), 772 (Barton).

meaning the power to bring a government to its knees – a power which it in fact exercised, in controversial circumstances, in 1975.[98]

In these ways, the framers of the Australian Constitution devised a federal structure of government reflecting a theory of the federal-state that can ultimately be traced to the views of Bluntschli and Freeman – as distinct from those of Jellinek and Burgess. On the Bluntschli-Freeman theory, both confederations and federations come into being through processes which resemble an agreement between the peoples of independent states. The difference between a *Staatenbund* and a *Bundesstaat* lies not in the location of sovereignty, but only in the precise scope of the executive and legislative powers conferred upon the federal organs of government. Relying upon and advocating such a conception of a genuinely 'federal government', the framers of the Australian Constitution drafted a document which provided for 'commonwealth of commonwealths', conceived especially in terms of its formative processes, representative institutions, configurations of power and amendment procedures. The Commonwealth of Australia accordingly emerged as a federation, not in the sense of Jellinek's *Bundesstaat* or Burgess's nationalist conception of the federal-state, but as a *Bundesstaat* in Bluntschli's sense, a kind of *Bund* or covenant between states. Bluntschli's conception was in this respect more flexible and more applicable to the circumstances of the Australian colonies, as well as more in tune with the ambitions and convictions of a majority of the Australian framers. While the divergent aspirations for Australian federalism exemplified by Isaacs and Higgins on one hand and Griffith and Baker on the other would probably still have existed without the Germans and their British and American interpreters, German *Staatslehre* contributed an additional rigour to the underlying conceptions of federalism that divided the two groups. For the Australian framers as a whole, the formation of the federation was an act of both idealistic political imagining and pragmatic political negotiation, and German state-theory contributed significantly to the conceptual world in which this occurred.

---

98   A prospect which Higgins acknowledged, and lamented. See Higgins, *Essays and Addresses*, 16–7.

Saskia Hufnagel

The Impact of the German Human Dignity Principle on the Right to Life and the Right not to be Subject to Torture

I. Introduction

The core question addressed within this paper is whether the right to human dignity – as established in Article 1 of the *Basic Law for the Federal Republic of Germany* (Basic Law)[1] – should exist as an 'absolute' human right, or if 'absolute' human rights in general, and the principle of human dignity in particular, should be limited in circumstances where such a limitation could facilitate the saving of lives of innocent persons. It will further be assessed whether the right to human dignity is a distinctive feature of German law or whether similar protection of human dignity is provided in common law systems, such as the United Kingdom (UK) and Australia. In particular the impact of the German human dignity principle on criminal law defences will be addressed focusing on justifications relating to infringements of the right to life and the right not to be subject to 'torture or cruel, inhuman or degrading treatment or punishment'[2]. Case studies considered herein are the 'shooting down of a hijacked aircraft' scenario, as discussed by the German Constitutional Court (*Bundesverfassungsgericht*) in 2006[3], and the 'ticking bomb' scenario. Using these two scenarios the impact of the human dignity principle on criminal law concepts, such as self-defence and necessity will be addressed. A comparison between German and Australian law will be employed to show the different possibilities of the protection of human rights in systems that, respectively, have and do not have an express principle of human dignity embedded in their constitutions. This comparison will also be employed to clarify the status of human dignity in the German context.

In light of the legal responses to terrorism since the attacks of 9/11, reasonable limits to human rights principles have to be re-examined, in particular

---

1   *Deutsches Grundgesetz* (1949); from here on 'Basic Law' or 'GG'.
2   See Article 7 International Covenant on Civil and Political Rights (ICCPR).
3   German Constitutional Court Decision BVerfG, 1 BvR 357/05 of 15/02/2006.

in relation to the right to life[4], human dignity[5] and the right not to be subject to torture[6] . The issue typically raised in this context is the balancing of the above mentioned human rights against security concerns.[7] It is generally possible and necessary to balance human rights principles, even the right to life[8], in cases where the public good is threatened. However, a problem arises when considering so called 'absolute' rights that cannot be limited. The right to human dignity could be regarded as one of the few 'absolute' human rights, at least in the German context. The importance of Article 1 Section 1 of the Basic Law, which proclaims that '*Human dignity is inviolable*', is displayed in the hierarchy of rights within the statute (first Article of the Basic Law) and has produced remarkable, brave and some might even say impracticable decisions. The point of view taken on these decisions – whether we classify them as impracticable or remarkable – often depends on which legal system and culture we have been raised in. Germany's history, in particular the influence of human rights developments after the 2nd World War, plays a major role in understanding the upholding of the human dignity principle in its current form. From the German perspective, the absolute right to human dignity and the consequential restriction of state power in relation to human rights infringements is a necessity with a view to the horrors of the Holocaust.

---

4   See Art 3 of the *Universal Declaration of Human Rights* (UDHR); Art 6(1) of the *International Covenant on Civil and* Political Rights (ICCPR); Art 2(1) of the European Convention on Human Rights (ECHR).

5   See the Preamle of the *Universal Declaration of Human Rights* (UDHR); Preamble of the *International Covenant on Civil and* Political Rights (ICCPR); Preamble of the European Convention on Human Rights (ECHR) and in particular Article 1 German Basic Law (Grundgesetzt) 1949.

6   Australia and Germany are signatories to the four Geneva Conventions of 1949, and their two additional protocols of 1977. Australia ratified the *Convention Against Torture* in 1989.

7   Lynch A, MacDonald E and Williams G (eds), *Law and Liberty in the War on Terror* (Federation Press, 2007) pp 137–164, "Human Rights and Terrorism: Is a Trade-Off Necessary"; Williams G, "Balancing National Security and Human Rights: Assessing the Legal Response of Common Law Nations to the Threat of Terrorism" (2006) 8(1) *Journal of Comparative Policy Analysis* 43; For a critique of balancing approaches, see Bronitt S, "Constitutional Rhetoric v Criminal Justice Realities: Unbalanced Responses to Terrorism?" (2003) 14 PLR 70; Zedner L, "Securing Liberty in the Face of Terror: Reflections from Criminal Justice" (2005) 32(4) *Journal of Law and Society* 507.

8   Gearty C, *Principles of Human Rights Adjudication* (Oxford University Press, 2004) pp 9–10; Security Legislation Review Committee (SLRC), *Report of the Security Legislation Review Committee* (2006) p 39.

The Kantian definition, that 'no specific human being shall be made an object, the mere means, a mere replaceable entity of state action'[9] has been accepted by the German courts since the 1950's and has so far resisted attempts of scholars and politicians to limit it. This resulted in the famous German Constitutional Court decision of 2006[10] where the court ruled that a hijacked plane threatening to crash into a building could not be shot down because (amongst other reasons) the human dignity of the innocent people on the plane could not be weighed up against the human dignity of the people in the building the plane is about to crash into. In other words, the people on the plane could not be made the means to the states' end to save the people in the building.

Countries that have not experienced human rights violations to the same extend as Germany, such as the UK and Australia, have less or no restrictions built into their constitutions to safeguard human dignity. From an Australian perspective, that the state cannot exercise control over human beings in cases where the life of another group of human beings is threatened might seem shocking and paradoxical. Why should more people die in the name of human dignity? In Australia, the law (Part IIIAAA of the Defence Act[11]) allowing the state to shoot down a hijacked plane – not only where human lives are directly threatened but even when only critical infrastructure is threatened – did not trigger the public outcry leading to judicial review as it did in Germany. It actually did not trigger much public response at all. This may be partially explained by the existence of human rights in a constitution leading to a greater culture of claiming those rights. Unlike Germany, Australia has no human rights catalogue included in its constitution, nor an independent federal human rights act. There is, therefore, no possibility to directly claim human rights infringements before a court. Furthermore, the possibility of a preliminary test of the legality of a law, the 'abstract assessment of rules' (*Abstrakte Normenkontrolle*), as prescribed in § 76 of the Federal Law for the German Constitutional Court (*Bundesverfassungsgerichtsgesetz*) does not exist in Australian law. A newly introduced law, as for example Part IIIAAA of the *Defence Act* allowing hijacked planes to be shot down, could not at the time of its enactment (and before its coming into force as allowed under Art. 82 Section 1 Sentence 1 Basic Law) be tested by the High Court upon the request of potentially affected citizens. Due to the lack of this possibility, and given that human rights in

---

9   See G. Dürig, 'Der Grundrechtssatz von der Menschenwürde' (1956) 81 *Archiv des öffent-lichen Rechts* 117 at 127.

10   German Constitutional Court Decision of 1 BvR 357/05 (2006).

11   *Defence Legislation Amendment (Aid to Civilian Authorities) Bill* 2006 (Cth), Revised Explanatory Memorandum.

Australia are only protected within statutes or else it is left to the judiciary, an active culture of complaint to the courts in relation to human rights has not developed. Further explanation for the difference in cultures might be provided by the considerable difference in costs involved in legal disputes in both entities. In Australia these costs are generally much higher than in Germany due to the more restrictive distribution of means through the legal aid system. It can therefore be concluded that apart from the existence of an 'absolute' human dignity principle, other factors influence the strong upholding of human rights by the German Constitutional Court, including the easy access to the court provided by procedural rules (§ 76 of the Federal Law for the German Constitutional Court (*Bundesverfassungsgerichtsgesetz*)) before and after the entering into force of a rule and advantageous legal aid provisions, as well as human rights being directly enforceable by individuals through their inclusion in the German Basic Law. When assessing whether the human dignity principle is in fact the distinguishing line between human rights protections in the German and common law systems, this needs to be taken into account.

One of the most prominent effects of the human dignity principle under German constitutional law is its impact on the balancing of the right to life in cases where, like in the 'hijacked plane' scenario, the right to life of one group of people needs to be weighed up against the right to life of another group of people. Unlike the right to human dignity, the right to life is generally not absolute[12]. The existence of legal concepts such as self-defence and necessity indicates that the right to life can be limited, for example in cases where a person acts illegally. In the 'hijacked plane' scenario, the court argued that the human dignity of the innocent people on the plane could not be balanced against the human dignity of the people on the ground, while the concept of self-defence would allow a plane occupied only by terrorists to be shot down.[13] This is similar in the 'ticking bomb' scenario, but here the application of the principle goes even further as the human dignity of the person acting illegally is also protected to the extent that it cannot be weighed up against the human dignity of his victim. In cases like the 'hijacked plane' (if civilians were on board) or 'ticking bomb' scenarios, the state representatives responsible for 'saving lives' by killing or torturing another person(s) would therefore face a conviction for manslaughter[14] or assault.

---

12   Gearty C, *Principles of Human Rights Adjudication* (Oxford University Press, 2004) pp 9–10; Security Legislation Review Committee (SLRC), *Report of the Security Legislation Review Committee* (2006) p 39.

13   German Constitutional Court Decision of 1 BvR 357/05 (2006).

14   In Germany this would be classified as manslaughter, while in a common law systems it would be classified as murder.

However, in Germany, like in any legal system, a disparity between the 'law in the books' and the 'law in action' can be observed. Even though the German Constitutional Court does not allow a hijacked plane occupied also by civilians to be shot down by the domestic armed forces and although German police are not allowed to torture a terrorist, the practice recognises that the absolute application of the human dignity principle would lead to overly harsh results. Although there is no German criminal law defence that protects a state representative taking on the responsibility of weighing up the confronting legal interests in those extreme scenarios, the blow of the principle can and has been softened in practice by applying the lowest possible sentences like for example in the *Daschner* case.[15]

It follows that the right to human dignity is to some extent limited even in the German context. Rather than at the stage where the guilt of a person is determined, the special circumstances that the accused had to weigh up confronting legal interests are taken into account at the sentencing phase. It could therefore be claimed that the value of human dignity under German law is reduced despite Germany's experience in history and is going down the 'slippery slope' again. As this statement would probably go too far, considering the strong influence of Constitutional Court decisions to the contrary, it should only be concluded that the 'absoluteness' of the human dignity principle under German law is to some extent diminished in practice.

This chapter will first give an overview of the applicable international and domestic laws protecting human rights in relation to the 'hijacked aircraft' and 'ticking bomb' scenarios. The right to human dignity will be discussed and it will be argued that it is protected in most systems, despite not having the prominent status it has been given in the German Basic Law. The chapter will then discuss self-defence and necessity defences in German law that could apply in relation to state representatives or private persons carrying out the use of lethal force or the act of torture and whether these defences could represent limits to the principle of human dignity.

The advantages and disadvantages of having the human dignity principle embedded in a constitution will be considered in the last part of the chapter. Although a definite answer to the question whether the principle of human dignity is a curse or a blessing cannot be given, the overall conclusion will support the latter as it offers a slightly broader protection of human rights than other systems.

---

15 See in more detail below – Decision of the Landgericht Frankfurt am Main decision Az. 5/27 Kla – 7570 Js 03814/03 (2004).

II. The Right to Life and the Right not to be Subject to Torture in an International and Domestic Context

Human rights lawyers typically disclaim any hierarchy of rights.[16] That said, some international human rights are absolute in the sense that these rights are non-derogable and are not subject to any exceptions (for example the right not to be subject to torture).[17] A distinctive German contribution to human rights law is the express articulation in the Basic Law that the right to human dignity should be regarded as paramount. Its primacy is reflected in its foundational place in the scheme of rights set out in the Basic Law: Article 1 Section 1 Basic Law. The right to human dignity is not expressly included in the Universal Declaration of Human Rights, ECHR and ICCPR[18], and there is no equivalent protection in the Australian Federal[19] or State Constitutions, or even in the recently enacted human rights legislation in the Australian Capital Territory or Victoria (despite being mentioned in their respective preambles).[20] Only few other countries have included the right to human dignity in their constitution, for example South Africa.[21]

The international laws applicable to torture are the Four Geneva Conventions and their Protocols and the Convention against Torture. The prohibition against torture is considered to be absolute. In terms of international law it is a peremptory norm or jus cogens[22], which distinguishes it from the right to life and the right to human dignity that have not required such a standard in international

---

16 See for example Theo von Boven, 'Distinguishing Criteria of Human Rights' in H J Steiner and P Alston, 'International Human Rights in Context – Law, Politics, Morals' (2nd ed, Oxford University Press, 2000) 154–157.

17 Article 2(2) *United Nations Convention Against Torture*, opened for signature 10 December 1984, G.A.Res 39/46 (entered into force 26 June 1987).

18 However, these human rights instruments are founded on the idea of human dignity, although not in the sense of Article 1 Basic Law. See in relation to international human rights instruments and human dignity C McCrudden, 'Human Dignity and Judicial Interpretation of Human Rights' *European Journal of International Law*, Vol. 19 No. 4 (2008), pp. 654–724.

19 See Commonwealth of Australia Constitution Act 1901 at http://www.aph.gov.au/SEnate/general/constitution/index.htm.

20 *Human Rights Act 2004* (ACT), A2004–5, Republication No 3, Effective: 2 January 2007, Republication date: 2 January 2007, Last amendment made by A2006–3 and *Charter of Human Rights and Responsibilities Act 2006* (Vic) (the charter), which was passed by Parliament in July 2006.

21 See Section 10 of the Constitution of the Republic of South Africa, 1996, Bill of Rights.

22 See for example Erika de Wet, 'The Prohibition of Torture as an International Norm of Jus Cogens and its Implications for National and Customary Law' *European Journal of International Law* 2004 15(1) pp. 97–121.

law. However, the right to life is protected in several international human rights instruments, like the Universal Declaration on Human Rights, the International Covenant on Civil and Political Rights (ICCPR) and the European Convention of Human Rights, and it is a right that requires special care when being balanced. The key principle in relation to weighing up the right to life when it comes to the use of lethal force is *proportionality*. Although states are being granted a 'margin of appreciation' in what is a necessary and proportionate response in the 'war on terror' states cannot exercise their discretion arbitrarily.[23]

In Germany, the protection of both, the right to life and the right not to be subject to torture, are cemented into the Basic Law. The right to life is protected by Article 2, Section 2, Sentence 1 Basic Law: 'Every person has the right to life and physical integrity'. In some cases where the right to life is balanced against an equal right, the prohibition of Article 1 Basic Law, the human dignity principle, will step in. In relation to torture Article 1 Basic Law, Article 2, Section 2, Sentence 1, Part 2 Basic Law: right to physical integrity, and Article 14 Basic Law: prohibition of coercive interrogation methods, protect from infringements. Of course these rights are also reflected in criminal laws and other statutes, like the right not to be subject to torture in §136a Criminal Procedural Code (StPO[24]), which prohibits the admissibility of evidence that has been gathered through the use of coercive interrogation methods. What needs to be emphasised in relation to both rights is that apart from their protection through specific provisions in the Basic Law, they are under certain circumstances also protected through Article 1 Sentence 1 Basic Law, the right to human dignity.

Should the state interfere with any of the before-mentioned rights, the state representatives executing the breach have to be held responsible under criminal law. In relation to the 'hijacked plane' scenario, no case has yet occurred that could be examined. However, the 'ticking bomb' scenario can be compared to the German *Daschner* case[25] in which police threatened the abductor of a boy with physical violence if he did not reveal the whereabouts of the boy. The responsible police officers were accordingly charged with assault and convicted. That the officers in the *Daschner* case were charged might already seem unlikely from the point of view of a common law system and the particularities of the German system are again prominent as state action is much more limited than in

---

23   Michaelsen C, "International Human Rights on Trial – The United Kingdom's and Australia's Legal Response to 9/11" (2003) 25(3) Sydney Law Review 275.

24   Deutsche Strafprozessordnung (German Criminal Procedural Law).

25   Decision of the Landgericht Frankfurt am Main decision Az. 5/27 Kla – 7570 Js 03814/03 (2004).

other systems. The scope for police and prosecutorial discretion differs between civil and common law systems and even between the different civil law systems. Unlike the executive authorities in most other countries, police and prosecution in Germany have to adhere to the principle of legality.[26] This means that the decision to investigate and prosecute is subject to very limited discretion and these limits are explicitly dictated by the law (the opposite to the principle of opportunity).[27] The prosecution needs to bring the charge if there are sufficient grounds to suspect that the person has committed an offence. Discretion is only allowed in relation to some petty offences (§ 153 StPO). In a scenario like the *Daschner* case[28] it is less likely that officials in a common law system, where discretion is the more prominent principle, would prosecute the police officers who threatened the abductor. Police and prosecution in a common law system could already at an early stage of the investigation take into account that the police officers were acting under particular pressure and had to weigh up competing legal interests and could therefore abstain from prosecution. It follows that in the German system not only the human dignity principle affords greater protection of the individual who suffers a breach of his human rights, but also criminal procedural rules like the principle of legality.

However, human rights protection should not generally be considered greater in the German than in other systems. In Australia the right to life is protected by common law principles and various federal and state laws. Examples for Australian federal laws affording protection from torture in the criminal justice system are s 23Q Crimes Act 1914 (Cth), s 84(1) Evidence Act 1995 (Cth), s 138 Evidence Act 1995 (Cth). This is very similar to the prohibition of torture as interrogation method and the inadmissibility of evidence gathered by means of coercive interrogation methods in the German system. State laws such as the ACT and Victoria Human Rights Acts further protect the right to life and the right not to be subject to torture at the state level, but they are the only human rights instruments (only two out of eight states and territories have enacted legislation) applying in Australia. One of the first decisions affording paramount protection to the right to life in the common law context is *R v Dudley and Stephens* (1884) 14 QBD 273. In this case, four sailors were shipwrecked on the high seas, and following the old maritime custom of cannibalism, decided to kill one of their number – the cabin boy – in order to avoid starvation. Two of the

---

26   See for example Julia Fionda *Public Prosecutors and Discretion: A Comparative Study* (1995), Oxford University Press, p. 167.

27   See Kühne Hans-Heiner, 'Chapter 5 – Germany' in *Criminal Procedure Systems in the European Community* Van den Wyngaert C (ed), Butterworths 1993, p. 146.

28   Decision of the Landgericht Frankfurt am Main decision Az. 5/27 Kla – 7570 Js 03814/03 (2004).

survivors were charged with murder. The Court of Queen's Bench held that necessity could not be pleaded as a defence to homicide. Lord Coleridge CJ emphasised the moral and practical difficulties in weighing competing interests involved if the defence was recognised:

> Who is to be the judge of this sort of necessity? By what measure is the comparative value of lives to be measured? Is it to be strength, or intellect, or what? It is plain that the principle leaves to him who is to profit by it to determine the necessity which will justify him in deliberately taking another's life to save his own.

In essence, the decision determines that life cannot be weighed up against life, even in situations where the life of another person can be saved. Dudley and Stephens were both convicted and sentenced to death. However, the circumstances of the killing were taken into account in the sentencing decision and the penalty of the two survivors was later commuted to six months imprisonment.[29]

As this decision stresses the importance of the right to life in the common law context and establishes a principle similar to human dignity in the German context, it might be seen to contradict the Australian legislation in relation to shooting down hijacked aircraft. Part IIIAAA of the Australian *Defence Act* allowing hijacked aircraft to be shot down in cases where human life on the ground and critical infrastructure are threatened could be just as illegal as § 14 Section 3 of the German *Aviation Security Act* if the *Dudley and Stephens* principle was still applicable. To a certain extent *Dudley and Stephens* protects human dignity similarly to Article 1 of the German Basic Law. It prescribes that a life cannot be taken to save another and that the state protects individuals from such breaches of the right to life. The judgement remains silent however on the relationship between the individual and the state in cases where competing legal interests have to be weighed up. Dudley and Stephens killed the cabin boy to ensure their own survival. This was considered to be a selfish act, disrespectful of another person's human dignity and worthy of punishment. If the state as an outsider would weigh up life against life, could this be considered less morally repugnant? The answer to this question has not been finally decided, but that a law like Part IIIAAA *Defence Act* remains unchallenged suggests that the state has more possibilities to interfere with the right to life of individuals than the individuals themselves. This is contradictory to the German human dignity principle, which clearly restricts state action in relation to the weighing up life against life.

It can be concluded that the principles protecting life and the right not to be subject to torture exist to a similar extent in the civil and common law systems.

---

29   *R v Dudley and Stephens* (1884) 14 QBD 273 at 287–288.

Although the human dignity principle does not expressly apply in common law systems, there are common law principles, international law provisions, statutes and case law implicitly protecting human dignity. However, the protection does not go as far as afforded in the German system by the human dignity and legality principles.

III. Application of Defences: Self-Defence and Necessity

The differences between the German and common law approaches to the right to life and the right not to be subject to torture can be further explored by examining the two relevant cases in the German jurisprudence. The first is the 2006 'shooting down hijacked aircraft'[30] decision of the German Constitutional Court and the second is the Frankfurt district court decision on the right not to be subject to torture[31] or the 'ticking bomb' scenario come true.

1. Shooting down Hijacked Aircraft

In 2006 a new section – Section 3 – was inserted into § 14 of the *Luftsicherheitsgesetz* (German Aviation Security Act), providing that a hijacked plane could be shot down by the German military on German territory if it threatened to become a danger to human life on the ground. Section 3 reads as follows:

'The direct use of force with a military weapon is only allowed if it can be expected under the special circumstances that the aircraft is supposed to be used to destroy the lives of human beings and if military force is the only means to prevent that imminent danger.'

The German Constitutional Court declared this section void.[32] Mainly, the decision was based on issues of competence under the Basic law. It was determined that the order to shoot the plane down could not be given by the Defence Minister after consultation with the Minister of the Interior as was determined in § 13 Aviation Security Act as this was contrary to Article 35 Section 3 Sentence 1 Basic Law. Also, competences of the Federal State and the Länder were determined to be a major barrier to the legality of Section 3 as the

---

30   German Constitutional Court Decision BVerfG, 1 BvR 357/05 of 15/02/2006.
31   Decision of the Landgericht Frankfurt am Main decision Az. 5/27 Kla – 7570 Js 03814/03 (2004).
32   German Constitutional Court Decision BVerfG, 1 BvR 357/05 of 15/02/2006, at 119–153.

military (federal competence) could under no circumstances be legally employed in state/Länder territory, other than to the extent the police could be employed (Article 35 Section 2 Sentence 2 Basic Law). The Constitutional Court also discussed, but did not predominantly base its decision on, the limits of the Article 1 (Right to Human Dignity) and Article 2 (Right to Life) of the German Basic Law. It did not base the judgement on these human rights provisions as the deficiencies in relation to competences had been sufficient to declare Section 3 void, but considered it crucial to make a statement in relation to human dignity in its decision. The Court determined that Article 2 Basic Law was subject to limitations and hence life could, under certain circumstances, be balanced against life. Article 1 Section 1 Basic Law however was considered to be 'absolute' and the right to human dignity was prohibited from being balanced. The Court went on to argue that where human dignity had to be balanced, the state had to refrain from action applying the Kantian definition of human dignity 'nobody shall be made the means to the state's ends'.[33] This reasoning was employed only in relation to the scenario in which the plane was hijacked by terrorists, but also occupied by civilians. The human dignity in question was that of the civilians and could not be balanced against the human dignity of the people on the ground. However, the court also discussed the scenario in which the plane is occupied only by terrorists. In those cases it determined that there can be a weighing up of life against life. As the terrorists represent a direct threat, their right to life can be restricted by the principles of necessity and self-defence, and the plane can therefore be shot down. The terrorist's right to life and human dignity, which has to be weighed up against the right to life and human dignity of the people in the building has therefore to be considered less worthy of protection in terms of proportionality.[34] If the court had applied the principle strictly in line with the Kantian definition it should also have considered the human dignity of the terrorists and not allowed the plane to be shot down. The Kantian definition strictly applies in the ticking bomb scenario. A terrorist would not be allowed to be tortured due to his human dignity as it

---

33   Another take on the subject is to focus on the Kantian definition and deny the fact that the passengers on the plane were *used to* stop the plane from killing more people. If the passengers were simply seen as 'collateral damage' the Kantian definition would not be fulfilled. See in this context Moller K, "On Treating Persons as Ends: The German Aviation Security Act, Human Dignity, and the German Federal Constitutional Court" (2006) Public Law 457.

34   German Constitutional Court Decision BVerfG, 1 BvR 357/05 of 15/02/2006, at 118, 122.

cannot be weighed up against the human dignity of the victim(s).[35] However, the reasoning the court employed in relation to the Aviation Security Act and the scenario where only terrorists are on board of the plane, is closely related to criminal law defences of necessity and self-defence under German criminal law. If there is a direct threat to a person, this person or a third party may take all reasonable and proportionate measures to avert this threat (§§ 32, 34 and 35 of the German Penal Code (StGB)). It follows that the right to human dignity can under certain circumstances be limited when a person acts illegally. This is an indication that the right to human dignity even under German law is not absolute and that there are ways to limit the right to human dignity.

It has to be noted, that the right to human dignity according to the Kantian definition is only limiting the right of the *state* to use a human being as a means to its ends. As we will discuss later, an *individual* not representing the state might under certain circumstances be allowed to shoot the plane down even if it was also occupied by civilians, provided a relative or a person close to this individual was exposed to the immediate danger of being killed on the ground. Obviously, this is an unlikely scenario, but for the purpose of the argument it shows how restricted 'state' action in Germany is. Going back to *Dudley and Stephens*, the common law principle prohibits the individual to interfere with another person's human dignity by weighing up life against life, however, the same principle does not seem to apply to the state while in Germany the principle applies to the state, but not the individual.

It can be concluded that the German criminal law provisions and the Basic Law distinguish between state action and the actions of civilians. Article 1 Section 1 of the Basic Law prohibits all state action that would require human dignity to be balanced. The 'excusing necessity' defence[36] limits necessity to the protection of 'relatives and close persons'. The wording of this defence makes it very unlikely that a state representative ordering the shooting down of a plane or the torture of a suspect can benefit from it. It follows that the human dignity principle is reflected in the criminal code necessity defences.

Looking more closely at the criminal law defences that can apply in the 'hijacked aircraft' and 'ticking bomb' scenarios, the three major provisions are §§ 32, 34 and 35 of the German Penal Code (StGB). The self-defence provision is § 32 StGB and states that:

---

35   See in relation to this criticism Moller K, "On Treating Persons as Ends: The German Aviation Security Act, Human Dignity, and the German Federal Constitutional Court" (2006) Public Law 457.

36   See § 35 of the German Penal Code (Strafgesetzbuch or StGB) Entschuldigender Notstand (excusing necessity).

(1) Whoever commits an act in self-defence does not act unlawfully.

(2) Necessary defence is the defence which is required to avert an imminent unlawful attack from oneself or another.

Shooting down a hijacked aircraft cannot be justified under self-defence. For self-defence to apply, the defence has to be necessary. It is only necessary if it is required to avert an imminent and unlawful attack. As the civilians on the plane are not carrying out an unlawful attack, the act of self-defence is not necessary and cannot be justified under § 32 StGB. A state representative could only be justified under the provision if the plane had been occupied by terrorists only. In this scenario the state representative would have the duty to provide for the defence of 'oneself or another'. It therefore limits the principle of human dignity for the terrorists, but not the civilians and is in line with the decision of the Constitutional Court.

§ 34 StGB is called the 'justifying necessity' provision and states that:

Whoever commits an act in order to avert an imminent and not otherwise avoidable danger to the life, limb, liberty, honour, property or other legally protected interest directed against himself or another does not act unlawfully if, taking into consideration all the conflicting interests, in particular the legal ones, and the degree of danger involved, the interest protected by him significantly outweighs the interest which he harms. This rule applies only if the act is a proportionate means to avert the danger.

If it applies, all actus reus and mens rea elements of the offence will be justified and thereby eliminated. The act will not be classified as 'illegal'. In contrast to 'justifying necessity' under § 34 StGB, § 35 StGB is the so-called 'excusing necessity' provision that states:

(1) Whoever, faced with an imminent danger to life, limb or freedom which cannot otherwise be averted, commits an unlawful act to avert the danger from himself, a relative or person close to him, acts without guilt. This shall not apply if the perpetrator could be expected under the circumstances, in particular in cases where he himself has caused the danger or where he was in a special legal relationship with the victim, to accept the danger without resistance. The punishment may be mitigated pursuant to § 49(1), if the perpetrator was not required to assume the risk with respect to a special legal relationship.

(2) If upon commission of the act the perpetrator mistakenly assumed that circumstances existed which would excuse him under subs (1), he will only be punished, if he could have avoided the mistake. The punishment may be mitigated pursuant to § 49(1).

This means the actus reus and mens rea elements are fulfilled and the act is considered 'illegal', but guilt cannot be determined. Excusing necessity is therefore considered to be a 'weaker' type of defence than justifying necessity.

Looking at both provisions in comparison – justifying and excusing necessity – § 34 StGB does not provide that the attack has to be illegal and could therefore justify the shooting down of the plane even if civilians were on board. However, § 34 StGB is ruled by the principle of proportionality. The defendant has to 'take into account all the conflicting interests, in particular the legal ones, and the degree of danger involved'. Also, the interest protected by the defendant has to significantly outweigh the interest which he harms. That the principle of proportionality applies has the consequence that the state has to weigh up all rights involved, including human dignity, and can therefore not shoot the plane down. This principle also makes it quite unlikely for a private person to shoot the plane down, as the requirements of proportionality are very strict and would not justify a balancing of lives.

The principle of proportionality is however not a requirement under § 35 StGB. Even if it were not proportionate, the shooting down of a plane occupied by civilians could be justified if a relative or close person to the defendant was inside the building the plane is threatening to crash into. It therefore does not give a defence to the state to shoot a plane down that is occupied by civilians, but could under certain circumstances justify a civilian doing so (but it is unlikely that he or she would have the means to do so).

Civilians could further be justified by mistakenly believing that a defence under criminal law exists.[37] This defence will not apply to the state representative shooting the plane down or ordering the plane to be shot down as it is very unlikely that the state would mistakenly believe it was justified when shooting the plane down, seeing that this issue has been in public debate in Germany since 2005.

It follows that the German criminal law provisions relating to defences are reflecting the principle of human dignity and do not give any justification or excuse to a state representative in the hijacked aircraft scenario. State action is therefore severely limited by the principle of human dignity.

The German approach displayed in the decision on the Aviation Security Act is different to other countries' approaches in relation to this scenario. The Polish Constitutional Tribunal had to consider the validity of a law allowing hijacked planes to be shot down and decided on 30th September 2008 that Article 122a of the Polish Airspace Law Act 2002 was unconstitutional.[38] The Court reasoned that the law lacked due precision and clarity in describing the circumstances as to when a plane could be shot down and therefore breached the principle of proportionality. Article 122a of the *Polish Airspace Law Act* 2002 determined that a plane could be shot down if it was in the interest of security of the state and the plane was to be used for unlawful aims. The court considered this

---

37   The so called, very debated 'Erlaubnistatbestandsirrtum' (ETBI).
38   Trybunat Konstytucyjny, judgement of 30.09.2008, Sygn.K44/07.

wording too vague to justify the breach of basic human rights by the state. Although the decision has the same effect as the German one (planes are not to be shot down) the Polish decision does not argue with the principle of human dignity or a similar constitutional principle. Should Article 122a of the *Polish Airspace Law Act* 2002 be amended and define precisely under which circumstances the plane can be shot down (if this is at all possible), the law might be considered constitutional and the shooting down of hijacked aircraft could be allowed. Despite coming to similar outcomes, the German decision is distinct due to the consideration of the human dignity principle.

In Australia Part IIIAAA of the Defence Act allows the shooting down of hijacked aircraft and the state representatives involved in shooting the plane down are protected from criminal prosecution as the Defence Act provides for an 'emergency' defence. This is not directly contradicting *Dudley and Stephens*, as this decision only determined that an *individual* cannot weigh up numbers when it comes to the right to life. The involvement of the state in balancing the right to life was not decided upon. However, one could claim that the decision should have an impact on state behaviour as well. Following this line of argument, even without the presence of the right to human dignity or the right to life embedded in the Australian constitution, in principle the state would not be allowed to shoot down a hijacked aircraft in Australia and the state representative responsible would not be justified by a defence as he or she, just like any civilian, would not be allowed to balance life against life. However, the principle is contradicted by domestic law as the Defence Act allows for the shooting down of a hijacked aircraft and provides for a special defence under the Act. As the legality of Part IIIAAA of the Defence Act has so far not been tested by the Courts, it remains to be seen whether the principle established in *Dudley and Stephens* would apply.

A similar approach to the Australian 'emergency' defence was considered in Germany. In 2007, the former German Minister of Defence (Franz Josef Jung) publicly stated that a hijacked plane would be shot down notwithstanding the court's ruling and that state action would be justified under the legal construct of 'suprastatutory state of emergency'. The ministerial statement provoked protest among the German Airforce Pilot Association, which put forward a statement that they would not follow his orders in a similar scenario.[39]

The concept of 'suprastatutory state of emergency' had initially been introduced by the German Imperial Court in 1927 to provide a legal basis for

---

39 Hefty GP, "Uebergesetzlicher Notstand – Jenseits von Gesetz undVerfassung", *Frankfurter Allgemeine Zeitung NET* (19 November 2007); See the arguments of the pilot associations commenting on the Aviation Security Act in Paragraphs 68 and 69 of the BVerfG judgment.

abortion in cases where the pregnancy or birth of the child would have threatened the life of the mother[40], but had been abolished by the Courts in 1949.[41] The attempt of the former Defence Minister to avoid the paramount principle of human dignity can be seen as a continuation of the German attitude towards terrorism in the 1970s when the untested legal doctrine of 'suprastatutory state of emergency', a concept which has never found recognition in the German Criminal Code, was last invoked. If this legal construct were employed in the 'hijacked plane' scenario, the 'law in the books' and the 'law in action' would diverge significantly, with *Realpolitik* and political pragmatism circumscribing the fundamental right to human dignity and life. It seems contradictory that in cases where the right not to be subject to torture is involved the human dignity principle *cannot* be limited by 'suprastatutory state of emergency', but in the 'shooting down hijacked aircraft' scenario the right to life in conjunction with the right to human dignity may be limited by reliance upon this broad and constitutionally untested doctrine.

In conclusion it can be said that the human dignity principle embedded in the German Basic Law is theoretically, but not practically, the distinguishing line in relation to deciding the 'hijacked aircraft' scenario. Both the German and the common law approach, one focusing on the right to life and the prohibition of weighing up numbers and the other through human dignity respectively, in principle prohibit the shooting down of an aircraft occupied by civilians. However, in common law systems, common law principles like *Dudley and Stephens* can be overruled by statutory law, like for example in the Australian scenario the Defence Act. *Dudley and Stephens* focused on the rights of the individual in relation to necessity, not the right of the state. A principle to limit state action was therefore not established. Also, there is a discrepancy between the 'law in the books' and the 'law in action' in Germany as the former German Defence Minister wants to evoke an emergency defence in the German context. Legal principles and political reality seem to significantly diverge in this case.

2. Ticking Bomb Scenario (Torture)

The outcome of the 'hijacked plane' scenario differs fundamentally from the ticking bomb scenario. In the *Daschner* case[42], a young boy was abducted by his

---

40   These cases would now fall under the exception of justifying necessity.

41   RGSt 61, 242; Similar in this respect to abortion: See *R v Davidson* [1969] VR 667 in S. Bronitt and B. McSherry (2005) 'Principles of Criminal Law' (Second ed.) 328.

42   LG Frankfurt am Main, Urteil vom 20.12.2004, Az. 5/27 Kls – 7570 Js 203814/03 –.

tutor and hidden in a place not known to police. When police identified the offender and took him in for the interview, he refused to reveal the whereabouts of the young boy. Desperate to find out where the boy was being held and to save his life, the commander of the police station (Daschner) where the offender was being interviewed. Daschner, desperate to bring the offender to reveal the boy's whereabouts and save the child, decided to torture the offender. He made inquiries and found a specialized police officer appropriately trained to carry out the procedure who was then flown in by helicopter. Together Daschner and 'the specialist' developed a 'three-step-plan' to coerce the offender into revealing the information. The first step was to threaten the offender with violence. However, after the first step of this procedure was enacted (carried out by 'the specialist'), the boy was found by police. It was later discovered that the boy had been killed before the offender was taken in. Daschner and the specialist officer were charged with assault and convicted. Both were sentenced to relatively high fines[43], but the execution of the sentence was subject to one year parole, a so called 'warning and conditional sentence'.[44] If the offenders did not commit any other offences within a year, they would not have to pay the fines. It has been suggested that the court chose these strikingly mild or virtually no sentences, as it wanted to balance the situation of necessity the officers had found themselves in. The sentences were indeed so low, that the officers were not prohibited from remaining in the police service. Despite this, after the incidence Daschner resigned from his service as a police officer. The low sentences applied indicate that there is a need to limit the overly harsh consequences of the 'absolute' human dignity principle in cases where those responsible have to weigh up competing legal interests.

In the criminal trial, Daschner tried to claim the defence of 'excusing necessity'. The judges refused to accept this defence as it requires the weighing up of rights – proportionality. Not only did the right to physical integrity of the offender have to be weighed up against the right to life of the boy, but – as torture is a breach of the right to human dignity – the human dignity of the offender had to be balanced against the human dignity of the boy. In these scenarios, the District Court confirmed the rulings of the German Constitutional

---

43   Daschner to 90 penalty units each valued at 120 Euros (10.800 Euros) and Ennigkeit 60 penalty units valued at 60 Euros see at LG Frankfurt am Main, Urteil vom 20.12.2004, Az. 5/27 Kls – 7570 Js 203814/03 –; Summary of the case in German language available at http://
www.lg-frankfurt.justiz.hessen.de/irj/servlet/prt/portal/prtroot/slimp.CMReader/HMdJ_15/
LG_LG_Frankfurt_Internet/med/acb/acb50880-b973-6411-aeb6-df144e9169fc,22222222-
2222-2222-2222-222222222222,true.pdf.

44   § 59 StGB (Verwarnung mit Strafvorbehalt).

Court, a balancing of rights was not possible and the state had to refrain from action. Here, the District Court went further than the Constitutional Court in the hijacking decision, as it did not claim that the offender gave up his right to physical integrity by acting illegally. These two decisions can therefore be considered contradictory. However, this outcome might be justified by the higher status of the right not to be subject to torture compared to the right to life.

Through the examination of the two scenarios above it can be concluded that the right to human dignity can be 'more' or 'less' absolute. If combined with an absolute right, a jus cogens protected by international law and carrying with it an inherent right to human dignity, Article 1 Section 1 Basic Law is 'more' absolute. If combined with a non-absolute right, like the right to life, that can be limited under certain circumstances like self-defence and necessity, Article 1 Sentence 1 Basic Law is 'less' absolute and the offender is not protected when acting illegally.

This is also reflected in the criminal law defences applying to it. Self-defence is not applicable in the torture scenario as there is no imminent attack. Justifying necessity is not applicable as the proportionality principle applies and human dignity cannot be balanced. Furthermore, excusing necessity would only protect the mother (close relative) threatening the offender to reveal the boys whereabouts but not the unrelated police officer.

The common law approach, even without taking recourse to the human dignity principle, is similar. Criminal and criminal procedural laws in common law systems generally prohibit the coercion of suspects during interviews. Common law countries are signatory to the four Geneva Conventions of 1949 and their two additional protocols of 1977. There are very limited possibilities to apply criminal law defences in relation to police officers in common law systems in torture cases. However, there are several decisions by higher courts in the United Kingdom that were issued in relation to the Northern Ireland conflict in the 1970's that took a different approach. Within these decisions security force operations against terrorists involving a reasonable degree of temporary hardship during detention and questioning, but not involving the application of force, was not considered to be torture or illegal coercion.[45] Further to this, the US has circumvented the application of criminal procedural laws and fair trial rights by claiming the state of war/emergency. Should Australian courts follow the UK

---

45 See also Neil James 'Torture: What is it, Will it Work and Can it be Justified?' (2007) *Law and Liberty in the War on Terror* (A. Lynch, E. MacDonald and G. Williams ed.), 153–164; There are also more recent House of Lords decisions in relation to extradition which point towards a more lenient attitude towards torture: See *RB et al (Algeria) v Secretary of State for the Home Department* (18/02/2009) [2009] UKHL 10 and *Secretary of State for the Home Department v OO (Jordan)* SC/51/2006.

example, the application of torture practices cannot be excluded. The threshold in common law countries therefore appears to be lower than in the German context. Also, unlike Germany, police and prosecution do not have to adhere to the 'principle of legality' in common law countries.[46] And so, the prosecution can exercise discretion whether to prosecute the police officer applying torture and could use this discretion in cases where the officer in charge is under extreme emotional stress.

The principle of human dignity applying in Germany and the general principles in relation to torture in common law systems within the ticking bomb scenario are similar. However, the common law has not created a protection that is as far reaching as the German Basic Law. The UK, the US and Australia have tried to justify torture under certain circumstances while Germany has made it very clear in the *Daschner* decision that there can be no justification. In this way it could be said that human dignity does to a limited extent become a dividing line between German and common law approaches. Even 'a little' torture is not allowed in the German context, whereas it can be an accepted exercise under the common law. Human dignity therefore does raise the bar in relation to human rights violations, in particular the right not to be subject to torture or cruel, inhuman or degrading treatment or punishment.

V. Conclusion

It can be concluded that the principle of human dignity as embedded in the German Basic Law and as defined by German Courts is not as much of a dividing line as might have been expected as the strict application of the human dignity principle is nearly impossible. The decisions of the German Courts show that there is 'more' and 'less' protection of the right to human dignity possible – depending on the rights concerned. In relation to the right to life, the terrorists can lose the protection under the Basic Law by acting illegally, but not in relation to torture.

In the hijacked aircraft scenario human dignity does signify a difference between the German and the common law approach. Both systems have principles prohibiting the weighing up of life against life, although they stem from different sources (Article 1 Section 1 Basic Law in the German context and the decision in *Dudley and Stephens* in the common law context). In theory both principles lead to the outcome that the plane should not be shot down, as the

---

46   See for example Julia Fionda *Public Prosecutors and Discretion: A Comparative Study* (1995), Oxford University Press, p. 167.

right to life cannot be balanced. Looking at the applying defences, however, the German law would allow for a civilian to shoot the plane down if he or she could save his or her own life or the life of a relative or close person. In this respect the common law principle goes even further as it does not allow the weighing up of life against life, even if the act could save ones own life (*Dudley and Stephens*). Yet, the common law principle can be overridden by statutory law as the Australian Defence Act shows and thus the state does not seem to be as restricted as the individual when it comes to the weighing up of competing legal interests. As the US, UK and Australia have special provisions in place that allow the shooting down of hijacked aircraft, they have thereby overruled the principle protecting the right to life. By having an explicit right to human dignity in the Basic Law, the German protection of the principle goes further, as laws enacted contrary to the principle can be and have been declared void.

In practice, however, the human dignity principle cannot be applied to the extent the theory requires. In Germany attempts have been made to limit the application of the human dignity principle through the concept of 'suprastatutory state of emergency'. In both the German and common law systems, the harsh consequences of the 'human dignity' principle (*Dudley and Stephens* and *Daschner* decisions) were balanced by the applied sentences. Both sentences were very mild to counteract the absoluteness of the principle adhered to. In both cases the legal principle and the statutory law and political realities diverge and have to be taken into account to prevent unreasonable results. The problem is again where the limits to these adjustments to the law lie. Would the Minister ordering a hijacked plane to be destroyed also be rewarded with a low sentence? In sum, the fact that the principle of human dignity is enforced and publicly discussed is the biggest advantage of its existence. It sets standards for the behaviour of state representatives, even if repercussions might be very mild for its breach.

The principles pertaining to the torture scenario applied in Germany are different compared to common law systems, although both are party to the same international covenants. Germany cannot justify torture, unlike the US, by evoking a 'state of emergency'. The 70's decisions show that in the UK torture is generally not yet outlawed and a 'little' torture might be justified. Due to Australia's colonial heritage, the common law applying to the torture scenario could rely on the UK decisions. The German approach here is very consistent. Even the threat of physical violence cannot be justified. This is where the human dignity principle actually becomes a distinguishing line.

Despite the existence of case law, it cannot be predicted what the courts will decide in the future. What can be concluded is that the human dignity principle in Germany is in fact not as absolute as it seems because of political and legal realities, while the common law – without having an explicit human dignity principle – could afford a very thorough protection to human rights and leads, in theory, to very similar outcomes.

Comparing the common law and the German systems in relation to the hijacked aircraft and ticking bomb scenarios, the major difference created by the principle of human dignity is not *whether* but *when* mitigating circumstances are taken into account. Without an explicit human dignity principle, the common law systems can evoke discretion and abstain from prosecution in the above-mentioned scenarios due to the particular circumstances the executing state representative found him or herself in. If prosecuted, the state representative can claim different defences in criminal law and the courts can determine that the behaviour was not illegal in the common law systems. A state representative acting in the two scenarios would therefore not be charged or not be found guilty under common law if he or she had to weigh up paramount competing legal interests. The state representative would not be criminally convicted or receive an entry in their criminal record and could therefore continue to serve the state.

In the German system, the explicit human dignity principle, the legality principle, and the lack of defences in criminal law will lead to a criminal conviction of the state representative. However, the blow of the principle will be softened in the sentencing phase. As we have seen in the *Daschner* decision, the officers could remain in the police service. While the common law system leaves the act legal, the German system has to condemn the act as 'illegal', but can balance the harshness of the principle through the sentence given. Although state representatives in both systems might not have a criminal record afterwards, it is important that in the German system they carry a much higher degree of accountability afforded by the human dignity principle. The main distinctive feature of the express right to human dignity in the German Basic Law is therefore that it considerably heightens the level of accountability of state representatives in these scenarios.

Simon Bronitt

The Common Law and Human Dignity: Australian Perspectives

Introduction[1]

The common law's approach to human dignity is essentially a reflection of a residual model of liberty. As constitutional lawyer, AV Dicey wrote in his late 19th century study extolling the virtues of an unwritten British Constitution,[2] it is the common law and the courts that provide the primary means for protecting civil liberties, an approach which contrasts favourably with the written bills of rights favoured in Continental Europe. It did not follow that fundamental values such as "human dignity" were not protected by the common law. But rather that these values found expression and protection within the fabric of the ordinary laws of the land, foremost criminal and tort laws, whether statutory or common law, which could be vindicated before the courts.

Dicey's model of constitutionalism borders on a form of legal nationalism. He manifests an acute historical myopia about the status of written codes, such as the Magna Carta, in the formation of British legal culture.[3] Indeed, it is wrong to assume that judicial review of legislation is a 'foreign' innovation alien to common law systems; indeed, within colonial jurisdictions, such as Australia, local statutes in the 19th century were regularly be held to be invalid as being incompatible with the traditional fundamental rights protected by the English common law.[4]

Having cast doubt on aspect's of Dicey's model, the basic thrust of his argument nevertheless stands true. Australia, at the national level, lacks an

---

1   This research for this chapter has been supported by Australian Research Council Grant monitoring legal changes post–9/11 (DP 451473) 'Terrorism and the Non-State Actor after September 11: The Role of Law in the Search for Security'. Email: s.bronitt@griffithu.edu.au
2   See AV Dicey, *Introduction to the Study of the Law of the Constitution*, 10th ed, Macmillan, 1959.
3   For a review of the Diceyan model, its purported virtues and vices, see S Bottomley & S Bronitt, *Law in Context* (3rd ed, Sydney: The Federation Press) (2006), Ch 2.
4   For a review of these distinctive aspect of colonial legal culture see I Holloway, S Bronitt and J Williams, "Rhetoric, Reason and the Rule of Law in Early Colonial New South Wales" in H Foster, B Berger and AR Buck (eds), *The Grand Experiment: Law & Legal Culture in British Settler Societies* (UBC Press, 2008).

entrenched bill of rights, and human rights standards are protected by ordinary domestic statutes including in some jurisdictions statutory Human Rights Acts, as in Victoria and the Australian Capital Territory.[5] The courts and the common law have a subordinate role to parliament under this model of human rights legislation: courts are placed under a duty to interpret legislative provisions to be consistent with these rights, or, if this is not possible, to make a declaration of incompatibility or inconsistent interpretation. Upholding the principle of parliamentary supremacy, the courts do not have the power to invalidate legislation on the grounds of inconsistency with the enumerated human rights.

This chapter explores the virtues and vices of these models of civil liberties. The absence of a prescriptive positive right in a constitutional law does not mean that human dignity, as a legal value, is unprotected in Australia: there are many examples where the importance of human dignity finds expression both in legislation but also in the judgments of our courts. There are of course many examples where the legal systems deviates or derogates from this standard. An important challenge for comparative law scholars is to move beyond the debate about determining the 'best' systems: as one leading comparative scholar notes debate between common law and civil law scholars, between adversarialism and inquisitorialism, is often reduced to a 'battle of slogans, without the protagonists really joining issue over anything particularly clear or precise'.[6] The more significant question to explore is the various ways in which, within legal systems each with their own distinct history and culture, the 'war on terror' has placed significant strains on the legal commitment to human dignity. With that scene setting, I turn to some specific examples to explore these issues from a comparative perspective.

Upholding Human Dignity through Statute and Common Law

Federal criminal procedure law in Australia, it could be argued, demonstrates a high level of commitment to human dignity compared with other common law systems. Federal law have specific rules of evidence excluding confession evidence obtained by use of torture, inhuman and degrading treatment, or by illegal or improper methods. More generally, there are also specific offences

---

5   The first human rights Act in Australia was modelled on the UK Human Rights Act 1998: see *Human Rights Act 2004* (ACT). Victoria has largely following the ACT model in *Charter of Human Rights and Responsibilities Act 2006* (Vic).

6   SJ Stoljar "Codification and the Common law" in SJ Stoljar (ed), *Problems of Codification* (Canberra: ANU Press, 1977) at p 2.

related to torture by public officials.[7] Indeed, the rule of voluntariness, evolved from the common law, place the so-called right to silence both before and during the trial as one of the cardinal principles.[8] The High Court of Australia, in limiting the privilege against self-incrimination to human beings (thereby excluding corporations from its protective remit), emphasised the important role the privilege plays in upholding human rights and specifically preserving human dignity.[9]

There is even a statement in general terms of the importance of human dignity during detention and custodial interviewing. The general statement contained in the *Crimes Act 1914* (Cth) in section 23Q comes to mind as an example. The section states that a person in police custody 'must be treated with humanity and with respect for human dignity, and must not be subjected to cruel, inhuman or degrading treatment'. It has been suggested that this provision of the *Crimes Act* was adopted in part to give force to the Article 10(1) of the International Covenant on Civil and Political Rights (ICCPR) that provides that all persons deprived of their liberty shall be treated with humanity and with respect for the inherent dignity of the human person. The values which find expression in the the ICCPR and 23Q reflect long standing concerns about the potential mistreatment of suspects held in custody. This had previously been highlighted in a series of regional United Nations (UN) meetings in the 1960s and 1970s.[10] Responding to these concerns, the UN drafted a soft law instrument called the *United Nations Code of Conduct for Law Enforcement Officials* (1979) (hereafter 'UN Code'), Article 2 of which provides:

---

7   Torture is an extra-territorial offence under federal law. The federal offence, which is intended to operate concurrently with State and Territory offences, carries a maximum penalty of 20 years imprisonment: see Criminal Code (Cth), section 274.2.

8   This may be contrasted with the erosion of the right to silence in the United Kingdom, where the law permits judges to direct the jury that they may, in certain cases, draw adverse inferences from an accused's silence in the face of questioning. For a review of the law in the Australian context, and rejection of the UK model of reform: see NSW Law Reform Commission, *The Right to Silence: Report 95* (2000).

9   See *EPA v Caltex* (1993) 178 CLR 477 where the High Court traced the evolution of the privilege as a means of protecting individuals from abuse, noting with approval Murphy J's earlier dicta in *Rochfort v Trade Practices Commission* (1982) 153 CLR 134 at 150 that "The privilege against self-incrimination is a human right, based on the desire to protect personal freedom and human dignity."

10 In 1963, the United Nations with the Australian Government convened a seminar in Canberra that brought together a group of senior lawyers and police from around the Asia Pacific region to discuss policing and human rights issues: *1963 Seminar on the Role of the Police in the Protection of Human Rights,* Canberra, 29 April to 13 May 1963 (1963, United Nations, New York), from the Australian Archives Series M1505/1 Item 133, Seminar Report 38; the report was adopted unanimously by the seminar at its final meeting 13 May 1963.

In the performance of their duty, law enforcement officials shall respect and protect human dignity and maintain and uphold the human rights of all persons.[11]

The Australian articulation of this duty in the federal *Crimes Act* 1914 however cannot really be presented as an unqualified success: section 23Q lacks 'normative bite' since it does not impose specific legal obligations on responsible custody officers to uphold these rights or provide effective remedies for any established breach. It may be viewed as human rights window-dressing, having never been discussed in any reported case dealing with the law governing police interviewing or treatment of suspects. This is part of wider marginalisation of human rights within law enforcement culture: although the UN Code was adopted more than 30 years ago, it has had limited impact on policing culture or policy. As a leading scholar of policing ethics, John Kleinig notes, the UN Code has had little impact.[12] As a form of 'soft law', it has exerted little influence on ethical debates on police education or scholarly discussions about the future direction of policing.[13] Clearly, much more could be done to educate policy makers (and our legislators) about the nature and scope of human rights in the policing context, a development that would serve to promote higher standards of human rights protection in the administration of criminal justice.

Having demonstrated how the prescriptive 'positive' legal rules in federal legislation have played a limited role in protecting human dignity, I turn now to consider how the common law, as developed by the courts, has approached these issued in *R v Benbrika & Ors*.[14] The defendants were charged with terrorism-related offences under the federal Criminal Code and applied to have the trial stayed on grounds of unfairness, arguing the conditions of incarceration and transport to and from Court adversely affected their right to a fair trial. Justice

---

11   Adopted by the UN General Assembly on 17 December 1979.

12   See J. Kleinig, *The Ethics of Policing* (Cambridge University Press, Cambridge, 1996), which devotes only one paragraph to the UN Code, concluding that "... in the member states it has never achieved the acceptance that was sought for it": at 237.

13   The negligible impact of human rights on policing practice and scholarship is apparent in B. Etter and M. Palmer (eds), *Police Leadership in Australasia* (Federation Press, Sydney, 1995). The volume pays scant attention to human rights and ethical matters, focusing instead on the future challenges to the police posed by white collar, hi-tech and transnational forms of crime: See also J. Kleinig, *The Ethics of Policing* (Cambridge University Press, Cambridge, 1996), which devotes only one paragraph to the UN Code, concluding that "... in the member states it has never achieved the acceptance that was sought for it": at 237. For an exception, which seeks to elevate the role of human rights in the conceptualisation of the police role, see S Miller, "Moral Rights and the Institution of Police" in T Campbell and S Miller (eds), *Human Rights and the Moral Responsibilities of Corporate and Public Sector Organisations* (2004).

14   *R v Benbrika & Ors (Ruling No 20)* [2008] VSC 80 (20 March 2008).

Bongiorno handed down a ruling in which he threatened to indefinitely postpone the six-week-old trial unless the state's prison authorities met a March 31 2008 deadline to change the high-security prison regime for 12 men charged with being members of an unnamed terrorist organisation. Most of the accused, and 10 others held on related charges in Sydney, had been incarcerated for more than two years in prolonged isolation. On March 31, the judge gave the go ahead for the trial to resume after receiving affidavits from state government and prison authorities promising that the changes he specified "have been or would be effected immediately". The defendants had argued that their imprisonment, daily transportation and repeated strip-searching during the trial were so onerous that they could not conduct their defence and were at risk of aggravated mental illness.

In his ruling, Justice Bongiorno noted the intolerable conditions in which the defendants were held: that for the first year of their detention inside the maximum security Acacia Unit, about 60 kilometres from Melbourne, the defendants had been kept locked in individual cells for up to 23 hours a day, with severe restrictions on receiving visitors and consulting with lawyers. From March 2007, prison authorities eased these conditions, marginally, in order to head off an initial legal application to halt the trial. Throughout the trial, the men were being woken at 6am and offered breakfast (which some of the prisoners refused for fear of motion sickness) before being strip-searched, handcuffed, shackled and loaded into small box-like steel compartments inside a totally enclosed van for the long drive – 80 minutes or more – to the court. The return journey each night was similar, complete with another strip-search. During the long hours of the trial each day, the men were obliged to closely follow the proceedings and read the transcripts of police telephone intercepts and listening devices, contained in seven lever arch folders. A number of expert doctors gave evidence that the defendants were likely to become depressed, irritable, anxious and fatigued.

Justice Bongiorno required the authorities to carry out a list of alterations in the incarceration. These included transfer to a nearby Melbourne city prison, with conditions no more onerous than those for ordinary remand prisoners awaiting trial, an end to daily shackling and strip-searching, and 10 out-of-cell hours per day when not attending court. Bongiorno rejected an extraordinary suggestion by the federal prosecutors that the prisoners be kept in the remote Acacia Unit, with their participation in their own trial restricted to a video-link. Such an arrangement would violate one of the most basic legal rights – to be present at one's trial to fully contest the charges and evidence. The judge noted: "None of the accused have, on any occasion, behaved other than impeccably in the courtroom and no other legitimate reason has been advanced as to why they should not be permitted to remain." There has been no previous case in Australia in which the conditions of detention were so oppressive and damaging to mental health that a judge felt compelled to shut down the proceedings. Bongiorno relied upon numerous judicial authorities for halting unfair trials, but none of these earlier High Court decisions had related to the detention regime imposed on the accused. This case reveals the generative capacity of the common law, and the right to a fair trial specifically, to offer immediate and effective protection against human rights abuses.

In the final section, I would like to turn to one of the paradigm leading cases of common law (see Chapter ??) which served to stimulate my interest in this topic. The traditional common law position in relation to the defence of necessity was unclear until the notorious cannibalism case that was tried in England in the late 19th century, *R v Dudley and Stephens*.[15] Dudley, Stephens, Brooks and a 17-year-old boy, Parker were cast adrift in an open boat 1600 nautical miles from land. On the 20th day at sea, nine days without food and seven without water, Dudley and Stephens agreed to kill Parker who was the weakest of the four and eat his flesh. Brooks refused to take part in the killing. Dudley then killed Parker and the three men survived by eating the boy's flesh. When they were subsequently rescued, Dudley and Stephens admitted what had happened, consistent with the established maritime custom of the sea,[16] and were charged with murder. The jurors declined to give their view as to whether the facts amounted to murder and asked for the advice of the Court of Queen's Bench. Lord Coleridge CJ in delivering the judgment of the Court held that the accused were guilty of murder and sentenced them to death. This mandatory penalty was later commuted by the Executive to six months' imprisonment. In holding that the defence of necessity was not available to a charge of murder, Lord Coleridge CJ stated:

> "To preserve one's life is generally speaking a duty, but it may be the plainest and the highest duty to sacrifice it. War is full of instances in which it is a man's duty not to live, but to die ... It is not correct, therefore, to say that there is any absolute or unqualified necessity to preserve one's life ... It is not needful to point out the awful danger of the principle which has been

---

15   (1884) 14 QBD 273.
16   For a detailed account of the case of *Dudley and Stephens* see AWB Simpson, *Cannibalism and the Common Law* (Chicago: The University of Chicago Press, 1984). In this book, Brian Simpson explores the clash between the customs of the sea, which traditionally accepted cannibalism as a measure of last resort for shipwrecked sailors, and the common law, which sought to label such practices as uncivilised acts of murder. Simpson provides elaborate detail of the practices and rituals relating to the drawing of lots and/or selection of victims for cannibalism, practices which were widely accepted as legitimate in sea-faring communities until the late 19th century.

contended for. Who is to be the judge of this sort of necessity? By what measure is the comparative value of lives to be measured? Is it to be strength, or intellect, or what? It is plain that the principle leaves to him who is to profit by it to determine the necessity which will justify him deliberately taking another's life to save his own ... it is quite plain that such a principle once admitted might be made the legal cloak for unbridled passion and atrocious crime".[17]

It has been questioned whether *Dudley and Stephens* should still applies in the post-9/11 context by scholars arguing that shooting down hijacked aircraft, killing innocent passengers, would be justifiable on the grounds of necessity.[18] There is a sound argument that such a blanket rule may be harsh in certain cases, and overlooks the State's duty to protect its citizens from unlawful criminal acts. Indeed, some scholars have argued that it should not apply.[19] Indeed, the availability of necessity as a defence to intentional killing, beyond the conventional scope of self defence and defence of others, has been accepted in the Model Penal Code in the United States.[20]

The necessity plea under the common law requires consideration of the nature of the threat, its imminence and proportionality (and to that extent would be consistent with the requirements of international human right law). But the problem in the hijacked aircraft scenario is that the person exercising the lethal force is not the person *in extremis* – but is another person calculating the least *worst* outcome. Weighing the numbers of lives in the balance in this context can be challenging. The difficulty is that in the real world the full extent of the likely harm involved and the respective death tolls in these situations is unknowable. Further, the human dignity point is very strong – as the *Dudley* case admits. Even where we can calculate the risks clearly, the principle of weighing harms remains problematic: does the status of the group being threatened with harm matter. Should we sacrifice a larger number of ordinary citizens to preserve the lives of a smaller number of politically significant individuals? How many

---

17 Ibid at 287–288.

18 For a review of the legal framework governing the use of force in this context, see S Bronitt and D Stephens, "'Flying Under the Radar' – The Use of Lethal Force Against Hijacked Aircraft: Recent Australian Developments" (2007) 7(2) *Oxford University Commonwealth Law Review* 265.

19 Some academics have doubted the continuing authority of the decision, though no authority is provided for this reversal: JC Smith and B Hogan, *Criminal Law* (London: Butterworths, 10th ed, 2002): 273–4; JC Smith, B Hogan and David Ormerod, *Criminal Law* (Oxford: Oxford University Press, 11th ed, 2005): 322; See also M Bohlander, "In Extremis – Hijacked Airplanes, 'Collateral Damage' and the Limits of Criminal Law" [2006] Crim. L.R. 579.

20 Section 3.02 of the Model Penal Code states that conduct which the actor believes to be necessary to avoid a harm or evil to himself or another is justifiable. Unlike the common law in England, there defence is available for cases of homicide.

innocent citizens would we potentially be prepared to sacrifice to save one member of the royal household!

Some academics, such as Bohlander, neatly dispose of the human dignity and autonomy interests of those on the hijacked planes by saying that they have, in effect, ceased to be human beings; either having become part of the terrorist's weapon, or a plane of putative corpses.

> "A harsh – but in my view ultimately correct – approach to that sort of case [the plight of passengers and crew on hijacked airplanes] would suggest that their doomed lives cannot be used as one side to the balancing exercise, when trying to decide whether necessity could be applied as a means of justification or excuse. The outwardly cynical but logically proper approach is that necessity does not enter into it at all because there is no balancing exercise; *they are, to put it bluntly, already dead.* If the lives of the passengers will be lost in any case, then it would be a mere academic exercise to weigh the relatively minor shortening of those lives by shooting down the plane against the possibility of saving the otherwise unendangered lives of the people on the ground".[21]

The problem with applying necessity or self-defence in these cases is that the risks involved are very hard to calculate – indeed they may well be incalculable. The best available information about the threat may be incomplete or indeed inaccurate. An excuse based on "sudden or extraordinary emergency", which is a recognised defence under federal criminal law in Australia,[22] may be more palatable, reflecting the highly pressured and immediate, perhaps even instinctual reaction. The *Criminal Code* (Cth) defence provides as follows:

10.3 Sudden or extraordinary emergency

(1)   A person is not criminally responsible for an offence if he or she carries out the conduct constituted the offence in response to circumstances of sudden or extraordinary emergency.

(2)   This section applies if and only if the person carrying out the conduct reasonably believes that:

        (a)   circumstances of sudden or extraordinary emergency exist; and

        (b)   committing the offence is the only reasonable way to deal with the emergency; and

        (c)   the conduct is a reasonable response to the emergency.

The defence operates as a complete defence to otherwise wrongful action. The scope of the defence was intentionally left open by the drafters, an approach that invites the jury to interpret the concept of sudden or extraordinary emergency as matters of ordinary words in the English language.[23] Although this defence has been intentionally left vague, there are some virtues in accepting this formulation

---

21   Ibid, 580 (emphasis added).

22   See *Criminal Code* (Cth), s 10.3; *Criminal Code* (ACT), s 41; *Criminal Code* (NT).

23   S Odgers, *Principles of Federal Criminal Law* (Law Book Co; 2007), p 109.

as a characterisation of how individuals react in emergencies. Indeed, it is simply fanciful to expect persons to engage in a calm, rational weighing of competing interests when faced by an emergency of this magnitude. From an explanatory perspective, basing a defence on emergency rather than necessity has the advantage of being more psychologically credible.

This indeterminacy of necessity under the common law or emergency under legislation may be contrasted with the new powers and defences conferred on members of the Australian Defence Force (ADF), who have been granted statutory powers to use lethal force under Part IIIAAA of the *Defence Act* 1903 (Cth) against hijacked aircraft to protect critical infrastructure. Part III AAA *Defence Act* 1903, which was inserted into the Act in 2000, amended last year and came into force shortly before the 2007 APEC Summit. The recent amendments to Part IIIAAA of the *Defence Act* 1903 create a legislative framework for prospective authorisation of force by the military in aid of civil power. It inter alia provides for 'the use of reasonable and necessary force when protecting critical infrastructure designated by the authorising Ministers'[24] and enables a 'call out' of the ADF to respond to incidents or threats to Commonwealth incidents in the air environment'[25] as well as ensuring that 'powers conferred on the ADF under Part IIIAAA can be accorded to the ADF in the course of dealing with a mobile terrorist incident and a range of threats to Australia's security'. Prior to these amendments, there was no legislative framework that provided specific powers to the ADF in protecting the State against domestic violence, nor was there any provision regarding the use of the ADF by the Commonwealth in protecting its own interests. A review of the powers to call out troops in 2004 noted that this was too reactive (modelled around a siege situation) and there needed to be a more proactive model, which led to the 2006 amendments.[26]

The scheme is different from other immunity schemes that have been developed, such as the scheme of prospective immunities granted to police and informers conducting undercover controlled operations.[27] Rather than a blanket criminal and civil immunity, Part IIIAAA gives a non-exhaustive list of powers

---

24   See Defence Legislation Amendment (Aid to Civilian Authorities) Bill 2006 – Revised Explanatory Memorandum.

25   *Id.*

26   For a comprehensive review of these powers see M Head, *Calling Out the Troops: The Australian military and civil unrest: the legal and constitutional issues* (Federation Press, 2009).

27   For a critical review of these prospective immunities, see S Bronitt, "The Law in Undercover Policing: A Comparative Study Of Entrapment and Covert Interviewing in Australia, Canada and Europe" (2004) 33(1) *Common Law World Review* 35.

given to defence personnel to do certain things. Section 51SE allows ADF members operating under orders given by the Chief of the Defence Force to do destroy a vessel or aircraft. The ADF member must conform to the requirements of s 51SE(2) or (3). Amongst other things, key requirements are:

- the order was not manifestly unlawful;
- the member has no reason to believe that circumstances have changed in a material way since the relevant order was given;
- the member has no reason to believe that the order was based on a mistake as to a material fact, and;
- taking the measures was reasonable and necessary to give effect to the order.

In addition, any action, or giving of orders, must have been authorised by a Minister beforehand (s51SE(4)), unless the ADF member believes on reasonable grounds that there is insufficient time to obtain the authorisation because a sudden and extraordinary emergency exists: s 51SE(5). The purpose of these provisions is to ensure that Defence personnel are under strict control, through a chain of command, when they are receiving orders. Subsections 51SE(2) and (3) draw heavily, according to the Explanatory Memorandum, on the principles of the defence of acting under lawful authority.[28] However, it is probably best described as a hybrid defence, melding elements of lawful authority and necessity.

Specific Powers to Deal with Aviation Security Incidents

The purpose of the new provisions in relation to aviation security incidents is to provide clear legal authority for the military to act (rather than engage in the deliberative exercise of weighing interests in necessity, stretch self-defence, or resort to the vagaries of Executive powers or the Defence head of power in the constitution!). The provisions seek to structure the decision making process and also to move beyond the reactive call out model, to designate a set of circumstances where the Chief of Defence is already pre-authorised or prospectively authorised to act (whether in Australia or offshore) – in these cases, the military can act without ministerial authorisation or Governor General order.

As noted above Section 51ST authorises the use of necessary force including the destruction of the aircraft. This action may be taken whether the aircraft is

---

28   Defence Legislation Amendment (Aid to Civilian Authorities) Bill 2006 – Revised Explanatory Memorandum.

airborne or not. Defence personnel must be acting within a command structure, giving/receiving orders: s 51 S T (1). These requirements perhaps reflect the concern of risks of excessive force in counter-terrorism operations. In relation to action under Div 3B, the action must be reasonable and necessary, but the further limitations are more relaxed than other powers:

Section 51T

(2B) Despite subsection (1), in exercising powers under subparagraph 51SE(1)(a)(i) or (ii) or Division 3B [action against aircraft], a member of the Defence Force must not, in using force against a person or thing, do anything that is likely to cause the death of, or grievous bodily harm to, the person unless the member believes on reasonable grounds that:

(a)   doing that thing is necessary to protect the life of, or to prevent serious injury to, another person (including the member); or

(b)   doing that thing is *necessary to protect designated critical infrastructure against a threat of damage or disruption to its operation;* or

(c)   doing that thing is necessary and reasonable to give effect to the order under which, or under the authority of which, the member is acting.

The new legislation goes even further as it provides for 'the use of reasonable and necessary force when protecting critical infrastructure designated by the authorising Ministers'[29]. This means that the right to life has not only to be weighed up against the life of people in the building at threat or on the ground, but also against the importance of an infrastructure that could be destroyed or even functioning impaired. It seems feasible that even if the plane threatens to crash into a nearly empty building (eg parliament house at night) the plane could be shot down, killing people on the plane although a greater number of people is not saved or even killing more people on the ground where the plane crashes.

Conclusion

In conclusion, from this brief survey drawn from both case law and statutory fields of Australian law, the concept of human dignity may have some important roles to play, even in a system which lacks a national bill of rights. I am mindful however of avoiding the form of legal nationalism so apparent in Dicey's theory of constitionalism outlined in my introduction. In that sense, I am much more attuned to the sociological perspectives of Professor Stoljar.[30] As one of the

---

29   See Defence Legislation Amendment (Aid to Civilian Authorities) Bill 2006 – Revised Explanatory Memorandum

30   Sam was the first ANU research professor of law (1954–1985) and for the first 6 years of his appointment was the *only* professor of law at the ANU until the establishment of the Law School in 1960. His appointment is testament to ANU's cosmopolitan outlook and

leading comparative law scholars of his generation, although removed from the heartland of his discipline, Stoljar was able to persuade many leading lights of the field – including Professors Andre Tunc, Coing and Zweigert – to visit Canberra in the early 70s to participate in a comparative law seminar. His reflections in the introductory essay examining the contours of the debates about differences seem particular pertinent today:

> "[C]ase-law forms an inevitable component of any system of law, at any rate to the extent that it emphasises the need as well as inevitability of an ongoing legal experience as this is nutured and sustained by judicial creativity; while the civilian or code-lawyer may say that codes represent a desire not so much for legal certainty as for structure or order, the need of rearranging or reordering an otherwise shapeless and unmanageable mass of legal results. *It follows that cases and codes, the former betokening experience, the latter form or structure, far from necessarily conflicting can in fact perform complementary roles*".[31]

Applying Stoljar's insight to the debates about protection of 'human dignity' suggests that our discussions should not be focused on which legal form – constitutional code or judge-made common law – offers the 'best' protection of human dignity. Rather our contributions should recognise that the two distinct legal domains of cases and codes, which are evident in both Anglo-American Common Law and European Civil Law Traditions, interact and perform complementary roles.

---

commitment to international perspectives at a time when most law schools were conceived as 'trade schools' for the local profession.

31   SJ Stoljar "Codification and the Common law" in SJ Stoljar (ed), *Problems of Codification* (Canberra: ANU Press, 1977) at p 3.

Torsten Stein

International Law and International Cooperation and Integration in the German Basic Law

In the preparation of this Conference it was agreed that we would place a special focus on the use of the armed forces, or, as Prof. Williams called it: The war power. Before I will come to that special focus, allow me to give a brief overview of the role and rank of international law in the German constitutional system.

One of the fundamental decisions of the Basic Law (the "Grundgesetz – GG") of the Federal Republic of Germany (FRG) of May 23, 1949, was to integrate the FRG into the international community. In contrast to the previous German Constitutions of 1871 and of 1919, the Basic Law obliges the relevant institutions to be open minded and prepared to participate in various forms of cooperation with other States and international organizations. This general attitude finds its expression in various provisions of the Constitution.

The preamble of the Basic Law underlines the will "to promote world peace as an equal partner in a united Europe". Art. 24 (1) authorizes the Federation to transfer sovereign powers to international institutions by legislation. On the basis of this article, the integration of the FRG into the European Community has taken place. Shortly after the reunification of Germany and in the course of the ratification of the Maastricht Treaty and the foundation of the European Union, European Integration was based on the new Art. 23, much more complicated and paying tribute to the federal character of the German State.

According to Art. 24 (2) GG, the Federation, with a view to maintaining peace, may enter into a system of mutual collective security and may consent to respective limitations on its sovereignty. This was at the time meant to cover accession to the United Nations (which occurred only in 1973), but today also membership in NATO, after the Atlantic Alliance has – somewhat reluctantly[1] – accepted to be such a system of mutually collective security and a regional organization in the sense of Art. 52 of the Charter of the United Nations. To facilitate international dispute settlement between States, the Federation will accede to agreements concerning international arbitration of a general, comprehensive and obligatory nature (Art. 24 [3] GG); only recently, in April

---

[1]   NATO was reluctant because of the reporting obligation under Art. 54 UN-Charter.

2008, Germany issued the declaration under Art. 36 para. 2 of the Statute of the ICJ[2]. In addition, Art. 25 incorporates the general rules of public international law as an integral part of federal law. Those rules shall take precedence over any law and shall directly create rights and duties for all inhabitants of the federal territory. Art. 26 (1) GG adds a ban on war of aggression and provides that acts, tending to and undertaken with the intent to disturb peaceful relations between nations, shall be unconstitutional.

Taken together, the constitutional provisions are an expression of a basic constitutional principle of cooperation with other States, organizations or the international community as a whole. Cooperation instead of autarky and isolation is one of the guiding principles of the Basic Law. Especially in the view of the present process of integration within the European Community or of cooperation in the framework of many world wide treaties, it appears that the principle of international cooperation is as important as the other basic structural principles laid down in the Basic Law which establish a democratic, federal and

---

2   The declaration reads as follows:

"1. The Government of the Federal Republic of Germany declares that it recognizes as compulsory ipso facto and without special agreement, in relation to any other state accepting the same obligation, the jurisdiction of the International Court of Justice, in conformity with paragraph 2 of Article 36 of the Statute of the Court, until such time as notice may be given to the Secretary-General of the United Nations withdrawing the declaration and with effect as from the moment of such notification, over all disputes arising after the present declaration, with regard to situations or facts subsequent to this date other than:

(i) any dispute which the Parties thereto have agreed or shall agree to have recourse to some other method of peaceful settlement or which is subject to another method of peaceful settlement chosen by all the Parties.

(ii) any dispute which

(a) relates to, arises from or is connected with the deployment of armed forces abroad, involvement in such deployments or decisions thereon, or

(b) relates to, arises from or is connected with the use for military purposes of the territory of the Federal Republic of Germany, including its airspace, as well as maritime areas subject to German sovereign rights and jurisdiction;

(iii) any dispute in respect of which any other Party to the dispute has accepted the compulsory jurisdiction of the International Court of Justice only in relation to or for the purpose of the dispute; or where the acceptance of the Court's compulsory jurisdiction on behalf of any other Party to the dispute was deposited or ratified less than twelve months prior to the filing of the application bringing the dispute before the Court.

2. The Government of the Federal Republic of Germany also reserves the right at any time, by means of a notification addressed to the Secretary-General of the United Nations, and with effect as from the moment of such notification, either to add to, amend or withdraw any of the foregoing reservations, or any that may hereafter be added."

The exclusion in (ii), (b) clearly has to do with the use of US-Airbases in Germany during the 2003 US-Iraq war.

social State governed by the rule of law[3]. From this concept the Federal Constitutional Court has deducted a *general rule of interpretation*: in a case of doubt, the Basic Law as well as all ordinary laws have to be interpreted as much as possible in conformity with the obligations of the FRG under public international law[4]. The underlying idea of this rule is twofold: the Constitutional Court attempts to follow the positive approach of the Constitution in regard to the international legal order and tries to avoid any possible conflict which could lead to an international responsibility of the FRG. Certainly, there are limits to this principle: it cannot correct or alter the specific decisions of the Constitution which determine the incorporation of the various rules of international law and their rank within the German legal order[5].

The Basic Law distinguishes between general rules and treaties, and lays down different rules for their incorporation.

According to Art. 25, general rules of international law shall be an integral part of federal law. As federal law overrides the law of the federated States, the *Länder* (Art. 31), the general rules have equally to be respected by them. Art. 25 thus provides for a general incorporation of general rules of international law which existed at the coming into force of the Basic Law or which will become part of the German legal order in the future.

"General rules" in the sense of Art. 25 are rules of *general customary law* as well as *general principles* of international law in the sense of Art. 38 (1) (c) of the Statute of the ICJ. The previous Constitution of Weimar of 1919, only referred to generally *recognized* rules[6]. In view of the different wording of Art. 25 GG, the Constitutional Court, supported by the doctrine, has stated that "general rules may only be those of a universal character; it is not necessary that the FRG has recognized a rule of customary law"[7]. However, a representative majority of affected States must have adhered to the relevant rule. The only condition is that the FRG has not formally protested against the formation of a general rule of customary law which would exclude a binding effect for the

---

3   Art. 20 (1) GG.
4   Cf. BVerfGE (Decisions of the Federal Constitutional Court) 74, p. 358 et seq.
5   Consequently, the rule "pacta sunt servanda", which as such is a general rule of international law taking precedence over any law (Art. 25 GG), does not give international treaties a higher rank in relation to subsequent statutes. And the interpretation of national law in conformity with international obligations of the state would end in the (very theoretical) case that the international obligation would violate basic principles of the German Constitution (BVerfGE 111, p. 307 et seq.).
6   Art. 4 "The generally recognized rules of public international law are binding part of the law of the German Empire".
7   BVerfGE 15, 25 (34). For a wider view cf. Steinberger, Handbuch des Staatsrechts, vol. VII, § 173.

FRG[8]. This concept of Art. 25 guarantees that the international obligations of the FRG under customary law are at the same time an integral part of national constitutional law.

Art. 59 (2) of the Basic Law provides a special procedure for the incorporation of treaty law[9]. In the case of treaties which regulate the political relations of the Federation and relate to matters of federal legislation a specific legislative act of consent by the competent legislative institutions is required. Administrative agreements are incorporated by legal acts of the executive.

The legislative act of consent has two major functions[10]: first, it authorizes the Federal President to ratify the treaty; and second, it incorporates the treaty into national law. As has been shown above, the treaty in its entirety becomes part of national law and has to be respected by all public authorities. Only an analysis of the various provisions of the treaty may reveal to what extent they may be directly applicable to individuals. An act of consent is necessary, however, irrespective of whether the pre-existing national legal order did already contain identical or parallel rules. The formal additional act of consent, which at the same time serves as a form of parliamentarian control over the executive, guarantees that the legislature may not change the pre-existing parallel rule as long as the international treaty is in force.

A "political treaty" in the sense of Art. 59 (2) GG is a treaty which may effect the existence of the FRG, its territorial integrity, its independence or its political position and weight within the international community[11].

In regard to decisions of international organizations, one has to make distinctions. In the case of the "transfer" of sovereign powers by legislation to a supranational organization, the same legislative act represents an anticipated incorporation of decisions of this organization. This holds true as long as the organization acts within the powers given to it and especially within the "program of integration" which is laid down by the founding treaty of the organization[12].

---

8   Herdegen in: Maunz-Dürig, Grundgesetz, Art. 25, marginal note 20.

9   For the following cf. Hilf, General Problems of Relations between Constitutional Law and International Law, in: Starck (ed.), Rights, Institutions and Impact of International Law according to the German Basic Law, 1987, p. 178 et seq.

10   Hilf, ibid., p. 187.

11   BVerfGE 1, 372 (381), and ever since.

12   Cf. in particular the "Maastricht" decision of the Federal Constitutional Court (BVerfGE 89, 155 et seq.), and most recently its decision on the "Lisbon Treaty" (BVerfGE 123, 267 et seq.); in both decisions the Court maintained that legal instruments of the European Union transgressing the limits of the previous "transfer" would be inapplicable in Germany.

As far as non-supranational organizations are concerned, decisions will have to be incorporated by an act of either the legislature or the executive, depending on which institution would be competent to adopt a corresponding rule of national law.

The general rules of international law shall – according to Art. 25 of the Basic Law take precedence over the laws. "Laws" in this context mean the ordinary federal laws or the laws of the Länder. Thus the general rules will not be able to override constitutional law. This is in the opinion of the prevailing doctrine and of the case law of the Constitutional Court[13].

The rank of treaties corresponds to the rank of the incorporating act. If a treaty is incorporated by a parliamentary act of consent, the treaty has the same rank as this legislative act. The lex posterior rule applies. This is at least the prevailing opinion of the doctrine. In regard to treaties in the field of human rights, a more recent opinion argues in favour of the concept of lex specialis. The general constitutional principle favouring the effective application of international obligations and the respect of the international legal order may equally lead to an application of the lex specialis rule in regard to all international treaties. In general it may not be supposed that the legislature wanted to violate prior treaty obligations. But it is recognized that the legislature can deviate from prior treaty law by adopting an internal law contrary to the relevant treaty rules, thus, however, accepting possible reactions/sanctions under international law. A deplorable practice of "treaty overriding" has become popular in the field of double taxation agreements[14].

This is the general framework. Let me now turn to what one may call "war powers".

For more than 10 years after the end of World War II, Germany had no armed forces and no provision in the Constitution relating to them. When such provisions were introduced into the Basic Law and new armed forces raised after fierce political debates and judicial struggles before the Constitutional Court[15] in 1956, the relevant provisions[16] made it very clear that the role of the armed forces should be limited to the defence of the country, that the armed forces could be deployed only in very few situations within the country (e.g. natural

---

13 This, according to Hilf (note 9, p. 188) is the prevailing opinion in the doctrine and the case law of the Constitutional Court.

14 Cf. Stein, Völkerrecht und internationales Steuerrecht im Widerstreit?, in: Internationales Steuerrecht 2006, p. 505 et seq.

15 For a historical overview cf. Dokumentation: Institut für Staatslehre und Politik (ed.), Der Kampf um den Wehrbeitrag, 3 vols., 1952–1958.

16 Amendments of the Basic Law of 19 March 1956, BGBl. (Federal Gazette) 1956 I, p. 111 and of 24 June 1968, BGBl. 1968 I, p. 709.

disasters), and that they were placed – as part of the executive – under the command of the government. Commander-in-chief is the Minister of Defence (always a civilian), and only in times of war (state of defence) the Federal Chancellor[17].

Art. 87a of the Basic Law, therefore, provides:

(1)   The Federation shall establish Armed Forces for purposes of defence. Their numerical strength and general organizational structure must be shown in the budget.

(2)   Apart from defence, the Armed Forces may be employed only to the extent expressly permitted by this Basic Law.

And those express permissions were only the already mentioned natural disasters.

For many years it was politically unconceivable to deploy units of the German armed forces beyond the national borders, remembrance of German uniforms in far away regions of the world being too fresh, even for UN peace-keeping operations.

But pressure on German governments from the side of its NATO allies as well as from the side of the UN, to contribute to peace-keeping operations, mounted constantly, and the old political arguments for not participating were no longer accepted.

Probably in the late seventies or early eighties, a subordinate lawyer in the Ministry of Defence (as it was rumoured) had the bright idea to say: Art. 87a of the Basic Law does not allow any deployment of the armed forces beyond the national borders; it would not be defence, and there is no explicit permission for that in the Basic Law. It is a somewhat typical German position to say "we have to", or "we are not allowed to", and not "we could, but we don't want to". This became the official position defended by all branches of government (of whatever political colour) and the vast majority of constitutional law professors[18].

But then came a dramatic change in German foreign policy, which during the Iraq-Kuwait conflict had still taken a very reserved stance and had confined itself to a – considerable – financial contribution to the "Coalition of the willing" efforts to liberate Kuwait. After the emergence of the crisis in the former Yugoslavia and in Somalia in 1992 and 1993, the German government decided

---

17   Art. 65a and Art. 115b of the Basic Law.

18   For the opposite view cf. Stein, Die verfassungsrechtliche Zulässigkeit einer Beteiligung der Bundesrepublik Deutschland an Friedenstruppen der Vereinten Nationen in: Frowein/Stein (ed.), Rechtliche Aspekte einer Beteiligung der Bundesrepublik Deutschland an Friedenstruppen der Vereinten Nationen (1990), p. 17 et seq.

to let German armed forces participate in various NATO and West European Union, as well as UN operations (monitoring activities in the Adriatic and assisting UNOSOM II in Somalia)[19]. Then – and until today, where troops are deployed in Bosnia, Kosovo, Afghanistan and some other countries –, conscripts and reservists only participate if they volunteer to do so.

The Social Democrats, the opposition in the Federal Parliament, but also the Free Democrats, the coalition partner of the governing Christian Democrats, took the view that any deployment of German armed forces "out of area" was in contravention of the Basic Law if not approved by Parliament in advance and – according to the Social Democrats – with a qualified majority of two-thirds of its members. Four applications were filed with the Federal Constitutional Court with the request that it should be decided that the Federal Government, by its decisions, had violated Parliament's and its members' rights to take part in any decision concerning the use of German armed forces outside the NATO framework.

Before I will come to the since then leading decision of the Constitutional Court, let me briefly mention the constitutional debate at that time[20].

The starting point of the debate is Article 87a paragraph 2 Basic Law[21]. At first glimpse, the wording suggests that this Article is close to the heart of the problem of deployment of German armed forces, whereas all other provisions of the Basic Law seemingly require broad interpretation to cover the question. However, the scope of Article 87a paragraph 2 has been controversial, and its applicability to the question at issue has been disputed. A number of constitutional scholars argue that it is strictly limited to domestic use of the German armed forces. There are some quite noteworthy arguments to be advanced in support of this opinion, the first of which is the position of Article 87a paragraph 2 in Chapter VIII of the Basic Law. Chapter VIII is entitled "The Execution of Federal Statutes and the Federal Administration" and deals with questions of federalism, i.e., with problems relating to the internal structure of the division of powers between the Federation and the Länder, not with external problems such as the deployment of the German armed forces abroad. Secondly, the drafting history points towards a limited scope of Article 87a paragraph 2. Replacing the former Article 143 Basic Law (which dealt with the use of the German armed forces in an internal emergency situation), Article 87a was

---

19   Cf. Heintschel von Heinegg/Haltern, The Decision of the German Federal Constitutional Court of 12 July 1994 in re Deployment of the German Armed Forces "out of area", in: Netherlands International Law Review 1994, p. 285 et seq.
20   For details see Stein (note 18).
21   Cf. for the following also Heintschel von Heinegg/Haltern (note 19).

included in the Basic Law in the framework of the 1968 "State of Emergency Amendment". From this context, some authors deduce that the scope of Article 87a paragraph 2 is equally confirmed to internal uses of the German armed forces. Another argument put forward is based on the 1956 version of Article 87a (which contained only para. 1) which in no way restricted the deployment of German armed forces abroad, and concludes that the 1968 amendment did not intend to curtail this freedom of action.

Others simply pointed at the wording of this Article, which provides no clue at all that the scope is to be limited to the domestic use of the armed forces.

Those scholars who came to the conclusion that any deployment of the German armed forces abroad constitutes a "use" in the sense of Article 87a para. 2 Basic Law without falling under the term "defence", have to deal with the legal consequences required by this Article: any lawful deployment necessitates the explicit permission by the Basic Law.

The central provision in the Basic Law in this respect is Article 24 para. 2, empowering the Federation to enter into a system of mutual collective security. But is that an "explicit permission", although it does not mention at all the deployment of armed forces?

The Constitutional Court[22], in contrast to the academic debate, did not consider Art. 87a para. 2 to be the starting point for a constitutional evaluation of an "out of area" deployment of the German armed forces, "out of area" meaning that forces were not engaged in defence operations within the NATO Treaty area.

Thus, the Court evades the problem of determining whether Article 87a para. 2 Basic Law only concerns the internal use of the German armed forces or whether it applies to any use, be it inside, be it outside the territory of the Federal Republic. According to the Court, neither a narrow nor an extensive interpretation of Article 87a para. 2 would exclude the use of the German armed forces within the framework of a system of mutual collective security to which the Federal Republic is a member State. The Court heavily bases its conclusion upon the fact that Article 24 para. 2 has been part of the Basic Law from the outset, whereas Article 87a para. 2 were only incorporated in 1968. The Court sees no reason to assume that the legislature, by amending the Basic Law, intended to modify the constitutional basis for the deployment of German armed forces within the framework of a system of mutual collective security, i.e., Article 24 para. 2 Basic Law. The 1968 amendment was not intended to reduce the possible participation of the Federal Republic in the UN system. In 1968

---

22 An English version of the decision (BVerfGE 90, 286 et seq) is published in International Law Reports 106 (1997), p. 319 et seq.

German accession to the UN was not then foreseeable. Thus, the impact of the amendment on Article 24 para. 2 lay beyond the legislature's intent. Rather, the legislature confined itself to the conditions required for the use of German armed forces in the case of an internal state of emergency. Article 87a para. 2 was thus neither aimed at establishing novel uses of the armed forces nor at reducing or modifying those already provided for in the Basic Law.

So the Court's choice fell on Art. 24 para. 2 in order to solve the case. That decision was very controversial within the Court, and on some questions the bench was split (4 : 4), which means that no violation of the Constitution could be established.

According to the Court, under Art. 24 para. 2 the Federation may enter into a system of mutual collective security. This does not merely imply that the Federation may enter into such a system and that it is entitled to consent to the respective limitations upon its rights of sovereignty. Moreover, Article 24 para. 2 Basic Law is the constitutional basis for the assumption of tasks typically connected with such a system, including the deployment of the German armed forces in operations that take place in the framework and according to the rules of the system. A system of mutual collective security regularly depends upon armed forces contributing to the fulfilment of the system's mandate. These forces, as an *ultima ratio* measure, may also be used against an aggressor State. The member States must, therefore, be prepared to make available military means to the system for the maintenance and for the restoration of peace.

But this "generosity" of the Constitutional Court had its price, a price that some nowadays see as very high, perhaps too high: The prior and constitutive consent of the Parliament to every detail of a deployment of armed forces abroad.

The use of the German armed forces "out of area" under a UN mandate does not require the Federal Government to acquire Parliament's prior and formal consent in the form of a bill of that effect. However, the Court was not prepared to leave the decision on the use of German armed forces to the executive alone. The German armed forces are not at the Government's disposal; they are an instrument within the democratic constitutional order. Hence, Parliament must have a decisive legal influence on the establishment, as well as on the use, of the armed forces. The Court, thus, by taking account of the legislative history, derives from the Basic Law the principle of a constitutive proviso of Parliament for the military use of the armed forces[23].

This is by no means a generally accepted reasoning. On the one hand, it may be doubted whether it is legitimate to rely that heavily on the legislative history,

---

23   Cf. for this and the following Heintschel von Heinegg/Haltern (note 19, p. 308).

especially when important questions like the use of the armed forces under today's circumstances are concerned. On the other hand, the examples the Court refers to relate to declarations of war. Under traditional international law and under the former German constitutions, a declaration of war was considered necessary for the creation of a "state of war". For that reason alone, a declaration of war was subject to the prior and formal consent of Parliament[24]. The use of armed forces abroad, in particular in connection with UN authorized peace keeping operations, is not necessarily (to say the least) comparable to a declaration of war. The truth is that the ever since by the Constitutional Court so-called "parliamentary army" is a "sovereign invention" by that Court, that had no serious basis in the Basic Law or any prior German constitutions.

This proviso is not limited to a deployment "out of area". Unless Parliament and the Federal Council have already determined the state of defence according to Art. 115a Basic Law, the proviso even applies if there is an attack against the territory of the Federal Republic or against a NATO ally, notwithstanding the "alliance clause" under Art. 5 of the NATO Treaty. The prior and constitutive consent of Parliament is, as already mentioned, also required if the German armed forces are to take part in operations decided upon by the UN Security Council. In this context, it is irrelevant whether they are entitled to take (military) enforcement measures or whether they have to confine themselves to traditional peace-keeping tasks. The Court reached this conclusion because it was unable to determine the borderline between the former and the latter. Moreover, in the case of a traditional peace-keeping operation the right to take measures in self-defence implies the right to meet by force any attempts aimed at preventing the peace-keeping forces from fulfilling their tasks. Only if members of the German armed forces are engaged in humanitarian assistance or other acts of assistance abroad, i.e., when they are not incorporated in armed operations, is prior consent by Parliament not required[25].

---

24   Art. 11 of the Constitution of the German Empire of 16 April 1871 states (my translation): "The Emperor declares war in the name of the Empire ... the declaration of war in the name of the Empire requires the consent of the Federal Council unless the federal territory or its coasts are attacked". Art. 45 (2) of the "Weimar" Constitution of 11 August 1919 states that (my translation): "A declaration war is to be effected by law". And, finally, Art. 115a of the German Basic Law (which does not know the "declaration of war" anymore) provides: "Any determination that the federal territory is under attack by armed force ... shall be made by the Bundestag with the consent of the Bundesrat ... and shall require a two-thirds majority of the votes cast ...".
Non of these provisions come only close to dealing with any other use of the armed forces.

25   See Heintschel von Heinegg/Haltern (note 19, p. 308 et seq.).

At the time of that first decision of the Constitutional Court in 1994 (repeatedly confirmed since)[26] we thought that it would not do much harm. Any government that would send troops abroad without having the support of its (simple) majority in the Parliament would not stay in office for long. But in the meantime (since March 2005) we have a "Law on the Participation of the Parliament on the Decision of the Deployment of Armed Forces Abroad"[27], according to which the Parliament (i.e. over 600 "strategic experts") decide upon the mission, the area of deployment, the legal bases of the deployment, the maximum number of troops and their capabilities, the duration of the deployment (seldom more than 6 months) and the expected costs and their basis in the State's budget.

One consequence is that even the German Navy needs prior parliamentary approval for taking action against pirates off the cost of Somalia or Yemen, actions which are an obligation under the UN Convention on the Law of the Sea, should a German Navy vessel in the area become aware of an attack by pirates against a ship flying whatever flag. Ironically, under the Constitution, the Special Forces of the Federal Police (GSG 9) do not need prior parliamentary approval if sent to free a German ship captured by pirates. Only some weeks ago, these Special Forces were sent to Kenya in order to prepare to liberate a German vessel, but disputes between the Ministries of Defence (Navy) and of the Interior (Federal Police) in the end led to end that operation before it began. This highlights another peculiarity of the German Constitutional system, the strict separation between the armed forces and the police, as well as between the different intelligence services and the police or the armed forces. This principle may have been understandable 60 years ago, at the moment of the adoption of the Basic Law, having the former "Gestapo" (the Secret State Police) in mind, which combined all investigating and executive powers. But today that principle of "separation" leads to absurd results and unnecessary failures.

International Cooperation and International Integration of the Federal Republic of Germany in the 60th year of the Basic Law is certainly a success story in many fields, but the self imposed "hand cuffs" for the deployment of armed forces in peace-keeping operations together with allies and/or under UN mandate in my opinion need to be reconsidered. Otherwise Germany's influence in international organisations will remain week or even shrink, as we see today in NATO.

---

26   The last one being Case 2 BVE 1/03 of 7 May 2008 on the participation of German Air Force soldiers in AWACS aircraft over Turkey during the Iraq war in 2003 (BVerfGE 121, p. 135 et seq.).

27   BGBl. 2005 I, p. 775.

George Williams

International Law and the War Power in Australia[*]

International Law and the Constitution

The Australian Constitution says very little about international law. The key sections that envisage some form of intersection with the international legal order are s 51(xxix), which grants the federal Parliament the power to enact legislation with respect to 'external affairs', and s 75(i) which vests the High Court with original jurisdiction in relation to 'matters arising under a treaty'. The Constitution makes no reference to three crucial issues: the method of Australia's entry into binding legal relationships on the international stage; the legal effect of international law within the domestic legal system; and the responsibility for enforcement of such obligations at the domestic level.

The decision not to define the relationship with international law in the Australian Constitution is based on two considerations. First, at the time of Federation in 1901, the British government had exclusive control over Australia's foreign relations. The drafters were concerned not to include any provision that might suggest that Australia was entitled to enter into treaties on its own behalf.[1]

The second consideration was a concern with the nature of international law. The debates in the Conventions of the 1890s[2] that drafted the Australian Constitution reflect a perception that international law was not law, but rather a discretionary set of norms that states could neglect at will. On the basis that there was then no effective enforcement regime operating in the international arena, it was seen as illogical to accord direct effect to international obligations in the domestic legal system. For example, at the Sydney Convention in 1897, the Premier of New South Wales George Reid stated:

---

[*] Parts of this article have been developed from Hilary Charlesworth, Madelaine Chiam, Devika Hovell and George Williams, 'Deep Anxieties: Australia and the International Legal Order' (2003) 25 *Sydney Law Review* 423 and George Williams, 'The Power to Go to War: Australia in Iraq' (2004) 15 *Public Law Review* 5.

[1] John Quick and Robert Garran, *The Annotated Constitution of the Australian Commonwealth* (1901) 770.

[2] *Official Record of the Debates of the Australasian Federal Convention* (1891–1898, reprinted 1986).

The treaties made by her Majesty are not binding as laws on the people of the United Kingdom, and there is no penalty for disobeying them. Legislation is sometimes passed to give effect to treaties, but the treaties themselves are not laws, and indeed nations sometimes find them inconvenient, as they neglect them very seriously without involving any important legal consequences.[3]

Against this backdrop, it is unclear why the reference to treaties was retained in section 75(i). Patrick Glynn, a delegate to the 1897–1898 Convention from South Australia, objected to the subsection because judicial decisions upon treaties 'might abrogate the Imperial law or polity upon the question at issue'.[4] However, other Members of the Convention, including Reid, argued for the retention of the subsection because treaties that specifically concern Australia might one day be entered into or that '[s]ome day hereafter it may be within the scope of the Commonwealth to deal with matters of this kind'.[5]

The modest view taken of the significance of international law in the 1890s failed to capture the changing nature of the international legal order since that time. International law has been transformed from an 'inter-state law of peaceful co-existence'[6] into a law that transcends individual state boundaries to affect domestic affairs and individuals. The globalisation process has brought with it increased co-operation among states in the regulation of economics and trade, human rights, the environment, communications, education, science, transport and so on. The lack of precision in the Australian Constitution means that it is able to accommodate such changes, although the manner in which is does so is not specified. The development of mechanisms to accommodate developments in international law has been left to the executive, legislature and judiciary.

Australia's constitutional structure assigns the executive a central role in determining the extent to which international law affects the domestic legal system. The powers of the executive are not defined, but are vested in general terms by s 61 of the Constitution in the Queen, and are exercisable by the Governor-General as her representative.[7] Nevertheless, it is clear that the executive power grants to the Executive an exclusive power to assume

---

3   *Official Record of the Debates of the Australasian Federal Convention* (Sydney, 1897), 240.

4   *Official Record of the Debates of the Australasian Federal Convention* (Sydney, 1897), 320.

5   *Official Record of the Debates of the Australasian Federal Convention* (Sydney, 1897), 320.

6   Luzius Wildhaber, 'Sovereignty and International Law' in Ronald Macdonald and Douglas Johnston (eds), *The Structure and Process of International Law* (1983), 438.

7   Section 61 states: 'The executive power of the Commonwealth is vested in the Queen and is exercisable by the Governor-General as the Queen's representative, and extends to the execution and maintenance of this Constitution, and of the laws of the Commonwealth.'

international obligations.[8] The executive also has the capacity to determine the manner in which international obligations are implemented domestically.

If the executive has determined that complying with Australia's international obligations requires the passage of specific implementing legislation, the Australian Parliament has the role of determining the form and content of that legislation. The power of federal Parliament includes, in s 51(xxix) of the Constitution, the capacity to pass laws with respect to 'external affairs'. This power has been interpreted broadly by the High Court to enable the Common-wealth to pass laws that implement any obligation that the federal executive assumes under an international treaty or convention.[9] The proliferation of treaties and conventions at the international level has made this power useful to the Commonwealth in a range of areas including industrial relations,[10] human rights[11] and the environment.[12]

Even apart from its treaty implementation aspect, members of the High Court have suggested that the external affairs power allows the Commonwealth to legislate for the criminalisation of certain offences, such as piracy, arising under international law that are recognised as being part of the 'universal jurisdiction' of all nations.[13] It is also arguable that the power enables the Commonwealth to legislate to implement international customary law in so far as it binds Australia.

When it comes to the role of the Australian judiciary, the following principles are generally accepted. First, treaties ratified by Australia have no direct effect in Australian law, unless given effect to by an Act of Parliament.[14] A limited exception is that individuals are entitled to a 'legitimate expectation' that Commonwealth decision-makers will take account of international treaties

---

8   *R v Burgess; Ex Parte Henry* (1936) 55 CLR 608, 644.

9   *Commonwealth v Tasmania* (*Tasmanian Dam Case*) (1983) 158 CLR 1.

10   See, for example, the provisions dealing with parental leave in Division 5 of Part VIA of the *Workplace Relations Act 1996* (Cth). They give effect to Australia's obligations under the Workers with Family Responsibilities Convention 1981 and the Workers with Family Responsibilities Recommendation 1981.

11   See, for example, the *Racial Discrimination Act 1975* (Cth) (implements the International Convention on the Elimination of All Forms of Racial Discrimination), the *Sex Discrimination Act 1984* (Cth) (implements Convention on the Elimination of All Forms of Discrimination Against Women) and the *Disability Discrimination Act 1992* (Cth) (implements International Labour Organisation Convention 111 – Discrimination (Employment and Occupation) Convention, the International Covenant on Civil and Political Rights 1966 and the International Covenant on Economic, Social and Cultural Rights 1966).

12   See, for example, the *World Heritage Properties Conservation Act 1983* (Cth), which gives effect to the Convention for the Protection of the World Cultural and Natural Heritage.

13   *Polyukhovich v Commonwealth* (*War Crimes Act Case*) (1991) 172 CLR 501 (Brennan and Toohey JJ).

14   *Kioa v West* (1985) 159 CLR 550, 570–1.

ratified by Australia but not implemented by legislation when a decision is made that affects their private rights.[15]

Second, customary international law and treaties reflecting customary international law are a source for the development of the common law. For example, in recognising 'traditional native title' in *Mabo v Queensland (No 2)*,[16] Brennan J stated: 'The common law does not necessarily conform with inter-national law, but international law is a legitimate and important influence on the development of the common law, especially when inter-national law declares the existence of universal human rights'.

Third, in the interpretation of legislation courts favour a construction that accords with Australia's international obligations, as set out in customary international law and treaties ratified by Australia prior to the enactment of the legislation. The use of international law in this way is authorised by s 15AB(2) of the *Acts Interpretation Act 1901* (Cth). As stated in *Chu Kheng Lim v Minister for Immigration*,[17] courts 'should, in a case of ambiguity, favour a construction of a Commonwealth statute which accords with the obligations of Australia under an international treaty'. Courts thus refer to sources of international law to confirm the meaning of a statutory provision, to construe general words, or to resolve ambiguity or uncertainty. Courts will also not impute to the legislature an intention to abrogate or curtail fundamental rights or freedoms (including those set out in international law) unless such an intention is manifested by unmistakable and unambiguous language.[18]

Fourth, despite the use of international law in statutory interpretation and in developing the common law, the High Court has been reluctant to use such norms in interpreting the Constitution. The extent to which international law may be used in interpretation of the Australian Constitution remains the subject of heated debate. On the one hand, Kirby J of the High Court has stated:

international law is a legitimate and important influence on the development of the common law and constitutional law, especially when international law declares the existence of universal and fundamental rights. To the full extent that its text permits, Australia's Constitution, as the fundamental law of government in this country, accommodates itself to international law, including in so far as that law expresses basic rights. The reason for this is that the Constitution not only speaks to the people of Australia who made it and accept it for their governance. It also speaks to the international community as the basic law of the Australian nation which is a member of that community.[19]

---

15   *Minister for Immigration and Ethnic Affairs v Teoh* (1995) 183 CLR 273.
16   (1992) 175 CLR 1 at 42.
17   (1992) 176 CLR 1 at 38.
18   *Coco v The Queen* (1994) 179 CLR 427.
19   *Newcrest Mining (WA) Ltd v Commonwealth* (1997) 190 CLR 513, 657–8.

On the other hand, most other judges of the High Court have rejected the use of international law in this way. For example, Callinan J has said:

> The provisions of the Constitution are not to be read in conformity with international law. It is an anachronistic error to believe that the Constitution, which was drafted and adopted by the people of the colonies well before international bodies such as the United Nations came into existence, should be regarded as speaking to the international community. The Constitution is *our* fundamental law, not a collection of principles amounting to the rights of man, to be read and approved by people and institutions elsewhere.[20]

The Power to go to War

Australia's controversial participation in the conflict in Iraq as part of the 'coalition of the willing' created debate about how the nation goes to war. Should the government of the day be able to direct the military to use force in hostile action outside of Australia without parliamentary approval? This question can be particularly acute where, as in the Iraq conflict, a government seeks to use force in a way that is apparently at odds with popular opinion and certainly at odds with the views of the upper house of the Australia Parliament, the Senate. The question can also be acute when force is used in a way that breaches international law.

It might be expected that the Australian Constitution would set out who can declare war for Australia. After all, there are few exercises of public power in the international sphere more important than committing a nation to war. Unfortunately, the Constitution does not expressly supply the answer.[21]

Section 51 empowers the federal Parliament to pass laws with respect to 'The naval and military defence of the Commonwealth and of the several States', while s 68 vests the Governor-General, as the representative of the Queen, with command of the defence forces. Section 61 describes the executive power in broad and undefined terms and says nothing directly on this topic.

The Australian Constitution is otherwise silent. It says nothing about who can declare war for Australia or the circumstances in which we might go to war, including whether Australia can use military force in breach of international law as part of a unilateral or pre-emptive strike. There is certainly nothing resembling Art 9 of the Japanese Constitution, which states that 'the Japanese people forever renounce war as a sovereign right of the nation'.

---

20   *Western Australia v Ward* (2002) 213 CLR 1 at 390–1.
21   See generally Geoffrey Lindell, 'The Constitutional Authority to Deploy Australian Military Forces in the Coalition War Against Iraq' (2003) 5 *Constitutional Law and Policy Review* 46

It is not surprising that much is again left unsaid in the Constitution. It is a document framed in the 19th century for governments operating according to the conventions and practices of the Westminster tradition of that era. That was not a time that contemplated popular or even parliamentary involvement in decisions about war, let alone that Australia might consider itself bound by the rules of a body like the United Nations. If we were bound in any way, it was to the foreign policy of the United Kingdom.

Without a clear answer from the text of the *Constitution* (or even from the *Defence Act 1903* (Cth)), some would argue that the decision to go to war against Iraq should be made by Parliament or the people. However, the unwritten practices of the Constitution inherited form the United Kingdom direct otherwise. They suggest that the decision is within the prerogative of the Prime Minister and Cabinet alone. The Prime Minister may have Parliament debate the issue or arrange for a popular vote. However, he or she need not consult Parliament or the people and the decision will ultimately be made in the secrecy of the Cabinet room. The Governor-General will then be informed as the Commander in Chief and by convention must follow the decision or face dismissal.

The situation is different in the United States, where President George W Bush was not as free to take his country to war. Article 1 of the United States Constitution vests the power 'to declare war' in Congress and not the President. On the other hand, Art 2 states that the President is the 'commander in chief'. Significantly, the President's power has been used without the approval of Congress to engage in undeclared wars in countries such as Vietnam and has given rise to an ongoing debate over which branch of government possesses the war powers of the nation.

The tension between Congress and President was resolved over whether to go to war in Iraq. In October 2002, Congress authorised the President, in its words, 'to use the Armed Forces of the United States as he determines to be necessary and appropriate in order to defend the national security of the United States against the continuing threat posed by Iraq'. The resolution enabled the United States to go to war with or without the backing of the United Nations Security Council.

Comparison with constitutional systems like the United States raises the question of whether Parliament or the people should play a role in Australia. The United Kingdom is in the middle of such a debate. Upon becoming Prime Minister in June 2007, Gordon Brown's first major announcement started a public debate on far-reaching changes to how Britain is governed. His Green Paper on *The Governance of Britain* calls for constitutional change that entrusts more power to Parliament and the British people. One of Brown's more contentious suggestions is to reform the power of government to deploy troops abroad to a conflict like that in Iraq. The proposal is to give Parliament the ultimate say on such decisions, perhaps in the form of a veto.

Such a decision should not be made by the people. A plebiscite is too unwieldy an exercise on such an issue, and for the same reasons that citizen-initiated referenda are not consistent with Australia's system of representative government, a popular vote on whether to go to war should be rejected. Parliament, on the other hand, should have a formalised role in Australia's decision to go to war. One reason for this is the obligations that Australia has assumed under international law. While Australia in 1901 had not submitted to an international jurisdiction that made illegal its use of force, this is not true today.

Australia has been a party to the Charter of the United Nations since 1945. That Charter has the status of a higher law in the international legal order, with Art 103 of the Charter providing that Member States' obligations under the Charter shall prevail over other international obligations. Australia's obligations under the Charter must be considered in light of the object and purpose of the Charter. The Preamble sets out the object of the establishment of the United Nations as being 'to save succeeding generations from the scourge of war, which twice in our lifetime has brought untold sorrow to mankind', with an overriding aim of ensuring 'that armed force shall not be used, save in the common interest'.

After the experience of two World Wars, the drafters of the Charter established a world order based on two interrelated underlying principles: first, to bring about the resolution of international disputes by peaceful means and, second, recognition that the use of force would only be justified as a last resort in the interest of the international community, and not individual States. Under this legal framework, the use of force is prohibited by Art 2(4), which states: 'All Members shall refrain in their international relations from the threat or use of force against the territorial integrity or political independence of any state, or in any other manner inconsistent with the purposes of the United Nations'. This cardinal principle of international law is subject to two exceptions, relating to Security Council authorisation under Ch VII and self-defence under Art 51 of the Charter, and possibly a third relating to humanitarian intervention.

The effect of this regime is that the use of force by Australia can raise different issues than were imagined at the time the Australian Constitution was drafted. A key question in the use of force by Australia in Iraq was thus whether

Australia breached its international obligations, as I believe it did.[22]. This question can have ramifications for the nation and its long term security and economic prosperity beyond the decision to use force in a particular case. Accordingly, international law is one legal reason why it is no longer appropriate for the decision to use force by the military to be left solely in the hands of the executive. This may especially be the case where there are serious doubts about the justification for the use of force as part of a unilateral pre-emptive strike.

The argument in favour of parliamentary involvement has been reflected in Australia in recent times in two ways. First, Australia did not use force in Iraq without parliamentary debate (albeit after troops had been pre-deployed in the region). The matter was brought before the House of Representatives on a motion by the Prime Minister and a vote held on 20 March 2003 that authorised the use of force.

While Prime Minister Howard recognised that the 'decision lies with the executive of government: the cabinet' he 'Nevertheless [thought it] appropriate that the parliament, at the first opportunity, have the chance to debate this motion. It is essential that the reason for that decision be made plain to the representatives of the people and that they have a full opportunity to debate them and to have their views recorded.'[23] That motion 'endorse[d] the Government's decision to commit Australian Defence Force elements in the region to the international coalition of military forces prepared to enforce Iraq's compliance with its international obligations under successive resolutions of the United Nations Security Council, with a view to restoring international peace and security in the Middle East region'.[24] A separate motion in the Senate 'call[ed] for the Australian troops to be withdrawn and returned home'.[25] The latter motion was ignored.

Second, it has been proposed that the power to go to war be changed by legislation. On 27 March 2003, a Bill was introduced in the Senate which would have amended the *Defence Act 1903* (Cth) to provide that members of the Defence Force could not be required to serve beyond Australia's territorial limits 'except in accordance with a resolution agreed to by each House of the Parliament authorising the service', or pursuant to an emergency proclamation by the Governor-General. In the latter case, if Parliament was not sitting when the proclamation was made, it was to be summoned to meet within two days

---

22   Devika Hovell and George Williams, 'Advice to Hon Simon Crean MP on the Use of Force Against Iraq' (2003) 4 *Melbourne Journal of International Law* 183

23   Australia, House of Representatives, *Debates* (18 March 2003), 12,506.

24   Australia, House of Representatives, *Debates* (18 March 2003), 12,505.

25   Australia, Senate, *Debates* (18 March 2003), 10,321.

thereafter. The Bill was debated in the Senate in 2005,[26] but was never put to a vote.

---

26   Australia, Senate, *Debates* (10 February 2005), 106–34.

Rolf Schwartmann

The Role of the Basic Law in Major Social Conflicts

I. Federal Constitutional Court as a special court of constitutional jurisdiction

First of all, I would like to thank you for the opportunity to speak here at the University House of the Australian National University in Canberra on this celebratory occasion, commemorating this great day for the German Constitution. It is my first stay in Australia and I really appreciate your invitation. I am more than delighted to attend this conference and I would like to express my gratitude for giving me this unique possibility to elaborate on the role of the basic law in major social conflicts just on the very day that marks the 60th anniversary of the German Constitution, the Grundgesetz.

Before my Australian counterpart, my honourable colleague Miss Katharine Gelber, will speak to you on behalf of the role of the Commonwealth Constitution concerning this very aspect, I would like to take this opportunity to talk about my understanding of the role of the German Constitution (Grundgesetz), the implemented basic rights (Grundrechte) and the role of the Federal Constitutional Court (Bundesverfassungsgericht) in major social conflicts.

Let me start out with something you most likely did not know about the German Federal Constitutional Court – unlike the High Court of Australia it is actually comparable to a *barbershop*. And I am not making this up but officially referring to a former President of the court. Nevertheless, I guess, I owe you an explanation now: Since there is no political question doctrine in German constitutional law, there have always been concerns about the Federal Constitutional Court deciding major social conflicts. Which has led to one significant question: Does this instance actually give the Federal Constitutional Court too much political power and at the same time downgrade legislature? Well, let me put it as Ernst Benda, a former President of the court, did when asked to describe its function and work: *"Our court is just like a barber shop – you come in, you get shaved. So if you want to stay unshorn, you better stay out."*[1]

---

1   Ernst Benda, quoted from Süddeutsche Zeitung, 12 December 2001, p. 8.

Nevertheless the German Constitution provides legal principles and merely sets a distinctive framework. To put it with my colleague, Horst Dreier, the Constitution is *"not the bible, political life is no high mass and the interpreter of the Constitution is certainly no high priest"*[2]. Therefore the Constitution cannot be regarded as an inexhaustible font of answers. One would certainly impose an unbearable burden on the Constitution if you ask for definite answers to all relevant and ethnical questions. As Dreier just recently phrased it in the German newspaper DIE ZEIT, it takes considerably more to solve these major social questions "than only to decipher the words of the constitution". And there is one fact you have to be aware of – the more you read into the Constitution the less clearance there is for legislature to solve major social conflicts independently.

However, as interpretation of the Constitution is essential and inevitable, the constitutional law in Germany is supplemented by interpretation by the Federal Constitutional Court, the Bundesverfassungsgericht – an instance which particularly comes to effect when major social conflicts and political questions arise. As the court's jurisdiction is limited to the interpretation of the Constitution, the so-called Basic Law, the court is often referred to as the "supreme guardian of the Constitution". As we will see later on, when I will highlight some significant decisions of the Federal Constitutional Court, over the past 60 years the court has elaborated rights that the constitution's authors never envisaged. We will have to determine to what extent these decisions have influenced the work of parliamentary legislature as well as the work of the courts until today. From these decisions, it becomes evident that the effects of the Federal Constitutional Court decisions live up to a sufficient extent to the task that is assigned to the Court by the Basic Law and to its importance in the constitutional system.

Although the Federal Constitutional Court is not a political body and its sole standard is the Basic law, its work undoubtedly does have a sustainable political impact[3]. With regard to the political and notional values of the constitution and with reference to the catalogue of basic rights the Federal Constitutional Court has constantly developed its own specific rules of interpretation. Thus it is the Federal Constitutional Court which merely determines the constitutional framework for political decision-making. As I mentioned at the beginning the question to be asked might be whether the Federal Constitutional Court even plays a bigger role than that, and – as some say –, in fact, dictate legislature what

---

2   Horst Dreier, "60 Jahre und kein bisschen heilig", DIE ZEIT, 7 May 2009, online available: http://pdf.zeit.de/2009/20/oped.pdf.

3   See *Landfried*, Impact of the German Federal Constitutional Court on Politics and Policy Output, in Government and Opposition, Vol. 20 (2007), p. 523–534.

to do. One instance must seriously not be queried though – the role of the basic law in major basic conflicts cannot be contemplated without taking a closer look at the impact and influence the Federal Constitutional Court's work has on questions of political expediency.

The court's competencies[4] are specified in the Constitution, the Basic Law, which was adopted in 1949 and complemented in 1990 on the occasion of German reunification. It has comprehensive competencies to control all three state powers on the basis of the Constitution. Therefore the Federal Constitutional Court reviews whether statutes, decisions of other courts and sovereign acts of German administrative authorities or German government are compatible with the Constitution. But one should always keep clearly in mind that the court must not make use of its competences at its own discretion. The Federal Constitutional Court may exercise its powers only if an application is brought to it appropriately. An application is always required – since the Court does not act *ex officio.*

The function of the Constitutional Court to make apparent rules of the Basic Law in concrete cases is based on a very explicit basis. In contrast to the inception of judicial review in the United States, derived by the Supreme Court in its landmark case *Marbury vs. Madison* through implication from basic postulates of the American System, the German Constitutional Court is expressly vested with that power by provisions in the Basic Law. Therefore the Court has to decide constitutional disputes in line with constitutional guidelines. This also applies to social conflicts, whose solving has been increasingly shifted to the judiciary.

The Federal Constitutional Court has developed the Constitution through a series of case rulings. The Court, as judicial body having ultimate responsibility for constitutional review, is concerned not only with the interpretation of the Basic Law but also with the incidence of its own work on the law. As it is to be expected, any *ratio decidendi, dictum* or even *obiter dictum* of such a court tends to invite application by legislative and executive authorities to different situations. In these circumstances it is the function of the Court to ensure that the constitutional evolution remains in accordance with the letter and the spirit of the Basic Law.

---

4   On the functions of the Court see *Limbach*, Das Bundesverfassungsgericht als politischer Machtfaktor, in Humboldt Forum Recht, Beitrag 12, 1996, p. 70 (online available: http://www.humboldt-forum-recht.de/deutsch/12-1996/beitrag.html#punkt1); *Hahn*, Trends in the Jurisprudence of the German Federal Constitutional Court, in American Journal of Comparative Law, Vol. 16 (1968), p. 570–573.

It is noteworthy to mention, that in many countries where a written constitution is implemented, constitutional development in the second half of the 20th century was dominated by concepts of human rights. Unlike Australian Constitution[5] the German constitution contains a significant catalogue of basic rights. These were not intended simply to be a catalogue of good intentions, but as Art.1, Paragraph 3 Basic Law states, the basic rights bind the legislature, the executive and the judiciary. The Federal Constitutional Court has elaborated a theory of human rights, which exceeds the jurisprudence of most other countries with constitutional jurisdiction. According to its jurisdiction, human rights are not merely subjective defensive rights of the individual against the state, but at the same time embody objective values and constitute the highest principles of the whole legal system. As consequence the Court drew the conclusion that the human rights govern the entire legal order, not only public law but private law as well.

II. Human rights as an "objective system of values"

The first decision to develop the notion of human rights as an **"objective system of values"** is the *Lüth* decision[6] of 15 January 1958. The question raised concerned the third-party effect of the human rights (*Drittwirkung*)[7], meaning whether provisions of the Basic Law could have effects between private parties. In their traditional understanding the basic rights are intended as a protection of individuals against the state and state authorities only[8]. It is, however, argued that basic rights stand at the apex of Germany's legal system and influence relations between individual and state as well as those between individuals.

The leading question is: How does the constitution become relevant in exclusively private conflicts? The foundations were laid in case *Lüth*, which is considered the landmark case in German constitutional history. The case, which originated in civil law, was brought to Federal Constitutional Court by Eric Lüth, chairman of the Hamburg Press Club. He called for a boycott of new film

---

5   On Australian Constitution and human rights see *Pittrof,* Grundrechtsschutz durch Verfassungswandel: die Kommunikationsfreiheit in Australien, 2001, p. 28–52.

6   BVerfGE 7, 198; see thereto *Odendahl,* Das "Lüth-Urteil", JA 1998, p. 933–937; *Fiedler,* in Menzel, Verfassungsrechtsprechung, p. 97–107; *Sachs,* Verfassungsrecht II Grundrechte, A4, para. 56–58.

7   See *Pieroth/Schlink,* Staatsrecht II Grundrechte, para. 76, 81, 173–185; *Sachs,* Verfassungsrecht II Grundrechte, A5, para. 30–43; *Lothar/Morlok,* Grundrechte, § 15, para. 478–485.

8   *Pieroth/Schlink,* Staatsrecht II Grundrechte, para. 73–75.

of Veit Harlan, who had directed anti-Semitic propaganda films during the Nazi period. The movie's distributors obtained a temporary order against Lüth based on a provision of the Civil Code (§ 826 BGB). The Court of Appeal (*Landgericht*) Hamburg has accepted that Lüth's call for a boycott could, if successful, cause substantial harm to the applicants. Against the Court order Lüth raised a constitutional complaint based on the right to freedom of speech (Art. 5, Paragraph 1 Basic Law). The Federal Constitutional Court held that the lower Court's decision limits Lüth's fundamental right of free speech. It confirmed that basic rights were primarily negative rights, providing protection of the individual against the state. The Court took, however, the decisive step. The fundamental rights of the Basic Law can also be regarded as an "objective system of values"; values which lie at the heart of Basic Law and influence all areas of the law and with which all law must comply (so called **"radiating effect"** – *Ausstrahlungswirkung*). The Constitutional Court has ruled that human rights can create an indirect effect (*mittelbare Drittwirkung*)[9]. The courts have to interpret the private law (usually general clauses) in the light of the human rights considerations and take the modified law into account. The reason is the fact that the civil court as a part of the judiciary is bound by the basic rights (Art 1, Paragraph 3 Basic Law). In case *Lüth* the civil court should have interpreted civil law provisions in light of the basic rights affected, *i.e.* the right to freedom of speech. Failure of the judge to take this "radiating effect" of basic rights into account will thus not only infringe the "objective system of values" but also the constitutional rights of the concerned individual[10]. The Constitutional Court has to check whether the ordinary court has appropriately assessed the scope of the fundamental right when interpreting the civil law provisions. It was required to balance the interest in the freedom of speech in calling for the boycott with the conflicting economic right to pursue a business and artistic right to display the film[11]. As Lüth had not directly pressurized anyone to follow his call for a boycott, it can be accepted that he had exercised his right within the usual limits of public discussion.

---

9 BVerfGE 7, 198 at p. 204–207. See also *Sachs*, Verfassungsrecht II Grundrechte, A5, para. 38–40; *Lothar/Morlok*, Grundrechte, § 15, para. 481–485
10 BVerfGE 7, 198 at p. 206–207.
11 BVerfGE 7, 198 at p. 207–211.

III. Development of the constitutional duty of the state to protect

The Lüth case can be seen as milestone for two developments in constitutional thinking generally accepted in German constitutional doctrine, i.e. indirect or radiating effect of constitutional norms and judicial balancing[12] of conflicting interests. But Lüth provides also the foundation for the constitutional duty of the state to protect (so called *Schutzpflicht*)[13]. I will illustrate this development in the following cases of the Constitutional Court, that deal with important social problems such as abortion, suppression of terrorism, homosexuality, etc.

IV. Social Conflicts and the Basic Law

1. Abortion

No other constitutional question was so intensely discussed as the problem of abortion[14]. The case began when the German Bundestag (Parliament) passed the Abortion Reform Act of 1974. Before then, abortion was illegal in all circumstances pursuant to German Penal law, with exceptions concerning the life and health of the mother. The reform of the abortion law was a complex process that involved numerous proposals. After four years of legislative wrangling the Bundestag passed the Abortion Reform Act. It amended Section 218 of the German Penal Code to allow abortions during the first twelve weeks of pregnancy with the exception of later abortion in case of certified medical necessity. An abortion up to the twenty-second week was possible to avoid the birth of a seriously defective child.

Shortly after the law was officially published the Act was attacked. One third of the Bundestag's members made use of the possibility provided by the Basic Law and challenged the constitutionality of the law. After eight months of judicial deliberation the Federal Constitutional Court issued its decision on February 25, 1975[15]. The Court interpreted the law according to the Basic Law.

---

12 See *Bomhoff*, Lüth's 50th Anniversary, in German Law Journal, Vol. 9 (2008), p.121–124.

13 *Pieroth/Schlink*, Staatsrecht II Grundrechte, para. 94–99.

14 On the reform of the abortion law see *Eser*, Reform of german abortion law, in American Journal of Comparative Law, Vol. 34 (1986), p. 369–378; *Kommers*, Abortion and Constitution, in American Journal of Comparative Law, Vol. 25 (1977), p. 258–264.

15 BVerfGE 39, 1. See thereto *Dederer*, in Menzel, Verfassungsrechtsprechung, p. 242–248; *Kommers*, Abortion and Constitution, in American Journal of Comparative Law, Vol. 25 (1977), p. 267–275; *Hunt*, A Tale of Two Countries: German and American Attitudes to

It rejected the trimester framework (so called periodic model – *Fristenregelung*) and stated in its decision that the law, which allowed abortion within the first twelve weeks of pregnancy, violated the Basic Law, specifically Art. 2, Paragraph 2 Basic Law, which stated: "everyone shall have the right to life and the inviolability of the person" and Art. 1, Paragraph 1, which proclaimed the "… inviolability of the human dignity" and charged the state with the duty to respect and protect it.

In contrast with Austria and the United States[16], in which the highest courts did not find constitutional support for such a right or favoured the mother's right during the initial phase of the pregnancy, the German Constitutional Court stated that life exists according to biological-physiological knowledge in any case from the 14th day after conception[17]. The fetus is "an autonomous human being" and the right to life should be extended also to the fetus, since the Constitution guaranteed it to "everyone". From the fundamental right to life derives not only the obligation of the state to refrain from direct interference with life but also the obligation of the state to protect and foster the life of the *nasciturus* even against the wishes of the mother[18]. Pregnancy belongs to the private sphere of the women, which is protected by the Basic Law (Art. 2 Paragraph 1 in connection with Art. 1, Paragraph 1 Basic Law). A pregnant woman has also the right to free development of her personality (Art. 2 Paragraph 1 Basic Law) including the right to decide against parenthood. This right however is not guaranteed without limits; it dos not include the right to violate the rights of others or, in our case, to kill that is already considered human life[19]. In the required balancing of the right of the pregnant women to free development of her personality and the right to life of the fetus, both constitutional values must be seen in their relationship to human dignity, which is the center of the constitutional value system. The pregnancy may be contrary to the women's choice and to her free development of personality. Nevertheless the interruption of the pregnancy

Abortion since World War II, UFL Conference Proceedings IV, 1994, p. 125–128 (online available: http://www.uffl.org/vol%204/hunt4.pdf)

16   On US milestone decision *Roe vs. Wade*, issued on 22 January 1973 (online available: http://www.law.cornell.edu/supct/html/historics/USSC_CR_0410_0113_ZO.html)   see *Kommers,* Abortion and Constitution, in American Journal of Comparative Law, Vol. 25 (1977), p. 256–258, 264–266.

17   BVerfGE 39, 1 at p. 37. On the similarities and differences between German and American decisions in the area of abortion see *Yonkers,* The judicial Treatment of Abortion in the United states and Germany, Paper presented at the annual meeting of the Midwest Political Science Association 20 April 2006, online available: http://www.allacademic.com/meta/p139 624_index.html

18   BVerfGE 39, 1 at p. 41–42. See also *Kriele,* Anmerkung, JZ 1975, p. 223–224.

19   BVerfGE 39, 1 at p. 43.

destroys unborn life. In these circumstances and according to the principle of carefully balancing competing constitutionally protected positions the court held that the *nasciturus's* right to life outweighs the right of the pregnant woman to self-determination for the entire duration of pregnancy[20]. This led to the conclusion that the state must consider the abortion to be unlawful. Therefore the court directed the legislature to reestablish abortion as a crime under the Penal Code, because, as the Court sees it, penal sanctions are more apt to prevent abortions and to protect unborn life that were the non-penal measures in the Abortion Reform Act. The law was not able to provide sufficient protection to the fetus's right of life as guaranteed under Article 2 of the Basic Law. For these reasons the Section 218 was declared unconstitutional.

The periodic model did not sufficiently satisfy the duty of the state to protect the fetus. The legislature reacted by adopting an "indication model" traced by the Federal Constitutional Court in its judgement. Abortion was still a criminal act, but in special conflict situations various exceptions to the prohibition of abortion exist. There are four categories of justifying indications: medical indication (danger to the life or health of the woman), eugenic indication (genetic abnormality of the embryo), criminal indication (the pregnancy was the result of rape or incest) and social indication[21]. After the German reunification in 1990 the majority of the German parliament held the view that the indication model had failed and in order to accommodate, both the East and West German positions, the Parliament passed the Pregnancy and Family Assistance Act in 1992. Abortion was legal during the first twelve weeks of pregnancy after a 3 day waiting period and a mandatory counselling session for the expectant mother.

As previously, the law was immediately attacked. In its second abortion decision from May 28, 1993[22] the Federal Constitutional Court declared the law unconstitutional. The Court reiterated the quintessence of its 1975 decision that pursuant to the Basic Law, the state has an obligation to protect the human life, including the life of the unborn child. The Court ruled that the abortion must remain illegal and that the pregnant woman has a legal duty to carry out the child. It continued to allow abortions during the first trimester procured for medical, genetic or criminological indications. The Court also stated that

---

20   BVerfGE 39, 1 at p. 43.

21   See *Eser,* Reform of german abortion law, in American Journal of Comparative Law, Vol. 34 (1986), p. 375–377.

22   BVerfGE 88, 203. See thereto *Dederer,* in Menzel, Verfassungsrechtsprechung, p. 248–252; *Geiger/von Lampe,* Das zweite Urteil des BVerfG zum Schwangerschaftsabbruch, Jura 1994, p. 20–30; critically *Hermes/Walther,* Schwangerschaftsabbruch zwischen Recht und Unrecht, NWJ 1993, p. 2339–2343.

abortion for reasons other than the above mentioned would not be punished under criminal law if the woman had attended counselling that encouraged her to carry out the child (consultation model)[23]. Therefore, the Court left the decision to the woman during the first trimester but stated that she must receive advice in favour of life[24]. The Court ruling was similar to its prior decision, while making some adjustments to it.

The first abortion decision is of significant importance. In this decision the Court developed the protective duty of the state, derived from fundamental rights as objective principles[25]. In their capacity as positive rights the fundamental rights require the legislature to take action in order to protect the constitutionally protected interests from violations by private parties. Following this judgement the legislative acts cannot only be declared unconstitutional if they limit fundamental rights too far but also if the legislature does not sufficiently protect a fundamental right against intrusions from others.

The question is to what extent the legislature is determined by the constitutional duty to protect fundamental rights. In its first abortion decision the Court counteracted a law passed in the Parliament and provoked criticism for overstepping the boundaries of its review powers[26]. The Court was not content with striking down the abortion law and leaving it to the discretion of the legislator for a new solution. Instead, it gave specifications for a constitutionally acceptable approach from its point of view with which the legislature later complied. This view, that the constitutional obligation may even include the means with which the legislature fulfils its duty, has not been upheld by the Court. Meanwhile it distinguishes, as is to be seen in the next case, between the "if" (Constitution) and the "how" (Legislature/Executive). However the Legislature has to make use of the means suitable to furnish adequate protection (*Untermaßverbot*).

---

23   BVerfGE 88, 203 at p. 264, 270–274.
24   BVerfGE 88, 203 at p. 267–270. See also *Hermes/Walther*, Schwangerschaftsabbruch zwischen Recht und Unrecht, NWJ 1993, p. 2338–2339.
25   On the duty of state to protect see also *Geiger/von Lampe*, Das zweite Urteil des BVerfG zum Schwangerschaftsabbruch, Jura 1994, p. 21–24.
26   See *Limbach*, Das Bundesverfassungsgericht als politischer Machtfaktor, in Humboldt Forum Recht, Beitrag 12, 1996, p. 70 (online available: http://www.humboldt-forum-recht.de/ deutsch/12-1996/beitrag.html#punkt1).

2. Schleyer Kidnapping Case – duty of state to protect in case of terrorist threats

The Federal Constitutional Court also emphasized the obligation of the state to take certain measures to protect the individual's life and physical integrity in the *Schleyer* case[27]. This is one of the important decisions made in the 1970s in reaction to terrorist activities by the Red Army Fraction (RAF). In 1977 some members of the "second generation" of the left-wing RAF terrorism group kidnapped the president of the federal association of employees Hans Martin Schleyer in order to obtain the release of eleven named terrorists from prison and guarantee their safe departure out of the country. In the light of the numerous terrorist attacks on the state (several assassinations in Germany between 1974 and 1977) and a tense situation within Germany, the government refused to comply with the demands of the terrorists. It rather relied on the police authorities to find and free the hostage.

After the drama lasted for a month Schleyer's son, acting on behalf of his father, petitioned the Federal Constitutional Court to issue a temporary injunction to force the Federal Government to release the named prisoners in order to avert the immediate danger to the life of Schleyer. He argued that the right to life stated in Art. 2, Paragraph 2 Basic Law included the duty of the state to go to any length to protect one's life. Thus, the Federal Government was obliged to comply with the terrorist's demands and save Schleyer's life. Furthermore, he argued that the state authorities may not sacrifice his father's life for the protection of some other legal interest of higher value because life itself is the highest legal value.

The Court rejected the complaint. It acknowledged the obligation of the state to protect life against unlawful interferences by others (in this case the terrorists threatening to kill the hostage) according to Art. 2, Paragraph 2 Basic Law. However the state authority enjoys far-reaching discretion as to the means to comply with its obligation to protect life effectively[28]. Even though the individual may, based on his fundamental right, demand state action, it has no claim as to the type of action. It is the task of the state authority to decide what protective measures are necessary to guarantee effective protection. The freedom of the state's authority in the choice of the means can only exceptionally be narrowed down to one particular mean, as in this case the release of the prisoners. Such a case was not at hand here[29]. The Court held that the

---

27 BVerfGE 46, 160. See hereto *Dederer*, in Menzel, Verfassungsrechtsprechung, p. 529–534.

28 BVerfGE 46, 160 at p. 164. See also *Pieroth/Schlink*, Staatsrecht II Grundrechte, para. 97.

29 BVerfGE 46, 160 at p. 164–165.

government's decision to rather try to find and free the hostage than to give in to terrorists' demands and release the prisoners was a sufficient state action. In order to protect life from life-threatening extortion by terrorists the protective measures have to be adapted to the specific situation[30]. The measures cannot be standardized first or cannot be derived from a basic right of individuals in a binding and standardized fashion. The Basic Law creates a duty to protect not only the individual, but also all citizens as a whole. Simply submitting to terrorists' demands would make the state's reactions predictable and the effective protection of its citizens impossible[31]. Schleyer was shot to death by his captors and found in the trunk of a car.

In contrast to the first abortion decision in *Schleyer* case the Federal Constitutional Court was not able to order the competent state organs to decide in a particular manner. It is within the discretion of the state authority to decide which measures are to be taken to fulfil their duty to protect. The Court held that in this specific case the state authority could not select the only one specific measure to effectively protect the life of the hostage, since the release of the terrorists would have considerable repercussions on the welfare of the citizens as a whole.

3. Homosexuality – legal equality of minority groups

Another social matter brought before the Constitutional Court was the constitutional problem of male homosexuality and its criminalization. Homosexuality was considered contrary to human nature and homosexuals were lying under social discrimination and harassment for centuries. Society's attitude toward homosexuality has however changed since the Federal Republic of Germany's beginnings[32]. At the time the Basic Law was passed and later until 1969 homosexuality was regarded as immoral and criminally prohibited through Art. 175 of the Criminal Code. In 1957, the question of the constitutionality of Art. 175 Criminal Code was brought before the Federal Constitutional Court[33]. The Court had to decide if Art. 175 was compatible with Art. 3, Paragraph 2 ("Men and women shall have equal rights..."), Art 3, Paragraph 3 ("No person shall be

---

30   BVerfGE 46, 160 at p. 165.
31   BVerfGE 46, 160 at p. 165.
32   On the history of homosexuality see *Linhart,* Decriminalization of Homosexuality, German Law Journal, Vol. 6 (2005), p. 945–948.
33   BVerfGE 6, 389. See hereto *Linhart,* Decriminalization of Homosexuality, German Law Journal, Vol. 6 (2005), p. 947–948; *Müller-Terpitz,* in Menzel, Verfassungsrechtsprechung, p. 91–96.

favoured or disfavoured because of sex, parentage, race, language, homeland and origin, faith, or religious or political opinions.") and Art. 2, Paragraph 1 Basic Law ("Every person shall have the right to free development of his personality..."). The Court found that the principle of equality between man and woman did not apply to the legislative distinction between female and male homosexuality[34]. It gave examples for differences between man and women that justified the different legal treatment[35]. However the Court did not show how those differences solely relate to the criminalization of male homosexuality. The Court found that homosexual conduct violated the moral code (*Sittengesetz*). As argument the Court cited the legislative history of the Criminal Code, which always had based the penalization of the homosexuality on the moral sense of the public[36]. The Court held that the decriminalization of homosexuality would lead to an increase of homosexual activities among adults in general which would lead to a higher risk for younger men. As consequence, the Federal Constitutional Court ruled that criminalizing male homosexuality was not unconstitutional.

Thus, the negative judgement of homosexuals was at first also confirmed by the Federal Constitutional Court. After an increase in criminal prosecution in the 1950s and beginning of the 1960s, in 1969 the homosexuality was decriminalized and the legal practice changed, gradually decreasing social stigmatization. However only in 1994 the criminal statute for homosexuality was completely abolished. The decriminalization of the homosexuality is the first necessary step toward the granting of further rights to homosexual couples. As far as the marriage is concerned, the Federal Constitutional Court found in a decision from 4.10.1993 that there is no right to same sex marriage[37]. The rejection of the register office (*Standesamt*) to a request of same sex partners to marry was confirmed by court decision.

The petitioner had filed a constitutional complaint against this decision. It violates the right to marriage as guaranteed under Art. 6 Paragraph 1 Basic Law, which provides an institutional guarantee for the protection of marriage and family. Consistent with its prior jurisprudence the Court defined marriage as "the union of a man and a woman". Thus from this fundamental right cannot be derived the right of marriage with a same sex partner[38]. Considering the numerous impediments to shaping the private life of the homosexuals the

---

34   BVerfGE 6, 389 at p. 422.
35   BVerfGE 6, 389 at p. 422–432. See *Müller-Terpitz,* in Menzel, Verfassungsrechtsprechung, p. 92–93
36   BVerfGE 6, 389 at p. 434–435.
37   BVerfG, BvR 640/93, NJW 1993, 3058–3059.
38   BVerfG, BvR 640/93, NJW 1993, 3058.

important question is, if the existing laws are compatible with Art. 2, Paragraph 1 (right to free development of one's personality) in connection with Art.1, Paragraph 1 (human dignity) and Art. 3 Basic Law (legal equality) and more specifically if the legislator has the obligation to provide the same-sex partners with a legal framework for their partnership.

These questions found no answer in this concrete case, because they were not object of the constitutional complaint. The legislator however granted same-sex couples some kind of legal recognition. In 2001 the legislator passed the Act on same-sex partnership (*Lebenspartnerschaftgesetz – LPartG*)[39]. It constitutes a new framework for the public recognition of homosexual relationships, governed by standards that have only been relevant to married, opposite-sex couples. The Act transfers some of these standards to homosexual couples through the institution of a publicly recognized relationship known as the registered lifetime partnership. According to the new law same-sex persons can for example enter into a partnership, owe care and support to each other, are free to choose a common name and bound to financially support each other.

Proceedings initiated by the Länder (Federal States) of Bavaria and Saxony before the Federal Constitutional Court to have the Act declared unconstitutional failed. They argued that allowing same sex marriage would damage the legal fundament of marriage. They claimed that the registered lifetime partnership discriminates because it is not equally available to heterosexual couples and other kinds of associations. The Court found however that the Act was in conformity with the constitution, specifically with Article 6, Article 3 Paragraph 1 and Article 3 Paragraph 3 of the Basic Law[40]. The Court saw no problem with the institutional guarantee of Article 6 since the Act was not concerned with marriage, but rather dealt with homosexual couples[41]. The Act does not bring any disadvantages for the institution of marriage, since the new law does not change its legal foundation. The Court saw also no violation of legal equality, as guaranteed under Article 3 Paragraph 1 and 3 – that states the equality of men and women and prohibits discrimination based on sex –, since there were sufficient differences between homosexual couples and other forms of common life[42]. Regarding heterosexual couples, this followed from the fact that

---

39   On the content of this law see *Scholz/Uhle,* Eingetragene Lebenspartnerschaft und Grundgesetz, NJW 2001, p. 395–396.

40   BVerfGE 105, 313. See hereto *Miller/Röben,* Constitutional Court Upholds Lifetime Partnership Act, in German Law Journal, Vol. 3 (2002), online available: http://www.german lawjournal.com/article.php?id=176; critically to the constitutionality of the law *Scholz/Uhle,* Eingetragene Lebenspartnerschaft und Grundgesetz, NJW 2001, p. 396–400.

41   BVerfGE 105, 313 at p. 342–351.

42   BVerfGE 105, 313 at p. 351–353.

homosexuals could not marry. After a draft for an amendment of the Act on same-sex partnership was introduced to the parliament in order to improve the situation for homosexual registered partnerships, the new law entered into force on January 1, 2005. In many important areas the situation of same-sex partnerships is now adapted to the law for heterosexual couples.

4. Freedom of faith and religious symbols in the public sphere

Another sensitive political and legal matter brought before the Federal Constitutional Court was the issue of religious symbols in the public sphere. Widespread public debate stimulated the Federal Constitutional Court's decisions on the presence of crucifixes and Islamic headscarves in the school system.

a. Ban of crucifixes in Bavarian schools

A Bavarian Law stated that there had to be crucifixes within all Bavarian elementary schools (§ 13 Paragraph 1 of School Ordinance for primary schools in Bavaria – Schulordnung für die Volksschulen in Bayern, BayVSO). A case was brought against this order by several pupils and their parents who adhered to an anthroposophical belief. They held that this provision violated their right to freedom of belief and upbringing of their children in accordance with their beliefs. Art. 4, Paragraph 1 Basic Law ("Freedom of faith and of conscience, and freedom to profess a religious or philosophical creed, shall be inviolable.") must also protect the freedom *not* to believe in Christian religion. Thus the state must refrain from intruding into this freedom. The question was whether putting up crucifixes constituted such an intrusion. The dissenting opinion of three judges stated that the crucifix did not have any missionary character[43].

The Court however ruled by majority verdict that the placement of a cross or a crucifix in classrooms of a state compulsory school, which is not a confessional school, violates Art. 4, Paragraph 1 of the Basic Law[44]. It held that the freedom of religion means that the decision for or against a faith is a matter for the individual, not the state. The state must neither prescribe nor forbid a religion to the individual. This fundamental right entails not only the freedom to participate in cultic activities of a faith, but also the freedom to avoid the cultic

---

43   BVerfGE 93, 1 at p. 25–37.
44   BVerfGE 93, 1. See hereto *Schulte zu Sodingen,* in Menzel, Verfassungsrechtsprechung, p. 575–580; see also *Caygill/Scott,* The Basic Law versus the Basic Norm?, Political Studies, 1996, S. 509–511.

activities of a faith one does not share[45]. The Court held that Art. 4 Paragraph 1 Basic Law entails also a positive duty of the state to guarantee the freedom of one's religious conviction[46]. Thus the state has the duty to secure a sphere of action in which the personality within the ideological-religious domain can develop, and to protect that sphere from attack by adherents to other religious faiths. The Bavarian crucifix order, as seen by the Court, was not compatible with this duty of the state. The court stated that the cross belongs to the specific symbols of Christendom and has an character apt to influence a child that has not yet formed its believes, since attendance in a public school is mandatory and so the child will be exposed for extended periods to the cross[47]. Furthermore the Court pointed out that Art. 4 Paragraph 1 and 2 and Art. 140 in connection with Art. 137 Paragraph 1 Basic Law require the state to be religiously and ideologically neutral. Thus the public schools have to refrain from preferring one religion or another.

The placement of crosses in classrooms violated the Basic Law's requirement of neutrality because the cross symbolizes Christianity[48]. There is no strict separation of church and state in Germany and the state is bound by principles of neutrality, rather than the strict forms of laicité. The Crucifix decision was intensely disputed[49], as the general perception was that the Church had enjoyed special protection of the state as representative of the beliefs of the majority of population. The decision however was one of consequence in the light of the constitutional principle of ideologically and religiously neutrality of the state.

b. Headscarf Debate

Another line of reasoning followed the Federal Constitutional Court in its seminal decision of September 24, 2003[50] on the headscarf of a Muslim schoolteacher[51].

---

45   BVerfGE 93, 1 at p. 15.
46   BVerfGE 93, 1 at p. 16.
47   BVerfGE 93, 1 at p. 19–21.
48   BVerfGE 93, 1 at p. 16–17.
49   On critical reactions against the Crucifix decision see *Schulte zu Sodingen,* in Menzel, Verfassungsrechtsprechung, p. 578–579.
50   BVerfGE 108, 282. See hereto *Sacksofsky,* Die Kopftuch-Entscheidung, NJW 2003, p. 3297–3301; *von Campenhausen,* The German Headscarf Debate, p. 676–685, online available: http://www.religlaw.org/docs/religlaw_1320.pdf
51   On the headscarf as a political threat in Germany see *Kahn,* The Headscarf as Threat?, bepress Legal Series, 2006, Paper 1504, p. 4–15, online available: http://law.bepress.com/expresso/eps/1504/

Headscarf decision is the culmination of a six-year legal battle before the German courts[52]. Fereshta Ludin was born in Afghanistan but has lived continuously in Germany since 1987, becoming a German citizen in 1995. In 1997 as Ludin neared completion of her pedagogical studies, the Stuttgart School Supervisory Authority (*Oberschulamt Stuttgart*) turned down her application for a position as a schoolteacher. Ludin's case failed of all levels of administrative appeal. She would not be found eligible to teach in the public schools so long as she refused to take off her headscarf while teaching. In response she filed a constitutional complaint by the Federal Constitutional Court, alleging that the regulation prohibiting her from wearing a headscarf while teaching violated her freedom of religion, as guaranteed under the Basic Law. Ludin argued that wearing a headscarf was not only a characteristic of his personality, but also an expression of her religious conviction.

The Federal Constitutional Court ruled with a majority of five judges that the Stuttgart school authority was wrong to reject Ms. Ludin's job application[53]. It held that a prohibition on a Muslim teacher from wearing a headscarf is theoretically permissible. The Court however found that the existing laws did not provide a "sufficiently clear legal basis" on which to justify an administrative decision to prohibit wearing headscarves while teaching. Proceeding from Art. 33 Paragraph 2, which states that every German enjoys equal access to every public office according to his eligibility, ability and professional qualifications, the Court noted that this access can be limited by subjective acceptance criteria. In setting these criteria the legislator has wide discretion. The Court stated that wearing a headscarf was covered by the scope protection of the freedom of religion as guaranteed under Art. 4 Basic Law[54]. As the constitutionally protected freedom of religion is guaranteed unconditionally, any limitations of this right must arise directly from the Basic Law. Such limitations of the freedom of religion require a sufficiently clear legal basis[55]. Potential rights that might collide with freedom of religion are, as identified by the court, the state educational mandate, the parents' right to upbringing and the negative religious freedom of the school children.

The Court ruled that the legislature, not the civil service, was best suited to balance Ms. Ludin's right to religious freedom with conflicting rights to a neutral classroom environment. In this case the Court found that a sufficiently

---

52   See also *von Campenhausen*, The German Headscarf Debate, p. 672–676, online available: http://www.religlaw.org/docs/religlaw_1320.pdf

53   Critically to the majority opinion see *von Campenhausen*, The German Headscarf Debate, p. 685–690, online available: http://www.religlaw.org/docs/religlaw_1320.pdf

54   BVerfGE 108, 282 at p. 298–299.

55   BVerfGE 108, 282 at p. 297.

clear legal basis, that might limit the unconditionally protected freedom of religion, was missing[56]. By returning the issue to the legislature the Court avoided taking a position on the religious question. As consequence the states were free to create their own laws on the issue. In its prior case law the Federal Constitutional Court had emphasized the primacy of protecting children from various dangers to their development. On this background the Court issued its Crucifix decision. As well as the placement of a crucifix in classrooms, the religiously motivated wearing of a headscarf from a schoolteacher could also have an improper effect on children's self-determination. This line of reasoning however did not play any part in the Headscarf decision.

V. Conclusion

In conclusion, the Basic Law established with the Federal Constitutional Court a special court of constitutional jurisdiction in order to grant protection against all infringements of constitutionally guaranteed rights. The Court's jurisdiction is mandatory, as the court may not refuse to hear a case brought before it through appropriate procedure – so we finally do have a difference to the barbershop I referred to at the beginning. In nearly 60 years of its existence, the Court, under explicit constitutional authority, reviewed the constitutionality of statutes and decided constitutional disputes. In reaching its findings and conclusions the German Court relied, as illustrated above, upon specific provisions of the Basic Law and their interpretation.

---

56   BVerfGE 108, 282 at p. 306.

Katharine Gelber

The Role of the Constitution in Major Social Conflicts

The effect of Australia's unique constitutional system of governance has been just as significant on social issues and conflicts, as on the other issues discussed in this volume. This is important to note because at first blush our Constitution has relatively little to say about how social issues ought to be resolved, and is focussed instead on the machinery of governing. It is devoid of a loftily-worded preamble such as exists in South Africa or the United States. It was drawn up in a peaceful process, and is a minimalist document which does not expressly cover some of the most important components of our system of governance, including for example the Prime Minister. Additionally it is a somewhat anachronistic document, which relies on unwritten Westminster conventions of operation, as well as interpretive principle, to be well understood.

The Constitution does have express provisions allowing for the Commonwealth's intervention in a range of social issues, including the aliens power,[1] marriage, divorce and custody arrangements,[2] immigration,[3] and industrial relations.[4] Other areas which have had a significant impact include the external affairs power[5] which has enabled the Commonwealth to legislate in areas subject to international treaties including those related to human rights, and the races power.[6] The thing that is remarkable about these references is that they do not specify *how* the Commonwealth ought to approach these issues, only that it may. Nor is there an overarching norm to which the Commonwealth is required or expected to conform, no keystone principle or principles other than the preservation of the constitutional system of government itself. An exception to this is the 'just terms' provision[7] which on the face of it requires that the Commonwealth deal justly and fairly with those from whom it is appropriating property. However in practice (as we shall see below) even this small mention of the word 'just' has proved ineffective in guaranteeing justice.

---

1   s 51 (xix)
2   ss 51 (xxi), 51 (xxii)
3   s 51 (xxvii)
4   s51 (xxxv)
5   s 51 (xxix)
6   s 51 (xxvi)
7   s 51 (xxi)

Australia's system of government is thus devoid of important and visible components which feature routinely in other constitutional liberal democracies including Germany. Most relevantly, our federal system is devoid of an express exogenously derived or constitutional statement of human rights. This lack, arguably, has a particular manifestation in a system of governance which is elsewhere and otherwise also reliant on unwritten, yet (to some) assumed components of good government.

Counter to this it could be argued that a constitution is not the framework from which to resolve all disputes and social conflicts. Nevertheless, since I have been asked to discuss the interaction between our constitutional system of government and social conflict, my focus will be on the relative weaknesses of that system in resolving those issues. When viewed against the equivalent chapter presented by my German counterpart, we can see that the Australian constitutional system has a significantly less visible role to play in resolving social conflicts than does Germany's, and also that its role is less determinative of rights-oriented solutions.

Over time the idea at the core of responsible government, that unwritten rules of governing ought to be accorded an equivalent weight to express provisions, has not been sustained as any analysis of increased Commonwealth intervention in policy areas not envisaged at the time of the Constitution's founding will tell. It is undoubtedly the case that the Commonwealth has been able to intervene in social issues not envisaged as within its purview at Federation (Kildea and Gelber 2007: 651–652). The reasons for this change are diverse and include changing expectations of government, changing norms of governance and demographic trends, as well as changes in constitutional interpretation that have permitted Commonwealth intervention in areas previously not considered to be within its remit. This lends additional weight to the argument that the provisions of responsible government, in so far as they have in the past been regarded as a mechanism capable of preserving rights (see eg Allan 2003), are weakening in this regard. The role of the High Court in interpreting the Constitution has been significant in expanding the areas the Commonwealth can intervene in. Since the late 1980s at least, political scientists in Australia have viewed the High Court as an institution of politics in the senses that it is part of the overall machinery of government, and that it reflects and adjudicates disputes in ways that have an impact on policy. This, of course, means that it helps to shape social policy in response to social conflict in Australian political culture (Galligan 1987: 3).

However in so doing, the High Court has also had to work within a framework which permits statements and interpretations of *what* powers the Commonwealth possesses, but is absent of clear rights-derived or -oriented principles guiding *how* policy might manifest. There have been moments when justices on the High Court have tried to move beyond these constraints, by among other things developing an implied rights jurisprudence[8] and interpolating principles of international law into their judgments.[9] But these forays have been counterweighted by the more frequent occasions on which an innovative jurisprudence and a progressive constitutional approach, as demonstrated by justices from Murphy to Kirby, have been thwarted by a legalistic approach to constitutional interpretation and a deference to the executive (see the chapter by Lynch in this volume). In relation to the positive resolution of social conflicts, viewed as a resolution in which the Constitution is able to provide a guide to enable the protection of human rights, all too often we have seen the limits of our constitutional framework, absent either an exogenous statement of principles or a more clearly elucidated constitutional text.

There are numerous examples of this. In 2004 the federal government amended the *Marriage Act* 1961 (Cth) to restrict marriages to a union between a man and a woman, and to prevent same-sex marriages conducted overseas being recognised under Australian law (Croome 2008: 63; Gelber 2005: 308) in a move that was undoubtedly constitutionally permissible, but against which there was no constitutional recourse. The rights of asylum seekers under Australian law have been widely found to be trampled on, resulting in some egregious instances of human rights abuses and even the overriding of the rule of law, and the executive's policy directions on this have been (at times regrettably[10]) affirmed by the High Court (see for example Gelber 2005: 311–315; Dunn and Howard 2003; Maley 2004; Prince 2004). In this chapter I will use indigenous rights as the primary lens through which to examine the Constitution's role in social conflict, or more specifically in being unable to provide a positive resolution to key social issues in Australian political life. This is because indigenous rights are paradigmatic in many ways of the challenges and difficulties faced in the Australian constitutional framework.

---

8   Especially in relation to an implied freedom of political communication, see Stone (2001, 1999); Blackshield and Williams (2006: 1293–1306).

9   eg Kirby J has argued that 'Australian courts and tribunals are accepting their new obligations [derived from international human rights standards] in a way that would have seemed astonishing even 20 years ago', cited in Kinley (1998: vi).

10   McHugh, for example, in finding indefinite detention constitutionally permissible described the outcome of the High Court cases as 'tragic' and argued that 'the Parliament ... must answer to the electors, to the international bodies who supervise human rights treaties to which Australia is a party and to history' (*Al-Kateb v Godwin* (2004) 219 CLR 562 at 581, 586).

Indigenous rights

The story of indigenous rights and the Constitution has been one of continuous frustration. Despite glimmers of hope in some important judgments, legislative enactments by parliament and subsequent developments in interpretation in the High Court have severely limited hopes for a constitutionally-derived comprehensive recognition of aboriginal rights in Australia. Moments of substantive recognition have been more than over-compensated for by the general inability of indigenous people to use the Constitution to secure their rights, and to seek to use the constitutional framework to assist in the resolution of long-standing, unresolved and deeply problematic social issues. As Sean Brennan has concluded, 'indigenous people [have looked] … largely in vain for constitutional protection of their rights in Australia's basic law' (Brennan 2003: 215–6). There are three primary areas I will focus on in showing this to be the case: the races power, implied constitutional jurisprudence and native title. It will not be possible to provide an exhaustive account of the fate of indigenous claims in the High Court in the period since Federation, and what follows is a necessarily selective account.

Races power

The races power in s51 (xxvi) of the Constitution is perhaps best-known as the basis of one of the two textual changes achieved in the historic 1967 referendum, which achieved the highest 'yes' vote in Australian history[11] (Attwood and Markus 2007: vi; Attwood and Markus 1998). The referendum made textual changes to the two explicit provisions in the Constitution related to indigenous people. These were the races power, which provided that the Commonwealth had the power to make laws with respect to 'the people of any race, other than the aboriginal race in any State, for whom it is deemed necessary to make special laws' (s 51 (xxvi)). The second was the provision that aboriginal people should not be counted in the census (s127). At the time of drafting the Constitution the inclusion of the races power had been advocated on grounds which by today's standards are clearly racist in their intention. The founders wanted to impose racially discriminatory laws in order to prevent people of non-Anglo races immigrating to Australia (Bottomley and Bronitt 2006: 279),[12] and to permit the

---

11   90.77% voted in favour nationwide, and a majority was achieved in every State and Territory.

12   The authors note, however, that even in the 19th century voices of dissent were raised against such views (Bottomley and Bronitt 2006: 279).

States to continue to impose racially discriminatory policies on indigenous people whom they considered 'inferior' (Blackshield and Williams 2006: 987) and a 'dying race' '(Attwood and Markus 2007: 1).

The government of the day became convinced that there was a perception of overt racial discrimination in the Constitution, and hence of the need for textual change[13] (Attwood and Markus 2007: 35). During campaigning, slogans used by indigenous activists included 'Remove Discrimination – Vote Yes', 'Vote Yes for Aboriginal Rights' and 'Vote Yes for Equality' (Attwood and Markus 1997: 47). Activists (erroneously) promoted the idea that a successful vote would force the Commonwealth to engage in major new policy to redress indigenous disadvantage, a 'real programme of equal rights and equal opportunity for Aboriginals' (Attwood and Markus 2007: 48, citing Faith Bandler). However the referendum did none of these things. It made it possible for the Commonwealth to develop indigenous policy by amending the races power, but it did not require the development of such policy, and the positive referendum result did not translate directly or rapidly into policy designed to redress indigenous disadvantage (Attwood and Markus 2007: 54–64).

The longer term understanding of the scope of the races power remains deeply ambiguous, at best. This became clear in the *Hindmarsh Island* case,[14] in which the exact meaning, intent and force of the races power were disputed. An aboriginal woman challenged the construction of a bridge to Hindmarsh Island[15] in South Australia, which was authorised by removing the Hindmarsh Island bridge area from the scope of the *Aboriginal and Torres Strait Islander Heritage Protection Act* 1984 (Cth) to preclude the possibility of preventing its construction on the grounds of aboriginal heritage . The power to enact the heritage legislation in question was derived from the constitutional races power. In judgment it was held that the races power may be used selectively for a sub-group of the designated racial group. It was also held that there is no limit to the races power other than that the measure have a consequence based on race (Blackshield and Williams 2006: 1000–1001). A discussion was had as to whether the races power can only be used for the benefit of a particular race,[16]

---

13   At the same referendum, a separate question regarding removal of the 2:1 proportional nexus between the size of the lower and upper houses (s 24) was also put, and defeated (Singleton et al 2006: 59).

14   *Kartinyeri v Commonwealth* (1998) 195 CLR 337.

15   *Hindmarsh Island Bridge Act* 1997 (Cth), s 4.

16   The idea of a 'special measure' derives from the International Convention on the Elimination of All Forms of Racial Discrimination [ICERD], which defines special measures to redress racial discrimination as those whose purpose is the 'advancement' of a racial or ethnic group (Blackshield and Williams 2006: 997).

and the justices were unable to reach agreement on this question. Although Gaudron J concluded that the section 'only authorises laws which operate to the benefit of Aboriginal Australians',[17] Justices Gummow and Hayne drew the contradictory conclusion that the section is not 'confined to laws which do not discriminate against a race'. In spite of the hopes of the indigenous activists who fought for the passage of the 1967 referendum to amend the races power, the High Court noted that 'the text is not limited in its operation by the 1967 amendment'.[18] The question was left undecided, and the possibility that the races power may be able to be used to disadvantage a particular race was not resolved (Williams 2004: 21–23; Williams 2002: 253).

Constitutional implications

The second area in which it appears neither the Constitution nor its interpreters have provided much succour for indigenous Australians is in the area of implied constitutional jurisprudence. Again, it will not be possible to canvass all the cases in which indigenous rights have been raised, but I will provide some emblematic examples.

In 1997, plaintiffs in the *Stolen Generations* case[19] argued that the ordinance[20] enabling the removal of indigenous children from their families to occur had been unconstitutional and therefore invalid on several grounds. Those most relevant to the discussion here include that the ordinance was contrary to 1) an implied constitutional guarantee of due legal process in accordance with Ch III of the Constitution; 2) an implied constitutional guarantee of legal equality; 3) an implied constitutional protection of freedom of movement and association; 4) an implied constitutional protection against genocide (whose definition was derived from the United Nations *Convention on the Prevention and Punishment of the Crime of Genocide* and involved the destruction in whole or part of a racial or ethnic group). The case followed the then recently-decided implied freedom of political communication cases,[21] in which it was found that a freedom of such communication was inherent in the constitutional framework and thus protected,

---

17   *Kartinyeri v Commonwealth* (1998) 195 CLR 337 at 338.
18   *Kartinyeri v Commonwealth* (1998) 195 CLR 337 at 338.
19   *Kruger v Commonwealth* (1997) 190 CLR 1.
20   *Aboriginals Ordinance* 1918 (NT), made pursuant to powers conferred by the *Northern Territory Acceptance Act* 1910 (Cth) and the *Northern Territory Administration Act* 1910 (Cth).
21   *Nationwide New Pty Ltd v Wills* (1992) 177 CLR 1; *Australian Capital Television v Commonwealth* (1992) 177 CLR 106.

in spite of the absence of express provisions doing so (Blackshield and Williams 2006: 1293–1306). In the immediate aftermath of these decisions, some hopes were raised that an implied jurisprudence may have been able to fill some of the interstices of constitutional text in relation to indigenous rights and other social conflicts.

However the *Stolen Generations* case failed and in judgment it was held that the ordinance and related legislation were not invalid on the ground of any of the imputed implied rights or freedoms contained within the Constitution, and that the Constitution does not create private rights enforceable directly by an action for damages.[22] More specifically, it was held that the Constitution contains no general guarantee of due process of the law, there is no constitutional requirement that all Commonwealth laws must accord equality before the law, there is no constitutional support for an implied freedom of movement and association, and since the ordinance did not display any intent to destroy a race, the acts committed under it did not constitute genocide.[23] This amounted to a clear declaration of the limitations of the Australian constitutional system and its absence of a statement of rights-oriented principles and norms.

Then in 2009 in *Wurridjal*[24] a legal challenge was mounted to elements of the federal government's intervention in the Northern Territory. The intervention was launched in response to a report delivered on 15 June 2007 by the Board of Inquiry into the Protection of Aboriginal Children from Sexual Abuse. The report noted that allegations of sexual abuse of indigenous children were not new, that sexual abuse was not a specifically indigenous problem, but that the classic indicia for abuse and neglect of children were unfortunately likely to be high in some indigenous communities (NTBI 2007: 5). The authors called for the report to be acted upon urgently, by both the federal and Northern Territory governments collaborating on addressing the issue, and by governments committing to consulting with indigenous communities (NTBI 2007: 7). These pleas were ignored, and instead the federal government announced it would intervene on 21 June 2007 (SLCAC 2007), only 6 days after the Report was handed down. On 25 June troops and federal police began arriving in the Northern Territory. On 6 August 520 pages of draft legislation were introduced to federal parliament. On 9 August five draft bills[25] were referred to the Senate

---

22   Other than an action for tort or breach of contract: *Kruger v Commonwealth* (1997) 190 CLR 1 at 3.

23   *Kruger v Commonwealth* (1997) 190 CLR 1 at 3–5.

24   *Wurridjal v The Commonwealth* (2009) 237 CLR 309.

25   Northern Territory National Emergency Response Bill 2007; Social Security and Other Legislation Amendment (Welfare Payment Reform) Bill 2007; Families, Community Services and Indigenous Affairs and Other Legislation Amendment (Northern Territory National

Legal and Constitutional Affairs Commmittee for Inquiry. A one-day hearing was held on 10 August and the Committee reported on 13 August, recommending the bills be passed.

The intervention *inter alia* involved imposing restrictions on the sale and consumption of alcohol, introduced pornography filters on publicly-available computers, provided for the immediate federal government acquisition of five-year leases over Aboriginal townships (while preserving pre-existing titles), imposed external administration of services, prohibited customary law from playing a role in bail and sentencing, introduced a new licensing regime for community stores, imposed income management on communities including quarantining 50% of welfare payments to be spent on essentials and linking income support to school attendance, abolished Community Development Employment Schemes, banned pornography in prescribed areas, and removed the permit requirement to enter Aboriginal land (SLCAC 2007: Chapter 1). In order to make this possible it suspended the *Racial Discrimination Act* 1975 (Cth).[26] Community leaders from Maningrida argued that the federal government's compulsory five-year takeover of Aboriginal townships[27] and removal of the requirement to obtain a permit for entry on to aboriginal land[28] were unconstitutional since they amounted to removal of property that was not 'on just terms' (s50 (xxxi)).

The claim that land had been acquired by the Commonwealth in contravention of the constitutional provision for 'just terms' failed. In judgment the High Court held that the compensation provisions in the legislation (mainly in the form of rental payments to the Land Trust) had been adequate to render the acquisition on just terms.[29] It is to be noted that the 'just terms' provision rests in the section of the Constitution devoted to the distribution of power between Commonwealth and State legislatures, making it difficult to define clearly what it means in terms of a property right (Allen 2000: 351). What is clear is that it was not intended, nor has it been interpreted, as commensurate with its provenance in the Fifth Amendment to the United States' Constitution, nor does it invoke a requirement to pay compensation (Allen 2000: 362; Blackshield and Williams 2006: 1288).

Emergency Response and Other Measures) Bill 2007; Appropriation (Northern Territory National Emergency Response) Bill (No. 1) 2007–2008; Appropriation (Northern Territory National Emergency Response) Bill (No. 2) 2007–2008.

26   *Northern Territory National Emergency Response Act* 2007 (Cth), s132.
27   *Northern Territory National Emergency Response Act* 2007 (Cth).
28   *Families, Community Services and Indigenous Affairs and Other Legislation Amendment (Northern Territory National Emergency Response and Other Measures) Act* 2007 (Cth).
29   *Wurridjal v The Commonwealth* (2009) 237 CLR 309.

The decision was not entirely negative in its potential effect on the rights of indigenous peoples. This is because in judgment it was held that the Commonwealth's power to make legislation to govern the Territories was limited by the just terms provision, in doing so overturning a long-held precedent.[30] The judgment also acknowledged that the property of the Land Trust had been acquired by the Commonwealth in the intervention (Horan 2010). Nevertheless, the loss of the claim on the question of whether just terms had applied put paid to hopes that the extraordinary scope of the intervention in its effect on indigenous people could be challenged through constitutional means. It is to be noted that, in dissent, Kirby J argued that,

[i]f any other Australians, selected by reference to their race, suffered the imposition on their pre-existing property interests of non-consensual 5-year statutory leases, designed to authorise intensive intrusions into their lives and legal interests, it is difficult to believe that a challenge to such a law would fail as legally unarguable on the ground that no 'property' had been 'acquired'. Or that 'just terms' had been afforded, although those affected were not consulted about the process and although rights cherished by them might be adversely affected.[31]

Thus, it is his argument that although the 'just terms' provision ought to be of some use to Aboriginal people in terms of a constitutional remedy for injustices sustained, without a broader appreciation of the particular needs of indigenous people in policy concerning their fate, such opportunities are lost.

Native title

Although the issue of native title relates primarily to the common and statutory law, it is also true that the Constitution has failed to provide a basis on which to shore up positive recognition of the native title rights of indigenous people. In the *Mabo* case, hopes of such recognition were raised by a Court that affirmed that the acts by which the 'dispossession of the Aboriginal peoples of most of their traditional lands' were carried out 'constitute the darkest aspect of the history of this nation [which will] ... remain diminished unless and until there is an acknowledgement of, and retreat from, those past injustices[32] (cited in Patapan 2000: 111–112). The confusion generated by the *Mabo* judgment's assertion that native title rights had not been extinguished by British settlement (Brennan et al 2005: 106), over how native title could be claimed and its implications for property entitlement (Butt et al 2001: 95–8) resulted in

---

30   Established in *Teori Tau v Commonwealth* (1969) 119 CLR 564.
31   *Wurridjal v The Commonwealth* (2009) 237 CLR 309 at 394.
32   *Mabo v Queensland* [No. 2] (1992) 175 CLR 1 at 109, per Deane, Gaudron JJ

legislative clarification in the form of the *Native Title Act* 1993 (Cth) [NTA] (Brennan et al 2005: 105–6). However the legislative recognition of native title was a tumultuous process. The second meeting of the Council of Australian Governments [COAG] in June 1993 was dominated by discussion of the judgment, but the response proffered to that meeting by then Prime Minister Keating was drafted without consultation with the States and Territories and agreement could not be reached on how to proceed (Galligan 1995: 211–212). The Commonwealth then decided to move ahead without the participation of the States and Territories, and although consultation with indigenous community representatives on the form of the *Native Title Act* did occur (Brennan et al 2005: 105), there were divisions among aboriginal people over its content. Some aboriginal activists argue that the representatives who were formally consulted were a small number of 'bureaucrats' who agreed to a more limited form of native title than should have been pursued (Maddison 2009: 131–3).

Two years later the High Court affirmed the validity of the NTA, held that the NTA overrode the authority of States and Territories on native title matters,[33] and simultaneously found s12 of the NTA invalid. This section had stated that the common law of Australia in native title had the force of a law of the Commonwealth, and was found invalid because *inter alia* the enactment of common law on native title was found to have no constitutional support in either s 51(xxvi) or (xxiv).[34]

After the *Wik*[35] decision six years later affirmed that pastoral leases did not automatically extinguish native title, but that if there were an inconsistency between the lessees' right to use the land and native title, the pastoral leases would prevail (Brennan et al 2005: 106), the ensuing furore and pressure resulted in further legislative intervention. The *Native Title Amendment Act* 1998 (Cth) delimited native title rights in a number of ways, including by spelling out the circumstances under which grants to land could extinguish native title and making it more difficult for native title holders to have the right to negotiate (Butt et al 2001: 109–113; Brennan 2003: 210). These changes incurred the wrath of the United Nations, which in 1998 subjected Australia to the Committee on the Elimination of Racial Discrimination's early warning procedures (the first Western government to be so subjected) and requested information concerning these changes. After considering Australia's report, in 1999 the CERD concluded that the amendments were racially discriminatory and

---

33   *Western Australia v Commonwealth* (1995) 183 CLR 373.

34   *Members of the Yorta Yorta Aboriginal Community v Victoria* (2002) 214 CLR 422 at 468 per McHugh J.

35   *Wik Peoples v State of Queensland* (1996) 187 CLR 1.

amounted to a contravention of Australia's obligations under the ICERD (Evatt 2001: 4; Gelber 2001: 2).

In the years following, there have been some important decisions that have recognised forms of native title, including the *Croker Island* case[36], *Yanner*[37] and *Blue Mud Bay*[38] (Patapan 2002: 249–250). Nevertheless, many other decisions have demonstrated the High Court's willingness to accept the approach of an executive with an indigenous policy hostile to native title. The Constitution has provided few rays of hope in this context. For example, in *Fejo*[39] it was held that where a freehold title had been granted and that land later reverted to crown land, the granting of the title had extinguished the possibility of a successful native title claim at any later time. In *Anderson*[40] and *Ward*[41] the meaning of co-existing native title on a pastoral lease was restricted and the NTA interpreted to permit partial extinguishment or suspension of native title rights. In *Ward* the possibility of raising the issue of indigenous spirituality in the context of the s116 prohibition against the Commonwealth making laws prohibiting the free exercise of any religion was raised by Kirby J, but has not yet been pursued with any vigour (Brennan 2003: 215–6).

In the important *Yorta Yorta* decision in 2002,[42] the threshold established in *Mabo* of demonstrating the maintenance of a 'traditional' connection to land which is subject to a native title claim was raised significantly to preclude a period of interruption, thus restricting the likelihood of successful claims (Brennan et al 2005: 105–7; Brennan 2003: 210–214). The outcome of the *Yorta Yorta* claim has been described as confirming the doubts of many aboriginal people concerning the utility of native title procedures (Maddison 2009: 134), and as penalising most 'those who have been most severely dispossessed' (Brennan et al 2005: 118; Patapan 2003: 307–308).

---

36   *Commonwealth v Yarmirr* (2001) 208 CLR 1, in which it was held that native title could be demonstrated over the sea, and that this did not permit the exclusion of others.

37   *Yanner v Eaton* (1999) 201 CLR 351, in which it was held that the *Fauna Conservation Act 1974* (Qld) did not extinguish native title rights established under the NTA.

38   Including the Blue Mud Bay case (*Northern Territory of Australia v Arnhem Land Aboriginal Land Trust* (2008) 236 CLR 24) in which it was held that indigenous owners of land including tidal waters did have the right to exclude fishers from that land.

39   *Fejo v Northern Territory* (1998) 195 CLR 96.

40   *Wilson v Anderson* (2002) 213 CLR 401.

41   *Western Australian v Ward* (2002) 213 CLR 1.

42   *Members of the Yorta Yorta Aboriginal Community v Victoria* (2002) 214 CLR 422.

Conclusion

The arguments I have presented here are not particularly novel, rather they are a summary of one perception of the weakness of the Australian constitutional approach, which is devoid of a prevailing and overriding rights-enhancing norm. I do not wish to suggest that should such a rights-enhancing norms, or set of norms, be adopted the problems identified here would be immediately resolved – indeed it is clear that in those jurisdictions in possession of such norms these kinds of problems persist. But in those contexts what does exist is an express framework within which to conduct those debates; in Australia that framework is diverse and indistinct.

There are also those who would disagree with the position I have put, and argue that the Australian framework is generally speaking robust and provides a good protection for basic liberties. On the whole Australia is undoubtedly a generally free and democratic society. However, the examples I have provided are I believe a clear reflection of the limits of the High Court's jurisprudence and approach on constitutional matters connected with indigenous rights, of the institutional limits on the court in a constitutional system with no bill of rights or exogenous platform from which to override executive decisions on rights-type issues, and of the concomitant jurisdictional limits in terms of the judges' own beliefs in the appropriate limits to their role.

Bibliography

Allen, Tom 2000. 'The Acquisition of Property on Just Terms', *Sydney Law Review* 22(3): 351–380.

Allen, James 2003. 'A Defence of the Status Quo', in *Protecting Human Rights: Instruments and Institutions*, T Campbell, J Goldsworthy and A Stone (eds), Oxford University Press, Oxford, pp. 175–194.

Attwood, Bain and Andrew Markus 1998. 'Representation Matters: The 1967 Referendum' in N Petersen and W Sanders (eds) *Citizenship and Indigenous Australians* Cambridge University Press, Melbourne, pp. 118–140.

Attwood, Bain and Andrew Markus 2007. *The 1967 Referendum*, 2nd ed, Australian Institute of Aboriginal and Torres Strait Islander Studies, Canberra.

Blackshield, Tony and George Williams 2006. *Australian Constitutional Law and Theory: Commentary and Materials* Federation Press, Sydney.

Bottomley, Stephen and Simon Bronitt 2006. *Law in Context*, 3rd ed Federation Press, Sydney.

Brennan, Sean 2003. 'Native Title in the High Court of Australia a Decade After Mabo', *Public Law Review* 14: 209–218.

Brennan, Sean; Larissa Behrendt; Lisa Strelein and George Williams 2005. *Treaty* Federation Press, Sydney.

Butt, Peter; Robert Eagleson; Patricia Lane 2001. *Mabo, Wik and Native Title*, 4th ed Federation Press, Sydney.

Croome, Rodney 2008. 'The Principle of Pre-Existence: or how the bible stole my rights, again', *Alternative Law Journal*, 33(2): 63–66.

Dunn, K and J Howard 2003. 'Reaching Behind Iron Bars: Challenges to the Detention of Asylum Seekers', *The Drawing Board: An Australian Review of Public Affairs* 4(1): 45–64.

Evatt, Elizabeth 2001. 'How Australia 'supports' the United Nations Human Rights Treaty System: Comment', *Public Law Review* 12: 3–8.

Galligan, Brian 1987. *The Politics of the High Court* University of Queensland Press, Brisbane.

Galligan, Brian 1995. *A Federal Republic: Australia's Constitutional System of Government* Cambridge University Press, Melbourne.

Gelber, Katharine 2001. 'Human Rights Treaties in Australia – Empty Words?', *Australian Review of Public Affairs: Digest*, posted 12 April, www.australianreview.net/digest/2001/04/gelber.html, accessed 28/04/09.

Gelber, Katharine 2005. 'High Court Review 2004: Limits on the Judicial Protection of Rights', *Australian Journal of Political Science* 40(2): 307–322.

Gleeson, Justin 2009. 'The Federal and State Courts on Constitutional Law: the 2008 Term', *Paper presented at 2009 Constitutional Law Conference*, Sydney, 20 February, http://www.gtcentre.unsw.edu.au/publications/papers/469.asp [9 May 2009].

Horan, Chris 2010. 'Wurridjal v The Commonwealth – The Intervention and the Acquisition', *Paper presented at 2010 Constitutional Law Conference*, Sydney, 19 February, http://www.gtcentre.unsw.edu.au/publications/papers/644.asp [23 Feb 2010].

Kildea, Paul and Katharine Gelber 2007. 'High Court Review 2006: Australian Federalism – Implications of the *WorkChoices* Decision', *Australian Journal of Political Science* 42(4): 649–664.

Kinley, David ed 1998. *Human Rights in Australian Law* Federation Press, Sydney.

Maddison, Sarah 2009. *Black Politics: Inside the Complexity of Aboriginal Political Culture* Allen & Unwin, Sydney.

Maley, William 2004. 'Refugees' in Manne, R ed *The Howard Years* Black Inc Agenda, Melbourne.

Northern Territory Board of Inquiry into the Protection of Aboriginal Children from Sexual Abuse [NTBI] 2007. *Little Children Are Sacred* NT government, Darwin.

Osborne, David and Ted Gaebler 1993. *Reinventing Government: How the Entrepreneurial Spirit is Transforming the Public Sector* Plume, New York.

Owens, Rosemary 2009. 'The Nature of s51(xx) – Corporations: A Reappraisal', *Paper presented at 2009 Constitutional Law Conference*, Sydney, 20 February, http://www.gtcentre.unsw.edu.au/publications/papers/469.asp [9 May 2009].

Patapan, Haig 2000. *Judging Democracy: The New Politics of the High Court of Australia* Cambridge University Press, Melbourne.

Patapan, Haig 2002. 'High Court Review 2001: Politics, Legalism and the Gleeson Court', *Australian Journal of Political Science* 37(2): 241–253.

Patapan, Haig 2003. 'High Court Review 2002: The Least Dangerous Branch', *Australian Journal of Political Science* 38(2): 299–311.

Prince, Peter 2004. 'The High Court and Indefinite Detention: Towards a National Bill of Rights?', *Research Breif No. 1 2004–2005* Parliament of Australia Parliamentary Library, Canberra.

Rhodes, R A W 1997. *Understanding Governance: Policy Networks, Governance, Reflexivity and Accountability* Open University Press, Buckingham.

Singleton, Gwynneth; Don Aitkin; Brian Jinks and John Warhurst 2006. *Australian Political Institutions*, 8th ed Pearson Prentice Hall, Sydney.

Senate Legal and Constitutional Affairs Committee [SLCAC] 2007. *Report of the Inquiry into the Social Security and Other Legislation Amendment (Welfare Payment Reform) Bill 2007, and four related bills concerning the Northern Territory National Emergency Response* 13 August, available http://www.aph.gov.au/senate/committee/legcon_ctte/completed_inquiries/2004-07/nt_emergency/index.htm [6 May 2009]

Stone, Adrienne 2001. 'Rights, Personal Rights and Freedoms: The Nature of the Freedom of Political Communication', *Melbourne University Law Review* 25(2): 374–417.

Stone, Adrienne 1999. 'The Limits of Constitutional Text and Structure: Standards of Review and the Freedom of Political Communication', *Melbourne University Law Review* 23(3): 668–708.

Tehan, Maureen 2004. 'Difference, Equality, Recognition and Justice: Indigenous Issues in the High Court Judgments of Justice Mary Gaudron', *Public Law Review* 15: 320–327.

Williams, George 2002. *Human Rights Under the Australian Constitution* Oxford University Press, Melbourne.

Williams, George 2004. *The Case For An Australian Bill of Rights: Freedom in the War on Terror* UNSW Press, Sydney.

Jürgen Bröhmer

The Legislative and Executive Branch versus the Federal Constitutional Court and the Judiciary – Conflict or Cooperation?

I. Background

The German Constitutional Court[1] took up its work in 1951, almost two years after the constitution came into effect. The reason for this was that the Court needed a procedural code and could not operate merely on the provisions contained in the Basic Law,[2] which had come into effect on 23 May 1949. That procedural code, spelling out the requirements and rules for the several procedures available at this court and the rules pertaining to the judges and the organization of the court, came into effect in 1951.[3]

The *BVerfG* is actually more than one court. It consists of 16 judges who are organized in two separate panels ('senates') of eight judges each.[4] The two senates are two separate decision making bodies of the court, each with specific tasks that are allocated to them. The full plenary of 16 judges is responsible mainly for organizing the work of the Court and becomes judicially relevant only when conflicts between the two senates in the treatment of a question of constitutional law arise.[5] Underneath the two senates, the court is organized in chambers of three judges[6], that deal with the admissibility of constitutional complaints, a specific procedure provided for individuals to bring matters to the Court. The sheer number of constitutional complaints brought to the Court has resulted in the necessity to institute this 'pre-screening' procedure to reduce the number of cases to be decided on the merits to a manageable level.[7]

---

1 Bundesverfassungsgericht (*BVerfG*), henceforth referred to as *BVerfG*.
2 Articles 92–94 Basic Law (Grundgesetz (GG), henceforth referred to as Grundgesetz or GG).
3 Gesetz über das Bundesverfassungsgericht (Bundesverfassungsgerichtsgesetz – BVerfGG) of 12 March 1951, BGBl. I 1473 (1993), last amended 22.12.2010, BGBl. I 2248 (2010).
4 § 2 BVerfGG.
5 §§ 1 sec. 3, 7a sec. 2, 14 sec. 4, 16 sec. 1 (dealing with the resolution of conflicts between the two senates), 105 sec. 2 and 5 (incapacity of judges).
6 § 15a BVerfGG.
7 §§ 93a to 93d BVerfGG. According to § 93d BVerfGG the admissibility decision requires no hearing and the decision need not be explained to the applicant. The procedure is therefore

1. Procedural Framework – The Jurisdiction of the BVerfG

The jurisdiction of the Court is enumerated in the *Grundgesetz* (Article 93 GG) and, with more detail, in the Statute Governing the Procedures at the *BVerfG*, the *Bundesverfassungsgerichtsgesetz*. There are four major procedures that can be brought to the *BVerfG*.[8]

a. Constitutional Complaints

Arguably, the most important procedure to the *BVerfG* is the constitutional complaint procedure (*Verfassungsbeschwerde*). The constitutional complaint procedure is by far the most numerous type of procedure brought before the Court. In the year 2009 alone, 6308 constitutional complaints were brought to the Court.[9] Between 1951 and 2009, almost 176,000 constitutional complaints were brought to the Court. The success rate for constitutional complaints is very small. In 2008, the *BVerfG* rendered a decision in 5911 constitutional complaints. Only 111 were successful (1.88%). In the past decade, the success rate for constitutional complaints has always been below 3%.

Constitutional complaints can be brought to the *BVerfG* only if regular judicial remedies have been exhausted to the last possible appeal.[10] That means that the *BVerfG* will only deal with constitutional complaints after the other 'regular' courts have rendered decisions in the matter. Obviously many constitutional issues are filtered out or remedied through this avenue.

b. Institutional Disputes

One of the core tasks of any constitutional court is the resolution of institutional disputes, i.e. disputes between the various organs of the state[11], and, in a federal system such as the Federal Republic of Germany, disputes between the constituent member states (*Länder*) and between the federal level and one or

---

similar to the certiorari procedure of the US Supreme Court (as introduced for this court by the Judiciary Act of 1891, 26 Stat. 826) without directly giving up the somewhat fictional notion that the *BVerfG* must hear all cases as a matter of right and cannot select the cases it is interested in.

8   Altogether there are 19 different procedures, which can be brought to the Court. All are enumerated in § 13 BVerfGG.

9   Statistical data cited in this paragraph pertains to the year 2009 and is taken from the *Statistik für das Geschäftsjahr 2009*, available on the Court's website at http://www.bverfg.de/organisation/statistik_2009.html.

10   § 90.2 BVerfGG.

11   So-called '*Organstreitverfahren*', see Article 93.1 No. 1, §§ 13 No. 5, 63–67 BVerfGG.

more of the *Länder*.[12] Such institutional disputes might be conflicts between a chamber of parliament and the federal government, between members of parliament and parliament itself, between parliament and the federal president or between the two chambers of parliament. Disputes between individual *Länder* are possible as well, although they have been very rare. Disputes between the federation and one or more *Länder* are more prevalent. In 2009 only two such institutional disputes between federal organs came before the court and between 1951 and 2009 the court decided 168 such disputes.[13]

c. Judicial Review

The *BVerfG* has the full power of judicial review. This means that the Constitutional Court has the – exclusive – power to quash any parliamentary statute on account of its unconstitutionality.[14] There are two distinct ways in which judicial review proceedings can be brought to the *BVerfG* as a principal – rather than incidental – matter. The first procedure is referred to as *abstract judicial review*.[15] The abstractness is a result of the fact that there is not a concrete case or dispute at issue in which the constitutionality of a norm arises as an incidental question. Rather, the constitutionality of one or more norms within a statute is the sole judicial matter brought to the court.[16] Such abstract judicial review proceedings can only be brought by the federal government, a state government or by joint application of one third of the deputies of the first chamber of parliament (*Bundestag*). If the constitutionality of a norm is challenged on the grounds of the federation having the power to legislate, the proceeding can also be brought by the second chamber of parliament, the *Bundesrat* and by a state parliament.[17]

---

12 So-called 'Bund-Länder Streit', see Article 93.1 No. 3, §§ 13 No. 7, 68–70 BVerfGG; there are other, similar procedures dealing with "federal" disputes, especially the new procedures concerning the exercise and limitations of concurring legislative powers (Article 72 GG), see Article 93.1 No. 2a and 93.2 GG, §§ 13 No. 6a, 6b, 76–79, 97 BVerfGG.

13 See supra footnote 9. The corresponding number for 2008 was 6. There have been no disputes between the federation and its *Länder* since 2006 and only 44 overall.

14 See infra footnote 19.

15 Article 93.1 No. 2 GG, §§ 13 No. 6, 76–79 BVerfGG.

16 The *BVerfG*'s power to judicial review is not limited to these two procedures of "*principal* norm control". The constitutional complaints procedure or any other procedure may lead to incidental judicial review of parliamentary statutes and the constitutional complaints procedure can itself constitute a form of principal judicial review in the exceptional case of a 'self-executing norm', i.e. when no further administrative act is involved in the alleged limitation of a fundamental rights' position of an individual.

17 See § 76.2 BVerfGG.

The second possibility for judicial review is referred to as a *concrete judicial review* of the constitutionality of the norm.[18] The concreteness arises from the fact that in these proceedings the constitutionality of a norm constituted the principal and decisive question in the regular court proceedings. However, regular courts do not possess the power to declare an act of parliament unconstitutional.[19] If a regular court comes to the conclusion that such an unconstitutionality exists and the decision of the concrete case is contingent on this unconstitutionality, the court must interrupt proceedings, prepare an opinion outlining in detail why it is convinced of the unconstitutionality of the norm and submit this opinion to the *BVerfG* who will then review the constitutionality of the norm in question. After that has happened, the regular court will then decide its case on the basis of the decision rendered by the *BVerfG*.[20]

Abstract judicial review cases can obviously be quite significant, but they do not happen very often. There were no such cases in 2008, only two in 2009 and a total of 165 cases between 1951 and 2009. Concrete judicial review under Article 100.1 GG is more prevalent with 47 cases brought in 2009 and a total of 3 457 cases brought between 1951 and 2009.[21]

2. The Judicial Framework

The German judiciary is organized as a complex system of different courts with defined jurisdictions. There are no less than five full supreme courts with a fully developed court system underneath each of them.[22]

The Federal Supreme Court[23] has jurisdiction in private and commercial law and criminal law cases. It is the court of appeal of last instance, exercising jurisdiction over the mid-level courts of appeal and the local and district courts. It is organized in various adjudicating units referred to as 'senates'. There are 13

---

18   Article 100.1 GG, §§ 13 No. 11, 80–82 BVerfGG.
19   The judicial review power of regular courts is therefore limited to 'pre-constitutional' norms, i.e. norms passed before the *Grundgesetz* became effective and the Bundestag began to operate and to non-parliamentary executive legislation such as regulations.
20   See Article 100.1 GG.
21   See supra footnote 9.
22   See Article 95 GG.
23   Bundesgerichtshof (BGH), see http://www.bundesgerichtshof.de. The Court has its seat in Karlsruhe. Information in English available at http://www.bundesgerichtshof.de/cln_134/EN/Home/home_node.html.

private law senates, 5 criminal law senates and a number of specialized adjudicating units, with a total of 129 judges.[24]

The Federal Labor Court[25] is the court of appeal in all cases that have to do with labor relations, employment contracts and issues arising from or connected to employment contracts. The Federal Labor Court is the last instance court of appeal and exercises jurisdiction over the first instance labor courts and the mid-level labor courts of appeal.[26]

The Federal Administrative Court[27] has jurisdiction over all general administrative matters. This court exercises jurisdiction over the administrative courts of appeal and the first instance administrative courts.

The Federal Social Court[28] has jurisdiction over welfare matters, such as public pension, health and unemployment insurance schemes. This court exercises jurisdiction over first instance social courts and mid-level social courts of appeal.

Finally, there is the Federal Tax (Fiscal) Court[29], which, as the name implies, has jurisdiction over taxation and customs matters. In contrast to the other courts, there are only two levels of tax courts, with the Federal Tax (Fiscal) Court acting as the court of appeal for the first instance courts.

These five federal supreme courts are, as the name implies, federal courts. The first instance courts and the mid-level courts of appeal below them are state (*Länder*) courts. In other words, the judicial system in the Federal Republic of Germany integrates federal and state courts into one hierarchal system of courts, rather than separating them into two distinct court systems, as is, for example, the case in the USA or Australia. The *BVerfG* itself is not part of this court structure. The *BVerfG* is not a court of appeal[30] and does not sit "above" the

---

24   Statistics taken from the Tätigkeitsbericht 2009, available at http://www.bundesgerichtshof.de/ cln_134/DE/BGH/Statistik/statistik_node.html.

25   Bundesarbeitsgericht (BAG), http://www.bundesarbeitsgericht.de. Information in English available at http://www.bundesarbeitsgericht.de/englisch/start.html.

26   The BAG has 35 judges organized in 10 senates and has its seat in Erfurt. For statistical information see http://www.bundesarbeitsgericht.de/statistik.html.

27   Bundesverwaltungsgericht (BVerwG). The Court is organized in 10 senates and has its seat in Leipzig; see http://www.bundesverwaltungsgericht.de. Information in English available at http://www.bundesverwaltungsgericht.de/enid/5d88c6098408b2dae10f346b48f46550,0/Aktue lles/Information_in_English_g0.html.

28   Bundessozialgericht (BSG). The Court is organized in 14 senates and has its seat in Kassel. See http://www.bsg.bund.de. Information in English available at http://www.bsg.bund.de/EN/.

29   Bundesfinanzhof (BFH). It is organized in 11 senates with a total of 60 judges http://www.bundesfinanzhof.de. Information in English available at http://www.bundes finanzhof.de/content/information-english.

30   For more detail see below II. The BVerfG as a "Super Court of Appeal"?

regular supreme courts. Rather the Constitutional Court is situated beside the regular courts with special jurisdiction for constitutional questions only.

As a constitutional court, it is itself part of a triad of constitutional courts, namely the Court of Justice of the European Union in Luxembourg[31] and the European Court of Human Rights as the court of the European Convention on Human Rights in Strasbourg.[32]

II. The BVerfG as a "Super Court of Appeal"?

As outlined above the *BVerfG* is not part of the vertical structure of the several court systems in the German judicial system. In a legal sense, the court is therefore not a court of appeal. The *BVerfG* does not have the right and the role to interpret regular statutory norms with definitive and final authority. Instead, the *BVerfG* is limited to the interpretation and application of norms of the *Grundgesetz*. The exercise of this task may reveal a conflict between a constitutional norm as interpreted by the *BVerfG* and a regular statutory or other norm as interpreted by the regular courts. The *BVerfG* will remand a case back to one of the regular courts – often one of the supreme courts – only if the interpretation of the regular norm by the other courts violated "specific constitutional law" by not taking into account at all or not sufficiently the impact of constitutional norms on the interpretation of that regular norm.

The procedural framework in which this usually becomes relevant is the constitutional complaint procedure. As explained above, the constitutional complaint procedure requires as one criterion for its admissibility that the complainant must have exhausted all regular court remedies. Consequently almost all constitutional complaints are raised against last instance regular court decisions.[33] In such a situation, a court of appeal could, if necessary, replace the "lower" court's interpretation of the statutory or other norm in question with its own interpretation. The *BVerfG, however,* will not do that. It will resolve the conflict by remanding the case back to the regular court together with the instruction on what the *Grundgesetz* requires.[34] The lower court will then have to decide the case in the light of this constitutional instruction.

---

31 See http://curia.europa.eu.

32 See http://www.echr.coe.int.

33 The only exception being constitutional complaints brought directly against a statutory or other norm which is only possible if that norm is self-executive, i.e. does not require a – challengeable – administrative act for implementation or if those affected cannot be expected to await such an act, such as, for example, in the case of criminal law norms.

34 See § 95.2 BVerfGG, http://www.gesetze-im-internet.de/bverfgg/__95.html.

However, this difference between the role of the *BVerfG* and the role of a regular appellate court is not always as clear as the theory behind it suggests. The *BVerfG* exclusively determines the scope of constitutional law *vis-á-vis* regular norms and their interpretation. It is therefore not surprising that at times the *BVerfG* has been criticized for behaving just like a super court of appeal going beyond its task of constitutional interpretation and interfering too much with the task of the regular courts of interpreting regular statutory law.

Two separate developments have abetted this potential danger of overreach by the *BVerfG*. The first is the *BVerfG's* own jurisprudence with regard to Article 2.1 GG. Article 2.1 states:

"Every person shall have the right to free development of his personality in so far as he does not violate the rights of others or offend against the constitutional order."

In plain language, this norm guarantees everybody the right to do what they want as long as they do not infringe on the rights of others, i.e. as long as they do not break the law: what is not expressly prohibited is allowed. The *BVerfG* has widely construed this guarantee to mean that any restriction of the right to do as one pleases, i.e. any restriction on private behavior or action instituted by law, must not suffer from any legal mistake. A faulty norm cannot limit the freedom of individuals regardless of the cause of the error.[35] Consequently, whenever courts render a decision on the basis of an interpretation of a regular statutory provision or other norm with which the *BVerfG* wanted to disagree, this could be construed as a violation of Article 2.1 GG or another more special right if applicable. This construction of fundamental rights protection in general and Article 2.1 GG in particular could therefore lend itself to potential overreach by the *BVerfG* in the sense of the Court taking on the role of a super court of appeal. The *BVerfG* itself has tried to counter that by applying a test under which the interpretation and application of regular, non-constitutional norms by the regular courts are subject to review only if the *BVerfG* comes to the conclusion that the regular courts failed to give due regard to relevant constitutional norms when deciding a case.

The second concept potentially conducing overreach by the *BVerfG* is the concept of indirect third party effect of fundamental rights. The application of the fundamental rights guaranteed in the *Grundgesetz* is not restricted to the relationship between government and individuals even if that defensive function has remained the primary function of fundamental rights. Over and above this function of defending the autonomy of individuals from governmental intrusion, *Grundgesetz* rights have also and consistently been held to have an *objective*

---

35   BVerfGE 6, 32 – Elfes, http://www.servat.unibe.ch/dfr/bv006032.html.

effect as well by affecting the interpretation of regular norms that determine the legal relationship between private individuals, i.e. the interpretation of private law norms. Defamation disputes between two private individuals may serve as an illustrative example. When assessing whether one individual defamed another and might therefore be liable for monetary damages, a regular court must take into account the significance of Article 5 GG, the free speech clause of the *Grundgesetz*. A regular court that failed to duly take into account the extraordinary significance of Article 5 GG as a cornerstone of a democratic society when assessing entitlements to damages in defamation cases would be in violation of the *Grundgesetz*. This indirect third-party effect of fundamental rights by way of extending the obligation under the fundamental right in question to the relationship between private individuals obviously has the potential of bringing private disputes to the *BVerfG* by way of the constitutional complaints procedure and thus creates another situation where the *BVerfG* might be tempted to act as a super court of appeal. Again, the Court attempts to limit this effect by applying its 'insufficient regard"-test rather than plainly overruling the regular courts. Whether the Court applies this test with sufficient respect to the judgments of the regular courts has been a point of contention.[36]

III. The BVerfG's Power of Judicial Review

1. The BVerfG as Guarantor of Basic Rights

One of the *BVerfG's* main roles is as guarantor of fundamental rights. The Court has no monopoly in this respect as the regular courts and indeed any and all state authority also have the obligation to respect and defend the Basic Law in general and fundamental constitutional rights and guarantees in particular.[37]

However, the *BVerfG's* role in this regard is obviously of great significance as it is the port of last resort for any disputes on the scope of these fundamental rights. The Court's interpretation and understanding of fundamental rights protected by the *Grundgesetz* has had a stand-out effect and shaped constitutional thinking perhaps even beyond the realm of the *Grundgesetz*.

---

36 See the instructive study of the – just retired – President of the Constitutional Court, Papier, Hans-Jürgen, Verhältnis des Bundesverfassungsgerichts zu den Fachgerichtsbarkeiten, DVBl. 2009, 473 et seq.

37 Article 1.3 GG reads: "The following basic rights shall bind the legislature, the executive and the judiciary as directly applicable law."

a. Human Dignity

The concept of human dignity and the significance attached to it in the *Grundgesetz* and in the jurisprudence of the Court is certainly one noteworthy aspect. The respect for and in fact the obligation of all state authority to actively protect human dignity is spelled out at the very beginning of the *Grundgesetz*[38] as a direct consequence of the inhumane and diabolic tyranny that had terrorized much of Europe from 1933 to 1945.

Human dignity has played a considerable role in cases large and small, despite the fact that one could, especially from a common law background, well dispute that human dignity constitutes an individual right in and by itself. The *BVerfG's* decision regarding life imprisonment is a good example.[39] The Court held that the criminal sentence of life imprisonment violates Article 2.2 GG (liberty of the person) in conjunction with Article 1 (human dignity), if life imprisonment clauses were construed to mean that a human being could be locked up without having any perspective of ever gaining freedom again. The consequence of this decision is that every life sentence has to be re-evaluated after 15 years and that only in very exceptional circumstances can a person be kept in prison for longer than 15 years.

A recent and very controversial decision concerned the air security legislation passed in Germany in the wake of the 9/11 attacks in New York and Washington. The legislation provided a legal basis for shooting down passenger aircraft in situations comparable to those in New York, i.e. when the aircraft is used as a weapon against buildings or other aggregations of people. The *BVerfG* held that the action of shooting down a passenger plane would violate the human dignity of innocent passengers on that plane, as they would become the mere object of a decision by state authority to be killed as a necessary consequence of the airplane being shot down.[40]

A "smaller" case not actually decided by the *BVerfG* but very much along the lines of the *BVerfG's* jurisprudence was concerned with the laser-tag game,

---

38   "(1) Human dignity shall be inviolable. To respect and protect it shall be the duty of all state authority."

39   BVerfGE 45, 187 – Lebenslange Freiheitsstrafe (life imprisonment), http://www.servat.unibe.ch/dfr/bv045187.html.

40   BVerfGE 115, 118 – Luftsicherheitsgesetz; English translation available at http://www.bverfg.de/entscheidungen/rs20060215_1bvr035705en.html. See also Lepsius, Oliver: *Human Dignity and the Downing of Aircraft: The German Federal Constitutional Court Strikes Down a Prominent Anti-terrorism Provision in the New Air-Transport Security Act*, 7 German Law Journal 762 (2006), available at http://www.germanlawjournal.de/index.php?pageID=11&artID=756.

where players wear an electronic vest and carry a laser gun with which they fire laser beams on each other and on other installed targets. A business planning to offer this game had been denied the necessary commercial license in Germany because the "simulated killing of human beings" was regarded as violating the human dignity clause which had been invoked by the authorities as part of the public order clause in the relevant commercial licensing statute. The European Court of Justice upheld this ban as a proportionate application of the public order exception to the freedom to provide services guarantee of what was then the European Community Treaty (ECT).[41]

b. The Principle of Proportionality

The second principle on which much of the Court's jurisprudence rests is the principle of proportionality, which serves as a major test of the constitutional legality of administrative and legislative acts.[42] The principle of proportionality is actually a three-pronged test. The first element of this test asks whether the measure in question is able to achieve the objective pursued. The second part of the test asks whether of all conceivable effective measures the measure in question is the one with the lowest impact intensity on the right in question. The final part of the test asks whether the impact of the chosen measure is proportional to the pursued objective, which, if answered in the negative, means that the government cannot act at all to remedy a given situation. This proportionality test will be applied to all cases brought under the fundamental rights and freedoms guaranteed by the *Grundgesetz*. All of these rights are subject to limitations spelled out in abstract terms in the *Grundgesetz* but these limitations are themselves limited by the application of the principle of proportionality.

c. Fundamental Rights Protection by Procedural Protection Frameworks

A third significant development in the jurisprudence of the *BVerfG* on the basic rights and freedoms was the development of the concept of fundamental rights

---

41 ECJ, C–36/02, 14.10.2004, Omega Spielhallen, ECR 2004, I–9609, http://eur-lex.europa.eu/LexUriServ/LexUriServ.do?uri=CELEX:62002J0036:EN:HTML. The decision giving rise to this preliminary ruling procedure was rendered by the Federal Administrative Court (*Bundesverwaltungsgericht, BVerwG*), BVerwG, 6 C3/01, 24.10.2001, BVerwGE 115, 189.

42 For broader discussion of the principle see Poto, Margherita, The Principle of Proportionality in Comparative Perspective, 8 German Law Journal (2007) 835, http://www.german-lawjournal.com/pdf/Vol08No09/PDF_Vol_08_No_09_835-870_Articles_Poto.pdf..

protection by having procedural protection frameworks in place. This aspect of the Court's jurisprudence towards a procedural approach to fundamental rights protection was significant in a decision concerning the legality of construction licenses for a nuclear power plant.[43] The Court pointed to previous decisions affording relevance to procedural norms when those procedural norms are manifestations of a balancing act between conflicting rights positions. In its *Mülheim-Kärlich* decision the Court brought these views together and applied them to the right to life and the nuclear power plant authorization procedure code and provisions therein whose purpose was to address dangers to the life and health of people who might be affected by such installations.[44]

The Court has used a similar approach for dealing with specific difficulties arising in the context of the freedom to demonstrate (Article 8 of the Basic Law) when such demonstrations are very large (so-called mass-demonstrations in emotionally charged circumstances such as the construction of nuclear power plants) and hence have a very large potential for violent disruptions, especially if intelligence implies that small groups might want to use that demonstration for non-peaceful purposes. In such cases, the Court has held that both the organizers of such large demonstrations and the police have an obligation to do what they can to protect the peaceful part of the demonstration and to minimize negative effects on third parties. This obligation can be discharged by way of cooperation between the organizers and the police, so long as this cooperation does not burden the organizers with policing responsibilities and does not lead to direct government involvement in the demonstration. The degree of this 'informal' cooperation will have an effect on the legality of any steps taken by the police against the demonstration. The more "trust-building" measures were undertaken the harder it will be for the police to disperse demonstrators or even stop the demonstration on account of violent behavior by some of the demonstrators.[45]

d. Duty to Protect

Fundamental rights are not only defense rights of individuals against government intrusion into a protected sphere of personal autonomy. Fundamental rights sometimes require active protection by governmental authority. In other words, fundamental rights protection cannot always be sufficiently afforded just by governmental inaction. Fundamental rights can also serve as a legal basis for an obligation of the government to act.

---

43 BVerfGE 53, 30 – Mülheim-Kärlich, http://www.servat.unibe.ch/dfr/bv053030.html.
44 BVerfGE 53, 30 (65) – Mülheim-Kärlich.
45 BVerfGE 69, 315 (355 et seq.) – Brokdorf, http://www.servat.unibe.ch/dfr/bv069315.html.

The right to life is an illustrative example. The defensive function of that right limits governmental action that poses a risk to an individual's life. The duty to protect on the other hand requires governmental action to protect individuals against life threatening behavior. Providing an appropriate legal order with criminal sanctions for the taking of life is one example. Whereas that might sound trivial as all legal orders will punish homicide and similar crimes it may well play a role when it comes to the negligent taking of life or even to the protection of unborn life. The decisions of the German Constitutional Court in the abortion cases are prime examples.[46] The Court stipulated that the duty to protect flowing from Article 2.2 of the Basic Law would bar the government from legalizing abortion and demand that some sort of protective system be put in place, for example counseling and support services that could persuade the mother to opt pro life.

The duty to protect often comes to life in trilateral constellations involving two colliding rights and the government as potential mediator. As fundamental rights do not directly obligate private individuals one can speak of the indirect third-party effect of fundamental rights.[47] The government cannot inactively stand by when private individuals infringe upon certain legal positions of others. In abortion constellations, for example, the concerned rights are the right of the mother to self-determination and the right to life of the unborn fetus. The duty to protect defines the legal minimum of protection for the unborn that the government must undertake. The defensive function of the self-determination rights of the mother describes the legal maximum the government can engage in to protect the unborn. The space between the minimum and the maximum defines the margin of appreciation the government has in this balancing act. Free speech is another example. The free speech guarantee does not obligate individuals in their legal relationships. However, the legal order must have due regard to free speech even when regulating contractual relationships between individuals. Free speech limitations in employment contracts, for example, must find a balance between the employer and employee and the same is true in constellations that pit free speech against personality rights.

The duty to protect is potentially problematic because fundamental freedoms become the legal basis for the restriction of freedoms. The protection of personality rights could, as implied above, lead to significant restrictions to free speech – the problem of delineating free speech from defamation has been

---

46   BVerfGE 39, 1, http://www.servat.unibe.ch/dfr/bv039001.html; BVerfGE 88, 203, http://www.servat.unibe.ch/dfr/bv088203.html.

47   Brinktrine, Ralf, The Horizontal Effect of Human Rights in German Constitutional Law, 4 European Human Rights Law Review (2001) 421.

controversial not only in Germany.[48] The German Constitutional Court has so far been successful in keeping a check on governmental duties to protect. The defensive function is and must be the prime function of fundamental rights.

e. Freedom of Communication – Free Speech and Broadcasting

Major controversies over the past 60 years have been around the concept of free speech (Article 5 GG), especially in constellations where free speech conflicted with the right to personal integrity and honor. Often it was politicians that were the object of harsh criticism that sometimes took on an insulting nature. Other cases concerned regular persons such as soldiers. One of the most famous – and controversial – decisions of the *BVerfG* dealt with the question of whether free speech protects referring to soldiers as "potential murderers" in the context of debates around pacifism.[49] The crime of "murder" (§ 211 German Criminal Code)[50] is among the most serious crimes and among the very few who carry a life sentence. In that sense the term "murderer" describes the most serious of criminals. The *BVerfG* deduced in favor of free speech in this case, arguing that the term 'murderer' cannot be taken at face value but must be put into the broader context of the debate and interpreted in that way. This exercise would have to reveal that characterizing soldiers as murderers is not necessarily an insult to people serving their country and – given the fact that Germany had compulsory military service – might even have been legally obligated to serve as soldiers, but could also be the mere expression of the idea that as a pacifist one inherently is of the view that war is unjust and cannot serve to justify the killing of others.

---

48   See the contribution of Craig Collins in this book for an Australian perspective on this topic. Specifically on hate speech see the instructive article of Winfried Brugger, The Treatment of Hate Speech in German Constitutional Law, 4 German Law Journal 1 (2003), available at http://www.germanlawjournal.com/pdf/Vol04No01/PDF_Vol_04_No_01_01-44_Public_Brugger.pdf. The European Court of Human Rights most recently addressed the matter in the case of Le Pen/France, ECtHR, Application No. 18788/09, 20/4/2010; see also Féret/Begium, Application No. 15615/07, 16/7/2009. Decisions of the ECtHR available at the HUDOC-database of the ECtHR, http://cmiskp.echr.coe.int/tkp197/search.asp?skin=hudoc-en.

49   BVerfGE 93, 266, http://www.servat.unibe.ch/dfr/bv093266.html.

50   § 211 of the German Criminal Code: "(1) Whosoever commits murder under the conditions of this provision shall be liable to imprisonment for life. (2) A murderer under this provision is any person who kills a person for pleasure, for sexual gratification, out of greed or otherwise base motives, by stealth or cruelly or by means that pose a danger to the public or in order to facilitate or to cover up another offence", see http://www.gesetze-im-internet.de/englisch_stgb/index.html (in this translation '§' are referred to as 'sections').

The Court has by and large always sided with free speech, especially when that free speech was somehow connected to what might be referred to as the public discourse in the broadest sense. It has, however, upheld personal integrity and honor if the speech in question could not be linked to a public discourse and hence remained on the level of a private insult[51] or if there was a power imbalance between those speaking and those affected by the speech.[52]

On an institutional level the Court's broadcasting decisions have defined the structure of the German media order. In an early decision the *BVerfG* held that broadcasting must remain a matter to be regulated by the *Länder* because the *Grundgesetz* does not allocate the requisite powers to the federal level.[53] This scuttled an attempt by the first Chancellor of the Federal Republic to institute a federal television station. In later years the Court in several decisions and in a very detailed fashion regulated the relationship between public sector television and private broadcasting and gave a constitutional guarantee to public sector television as absolutely necessary to maintain plurality in the media order.[54]

f. Other Controversies

Serious controversy arose, perhaps unsurprisingly, from the Court's decision on religious freedom in a case concerning the right of a *Land* (in this case Bavaria) as the entity with jurisdiction for the schools to mandatorily require Christian crosses in the classroom of some public schools.[55] The Court held that the negative freedom of religion, i.e. the freedom not to be religious, is violated if a pupil is forced "to learn under the cross"[56] and that therefore the cross must be removed if no other solution can be found.

---

51   BVerfGE 86, 1 (13) – Titanic, http://www.servat.unibe.ch/dfr/bv086001.html. In this case a satirical magazine had named a paraplegic man in a list of the most embarrassing people because he wanted and had succeeded in being called for a military reservists' exercise despite his disability. The man had been named and referred to as a "cripple".

52   BVerfGE 25, 256 – Blinkfüer, http://www.servat.unibe.ch/dfr/bv025256.html. This decision concerned an action for damages by a small magazine publication against one of the largest publishing houses of Germany because the latter had asked for a boycott against any publication, such as the plaintiff's, which continued to publish the TV schedule of communist East-Germany, and had supported its boycott by threatening to withhold its widely circulated newspapers and magazines from anyone still willing to sell the boycotted publications. The regular courts had decided for the defendants and against damages on the basis of free speech but the *BVerfG* held that this type of extortionist speech goes beyond a mere competition of ideas and opinions.

53   BVerfGE 12, 205 (243 et seq.), http://www.servat.unibe.ch/dfr/bv012205.html.

54   See BVerfGE 31, 314; 57, 295; 73, 118; 74, 297; 83, 238; 87, 181; 90, 60.

55   BVerfGE 93, 1 – Kruzifix, http://www.servat.unibe.ch/dfr/bv093001.html.

56   BVerfGE 93, 1 (18) – Kruzifix.

The case of a female teacher who was denied a teaching position because she insisted on wearing the Islamic headscarf in school[57] concerns a constellation that has arisen in many jurisdictions[58] and goes to the extremely sensitive relationship between religion and state and between occidental and Islamic traditions. However, the real difficulty lies in the distinction between those who aim to politicize Islam and foster Islamic religious extremism, which, with its inherent and stark discrimination against women, its lack of tolerance against others, and its anti-democratic philosophy is *per se* incompatible with liberal western constitutional values, and those who simply want to practice their religion.

As in many other jurisdictions, the abortion problem has repeatedly been brought to the *BVerfG* and also as in many other jurisdictions, the court's approach to the abortion issue, somewhat restrictive in comparison from the point of view of the right to chose, was subject to great debate. What it reflects and illustrates is the fact that the German Court's understanding of rights, especially the concept of the duty to protect, demands that conflicting rights be balanced and the abortion decisions of the *BVerfG* are good examples for such balancing exercises.[59]

Finally, industrial relations law has given rise to some very profound controversies. The first change from a conservative government to a center-left government in 1969 subsequently led to a number of political reform projects.[60] One of these projects dealt with industrial relations and especially the intention of the new center-left coalition to introduce 'workers co-determination', by which certain companies and their management were to be supervised by a supervisory board composed not only of the owners of the company in question, i.e. the shareholders, but also and (almost) equally[61] by representatives of the employees. This caused some very profound and equally controversial debates about the scope of the property protection clause (Article 14 GG) and the freedom of association clause (Article 9.1 GG) of the *Grundgesetz*.

---

57   BVerfGE 108, 282 – Kopftuch, http://www.servat.unibe.ch/dfr/bv108282.html.
58   See, for example, ECHR, Appl. No. 44774/98, 10.11.2005, Leyla Sahin/Turkey.
59   BVerfGE 39, 1, http://www.servat.unibe.ch/dfr/bv039001.html; BVerfGE 88, 203, http://www.servat.unibe.ch/dfr/bv088203.html. See also supra, text around footnote 46.
60   Abortion law reform was one of those reform projects and the first abortion decision of the *BVerfG* (see previous footnote) quashed that reform effort at least to some degree.
61   The chairperson of the board has the tie-breaking vote.

2. The BVerfG as Institutional Arbitrator

One of the important tasks of the Court is institutional arbitration, i.e. the resolution of disputes between the various organs of state and government. The relevant procedure is the institutional complaint procedure or a specialized version thereof, the so-called *Federation-Länder*-dispute[62], under which enumerated governmental institutions (chambers of parliament, the federal government, the *Länder*) can bring a conflict directly to the *BVerfG*[63]

a. Deployment of Military Forces Abroad

The disputes surrounding the deployment of German military forces abroad had to be settled by the Court and have, inter alia, led to the very special German invention of a "parliamentary army" requiring a full and detailed parliamentary mandate for any and all use of force abroad.[64]

b. Party and Campaign Financing

The Court has also regulated campaign and party financing in painstaking detail and with shifting positions to the fundamental question of whether parties can only be entitled to be reimbursed for their role in the conduct of elections or if they can be paid general operating subsidies for their general role in a democratic system.[65] The Court's decisions in this area are illustrative examples of what could be regarded as overreach, albeit arguably with beneficial effect in the German democratic system. The Court, for example, determined an absolute sum of money that political parties can legally receive from state coffers under party and campaign financing schemes.[66] All of that the Court deduced from the very general democracy principle in the constitution in conjunction with Article 21.2 of the Basic Law where the role of political parties is outlined in very general terms.

---

62   "Bund-Länder-Streitigkeit". See BVerfGE 103, 81 (86 et seq. and 88 et seq.).

63   See supra footnote 11.

64   See BVerfGE 90, 286, http://www.servat.unibe.ch/dfr/bv090286.html; see also BVerfGE 100, 266; 108, 24; 118, 244; 121, 135 and the contribution of Torsten Stein in this volume.

65   See BVerfGE 20, 56 for the original position.

66   BVerfGE 85, 264 (285 et seq.), http://www.servat.unibe.ch/dfr/bv085264.html. In this decision the *BVerfG* stipulated that the maximum sum of money available for political parties for party and campaign financing must not exceed the average sum of monies paid out between 1989 and 1992, subsequently to be adjusted for inflation. At the time that was roughly DM 230 Mio.

c. Dissolution of Parliament After Intentional Loss of Confidence Vote

One of the consequences of the Weimar Constitution was to make the dissolution of parliament (*Bundestag*) very difficult. A vote of no confidence (Article 67 GG) cannot lead to dissolution under the *Grundgesetz* because it requires a new chancellor to be elected and hence installs a new government with a parliamentary majority. The only way to dissolve parliament is if the Chancellor applies for a vote of confidence (Article 68 GG). If such an application for a vote of confidence does not find an absolute majority in the parliament, the Federal President, acting on a proposal of the Chancellor, "may" dissolve the *Bundestag* if he determines that this is necessary for the effective functioning of government.

In the past, this has led the incumbent Chancellor to apply for a vote of confidence and instruct his supporters to abstain so as to intentionally lose the vote and achieve dissolution. This happened for the first time in 1982 after former Chancellor Helmut Schmidt had been voted out of office by a vote of no confidence. The new Chancellor, Helmut Kohl, soon instituted a vote of confidence to achieve dissolution, hold new elections and gain a new democratic mandate in the light of very difficult and even more controversial decisions which had to be taken concerning the stationing of nuclear missiles in Germany by NATO to counter similar deployments by the then Soviet-Union (USSR). The majority carrying the new government was instructed to abstain and the confidence vote was lost as planned. In a way this was a clear circumvention of constitutional principle and an abuse of the vote of confidence, whose purpose it was to "rally the troops" and show that the government is still in control but not to create dissolution and put the election term at the disposal of the government.[67] However, the *BVerfG* decided that proceeding in this manner was constitutional.[68] The Court held that the interpretation of the Basic Law cannot be conducted completely independently from the political realities of the day and that the court must take into account the broader context and the constitutional convictions of the other constitutional organs involved.[69] After all, both the Federal Government and the Chancellor, and the Federal President had regarded

---

67   As is traditionally possible in Westminster parliamentary systems.
68   BVerfGE 62, 1, http://www.servat.unibe.ch/dfr/bv062001.html.
69   BVerfGE 62, 1 (38–9). Equally clear in the second decision on no confidence dissolution, *BVerfG*, 2 BvE 4/05 of 25.8.2005, para 160, http://www.bverfg.de/entscheidungen/es20050825_2bve000405.html. See also Bröhmer, Jürgen, Containment eines Leviathans – Anmerkungen zur Entscheidung des Bundesverfassungsgerichts zum Vertrag von Lissabon, ZEuS 2009, 543 criticizing that the Constitutional Court did not use this concept in regard to European integration.

this as a way forward in the light of the concrete political situation. Absent any intentions to manipulate elections and voter decision such an intentional loss of a vote of confidence can therefore be a potential possibility for dissolving the German parliament. What the Court did in these decisions could be a referred to as a mild application of what elsewhere is known as the political question doctrine.[70]

d. Federalism

The Court's record on federalism issues is a mixed one. Early on it gave an extensive interpretation to those provisions of the *Grundgesetz*, especially Article 84.1 GG, dealing with the so called "assent legislation."[71] Assent legislation is legislation, which requires the full proactive assent of the second chamber of parliament, the *Bundesrat* as the chamber of the German *Länder*. By broadening the scope of this assent legislation, the *BVerfG* considerably strengthened the federal element in the legislative process. The Court also remained relatively strict on issues of fiscal federalism, thus avoiding a situation comparable to that in Australia, where the states are very much dependent on federal financial assistance.[72]

Contrastingly, the Court was, for a long time, very lax in the interpretation of Article 72.2 GG by giving parliament almost unlimited discretion in determining whether the conditions prescribed there for exercising federal concurring

---

70 On this doctrine, which has never really had a strong foothold in Germany, see Supreme Court of the United States, *Baker v Carr*, 369 U.S. 186 (1962), http://www.law.cornell.edu/supct/ html/historics/USSC_CR_0369_0186_ZS.html (3.11.2009). See also *Barkow*, The Rise and Fall of the Political Question Doctrine, in: Mourtada-Sabbah/Cain (Hrsg.), The Political Question Doctrine and the Supreme Court of the United States, 2007, S. 23 ff.

71 BVerfGE 24, 184 (194 et seq.), http://www.servat.unibe.ch/dfr/bv024184.html.

72 See especially the decisions of the *BVerfG* concerning vertical and horizontal fiscal equalization, BVerfGE 72, 330, http://www.servat.unibe.ch/dfr/bv072330.html; 86, 148, http://www.servat.unibe.ch/dfr/bv086148.html and 101, 158, http://www.servat.unibe.ch/dfr/ bv101158.html. In Australia and the United States of America the federal governments effectively control policy areas otherwise in the jurisdiction of the respective constituent entities by giving financial grants tied to political conditions. This undermining of federalism has not taken place in Germany in any comparable way because of a constitutional reform in 1969 and the introduction of Article 104a.1 GG, which separated the expenditure responsibility between the federal level and the Länder. See also Ress, Georg/Bröhmer, Jürgen, Legal Opinion on the Question of the Extent of Constitutional Entitlements of the Free Hanse City of Bremen Against the Federal Republic of Germany and/or other Länder of the Federation to Overcome Budgetary Emergencies, submitted 2006 on behalf of the Senator for Finance of the Free Hanse City of Bremen, available at http://finanzen.bremen.de/sixcms/ media.php/13/Gutachen_Ress_Broemer.pdf (9.12.2009).

legislative power are fulfilled[73] and it was not until after a constitutional amendment of Article 72.2 that these criteria were reinvigorated.[74]

IV. The *BVerfG* as Controller of Foreign Policy and International Integration

Foreign policy in general and the integration of Germany into international and supranational bodies has repeatedly been the subject of decisions by the *BVerfG*. The first major issue brought before the Court was the *Ostpolitik* of détente instituted by former Chancellor *Willy Brandt* and his foreign minister *Walter Scheel*. One of the results of this new policy was an international treaty signed with the former German Democratic Republic.[75] This was highly controversial as the opposition claimed that this would stifle reunification of the two Germanys by recognizing East-Germany as a legitimate country. The Court disagreed recognizing in essence that the exercise of foreign policy requires some degree of political discretion.[76]

Germany's participation in European integration has been the subject of a number of very significant decisions of the *BVerfG*. The first – as it is commonly referred to – "as long as No. 1" decision of the court in 1974 stipulated that the *BVerfG* would remain active as a guardian of fundamental rights and freedoms in Germany for as long as the European Community itself did not possess a catalogue of rights and freedoms of similar quality as the German one.[77] This decision arose out of the increasing relevance of European Community legislation for fundamental rights and freedoms. This effect of dynamic integration had not been foreseen when the founding treaties had originally been concluded in 1952 and 1957 respectively. Property rights of farmers, for example, became an issue in the context of legislation in the common agricultural policy.[78]

---

73 See, for example, BVerfGE 2, 213 (244–5); 78, 249 (270) and, recapitulating, BVerfGE 106, 62 (136 et seq.).

74 See BVerfGE 106, 62; 110, 141; 111, 10; 111, 226, 112, 226.

75 On the other two treaties signed with the USSR and Poland, the treaties of Moscow and Warsaw, see BVerfGE 40, 141, http://www.servat.unibe.ch/dfr/bv040141.html.

76 BVerfGE 36, 1, http://www.servat.unibe.ch/dfr/bv036001.html. However, this is a results based assessment. The Court went through great length to assert its power, criticizing Parliament and the Federal President for putting the Treaty into effect before the Court had rendered its decision.

77 BVerfGE 37, 271, http://www.servat.unibe.ch/dfr/bv037271.html.

78 One of the leading cases in this respect was Case 44/79, ECR 1979, 3727 – Hauer, concerning the prohibition in a Community legislative act of using land for growing vines (wine grapes), http://eur-lex.europa.eu/LexUriServ/LexUriServ.do?uri=CELEX:61979J0044:EN:HTML.

Twelve years later and after the European Court of Justice had in the meantime developed fundamental rights as part of the general principles of European Community law, the *BVerfG* decided in its "as long as No. 2" decision that it will no longer act as a guardian of fundamental rights and freedoms against actions stemming from European Community authority as long as these actions are subject to an effective rights control by the European Court of Justice in Luxemburg.[79]

Later the Court had to decide on the constitutionality of the Maastricht Treaty, which broadened the scope of the European Community towards the development of a common currency and culminated in the creation of the Euro[80] and founded the European Union with its Common Foreign and Security Policy and the Cooperation in Justice and Home Affairs. The Court held the Maastricht Treaty to be compatible with the *Grundgesetz* if and so long as the subsidiarity principle limiting the exercise of legislative powers by the European Communities was effectively applied and the powers attributed to the European Union were not interpreted too broadly thus leaving substantial decision making powers with Germany and the *Bundestag* in particular.[81]

Just recently the Court opined that the new Reform Treaty of Lisbon is also compatible with the German constitution, again emphasizing that any further integration steps must take into account that the democracy principle of the *Grundgesetz* requires that fundamental decision making powers, for example in the area of social policy, budget or military action, must remain with Germany and cannot be transferred away to the European Union.[82]

V. Conclusions

In summary I would like to present the following four main conclusions for the role of the Federal Constitutional Court within Germany's constitutional structure:

---

79   BVerfGE 73, 339, http://www.servat.unibe.ch/dfr/bv073339.html.
80   Technically in 1999 with the coming into force of permanent exchange rates between the participating currencies, in essence creating one currency with many different denominations and in then 2002 with the visible transfer from the "old" money to the newly issued Euro bills and coins, see http://www.ecb.int/ecb/10ann/history/html/index.en.html.
81   BVerfGE 89, 155, http://www.servat.unibe.ch/dfr/bv089155.html.
82   *BVerfG*, 2 BvE 2/08 of 30.6.2009, http://www.bverfg.de/entscheidungen/es2009 0630_2bve000208en.htm. See also the special issue of ZEuS 2009, 491 et seq. (Volume 12/4) with a number of articles pertaining to that decision, including Bröhmer, Jürgen, Containment eines Leviathans – Anmerkungen zur Entscheidung des Bundesverfassungsgerichts zum Vertrag von Lissabon, ZEuS 2009, 543.

1. The Federal Constitutional Court has played an instrumental role in shaping all aspects of the socio-political context in Germany.
2. The Federal Constitutional Court has been a court of both forceful intervention and judicial restraint. Whereas it has not shied away from "constitutional law making" in the sense of political activism, it has mostly, albeit not always painlessly, respected the democratic process when it came to fundamental questions of reform, ranging from European integration to abortion, from workers' co-determination rights to military deployments of the armed forces outside Germany.
3. The Federal Constitutional Court has shaped and is shaping the legal political environment not only by its decisions and rulings, but considerably also by having created an atmosphere of anticipatory compliance. The "will it stand in Karlsruhe?" question has become a hallmark test of the German political process.
4. The Federal Constitutional Court is itself part of a triad of constitutional courts, the European Court of Justice and the European Court of Human Rights and regards itself as standing in a cooperative relationship with these two courts on the European level.

Andrew Lynch*

The Legislative and Executive Branch vs. The Constitutional Court and the Judiciary – Conflict or Cooperation?

The High Court of Australia

No human relationship – even the most loving or hateful – can be appreciated stripped of all nuance and complexity. Similarly, the dealings between the judicial and political arms in any constitutional system defy simple classification. The constantly changing composition of institutions, the steady evolution of political and legal ideas and techniques, and the shifting social, moral and economic context in which this is all taking place frustrate any attempt to capture the relationship and designate it as one thing and not another. Inevitably, the judiciary play a role marked by notable instances of both obstruction and accommodation, rather than an unwavering course of one or other of these. Indeed, grave fears would be sensibly held for the health of any state in which the judicial branch was either trapped in perpetual conflict with, or was monotonously obliging towards, the other institutions of government.

This is not to say that any attempt to characterise the relationship between the courts on one hand and the executive and legislature on the other is entirely futile. But certainly some acknowledgment is required that what will be most revealing in this regard will be those cases which transcend their immediate factual concerns to more generally set the parameters within which judicial power will be exercised in the state and what this means for governmental power in the ordinary run of things. Additionally, some consideration of what the terms 'co-operation' and 'conflict' might indicate in a particular jurisdictional context is necessary. Failure to be explicit about these concepts renders their application in assessing the relationship between the three arms of government in Australia

---

*   Director, Gilbert + Tobin Centre of Public Law and Associate Professor, Faculty of Law, University of New South Wales. I express my gratitude to Professor Jürgen Bröhmer and all participants at the 60 years Deutsches Grundgesetz – The German Constitution turns 60: Human and basic rights through the eyes of Germany and Australia, Australian National University, Canberra, 22–23 May 2009 for their stimulating conversation and enthusiasm for comparative dialogue on constitutional issues between our two countries.

of limited utility – especially for the purposes of fostering the kind of comparative exchange which is the aim of this collection.

With those qualifications duly noted, it makes sense to embark on a discussion of these issues by positing some basic assessment offered at the outset of the Australian judiciary's interaction with the political arms of the national government. For reasons which I shall go on to elaborate, I do believe that this is possible and a worthwhile venture. Additionally, it provides a base from which to tease out the values implicit in labels such as 'conflict' or 'co-operation'. Essentially, in this chapter I shall argue that the High Court of Australia's relationship with the Commonwealth Parliament and executive government has overwhelmingly been marked by a spirit of co-operation rather than conflict. Indeed, at times, the Court might be seen as having been, accommodating of the national government to the point of indulgence.

However, in stating the reasons for my view that 'co-operation' is, in the main, the appropriate description for the part played by the judiciary in relation to the legislature and executive, the bluntness of that simple assessment must be tempered by highlighting those occasions which have exposed where the limits of the courts' co-operation lie. These are not, as shall be seen, insignificant and have been crucial to securing the Court's high standing in the Australian political system.

Finally, just why it is that the High Court has tended to accommodate rather than hinder the ambitions of the national government requires some consideration. I argue that the strong positivist tradition of the Australian legal profession, reinforced by the absence of entrenched legal protection of human rights, is crucial to understanding the tenor of the High Court's relationship to government. Both the founding of the Australian constitutional system and the prevailing judicial attitude since has been deeply reflective of a core faith in the Westminster doctrine of responsible government as a check on power.

The only era in the High Court's history which clearly defies classification as 'co-operative' in tone is the period of Sir Anthony Mason's tenure as Chief Justice.[1] The so-called Mason Court was marked by the embrace of a legal methodology far more explicitly policy-oriented than that practiced by the court before or since and which led it to make a succession of high-profile decisions challenging the traditional relationship of the Court to the other arms of government. Examining the tensions of the Mason era helps illuminate the judicial approach which has traditionally sustained the non-confrontational relationship of the Court to the legislature and executive, while also suggesting that things might be otherwise.

---

1   Sir Anthony Mason was Chief Justice of Australia between 1987–1995.

'Conflict' and 'Co-operation'

Clearly both 'conflict' and 'co-operation' may mean rather different things in different jurisdictions. Consequently, to describing the High Court as 'co-operative', might mean anything along a rather vast spectrum. An obvious and generally uncontroversial example is the tendency of courts to afford government much more leeway during times of existential crisis than would normally be the case. Outside times of real emergency or war, a positive use of the label 'co-operation' might signify that the judicial institution is duly appreciative of the context of national priorities and changing social circumstances in which its decisions are made and into which they will be received.

In that sense, the eventual abandonment by the United States Supreme Court of the laissez-faire constitutionalism which marked the *Lochner* era[2] so as to uphold key components of President Roosevelt's New Deal might be identified as a clear example of a 'co-operative' court. Of course the Court's move in favour of Roosevelt's agenda was hardly unprompted 'co-operation' but came after the threat of the court-packing plan and by replacing those retiring judges who had obstructed the President with candidates who were seen as likely to be supportive of his solutions to the nation's problems.[3] In other countries, at other times, judicial 'co-operation' may be even more ruthlessly secured and be little more than a euphemism for a weakened, compromised or entirely corrupt judiciary.

So it must be recognised that neither term is neutral but inevitably invites consideration of its desirability. It is obvious that too much of either is a bad thing with the potential to destabilise the constitutional settlement. Thankfully, a discussion of 'conflict' or 'co-operation' in respect of the Australian courts avoids such extremes. The federal judiciary has guarded its independence and the purity of its own power with a zeal that has occasionally produced distinctly inconvenient results.[4] But the fact that our courts are generally not cowering under the threat of governmental interference and are suitably impartial and independent does not prevent classification of the course of their decisions as either 'co-operative' or in 'conflict' with the prevailing political agenda. It just means that their motivations for so acting come from a more complex place.

---

2   *Lochner v New York* 198 US 45 (1905).
3   See Marian McKenna, *Franklin Roosevelt and the great constitutional war: the court-packing plan of 1937* (New York: Fordham University Press, 2002).
4   See particularly *R v Kirby; Ex parte Boilermakers' Society of Australia* (1956) 94 CLR 254; *Brandy v HREOC* (1995) 183 CLR 245; and *Re Wakim; Ex parte McNally* (1999) 198 CLR 511.

Advancing that view is not to deny the political context in which the judiciary functions. While the executive's unconstrained power of judicial appointment may not have been used in Australia as overtly as in some other jurisdictions to secure a more obliging court, no appointment can ever be simply apolitical.[5] Appointment to the High Court is inevitably politicised even though political actors rarely admit as much and the announcement of new judges rarely meets with anything but universal approval. Occasionally, however, the facade falls away and the reality of this power receives explicit recognition – most memorably when in the late 1990s the Deputy Prime Minister expressed the government's desire to place on the High Court a 'conservative with a capital C'.[6] But while of course this is a factor, over-emphasising the significance of appointments as an explanation for the nature of the Court's relationship with government is something of which we should be most wary.

How then am I using the two terms 'co-operation' and 'conflict' in my discussion of the High Court in this chapter? The usefulness of these labels appears to be as a kind of shorthand for describing the extent to which the court has, through application of an articulated legal methodology and from a position of real independence, been willing to accommodate or frustrate the exercise of power by the legislature and executive. Another, rather more general, way in which this might be expressed is to ask whether the Australian judiciary is essentially trusting of political power or whether it perceives its role as requiring the aggressive policing of the other arms of government.

Framing the issue in this way draws attention to the relevance of historical circumstance in understanding the central question. Australia's development from a British penal colony to a functioning democracy took place without revolution and with a sustained commitment to representative and responsible government. While Australians may not be overly enamoured of their elected leaders, our political culture is not one marked by a trauma which has required the judiciary to define itself by scepticism and distrust of the arms of government from which it is separate. Consequently, judicial power has generally been exercised with the kind of restraint one would expect in a polity whose constitutional ethos is committed to political, rather than legal, solutions to abuses of power.

---

5   Rachel Davis and George Williams, 'Reform of the Judicial Appointments Process: Gender and the Bench of the High Court of Australia' (2003) 27 *Melbourne University Law Review* 819.

6   See Haig Patapan, *Judging Democracy – The New Politics of the High Court of Australia* (CUP: Cambridge, 2000) 166.

Co-operation as accommodation

The assessment of the High Court as having tended to strongly enable and accommodate the powers of the Commonwealth government and parliament rather than curb or frustrate them, rests on two interrelated strands in its constitutional jurisprudence stemming from the virtually unimpeded ascendency of the Commonwealth over the Australian states since the decision of the Court in the *Amalgamated Society of Engineers v Adelaide Steamship Co Ltd (Engineers' Case) of 1920.*[7]

First, and most simply, the High Court, in its capacity as the umpire of federal disputes, has since that time exhibited a virtually unyielding tendency to favour the national government at the expense of the States. This has meant that it has directly facilitated, rather than thwarted, the ambitions of the Commonwealth legislative and executive. The stark unbalancing of our federal system which has attended these successive victories for the national government has been extensively documented. That this outcome was definitely not intended by the Constitution's authors nor the people who voted for its adoption suggests that the Court's contribution has been significant in producing the current state of affairs. That a rather less 'co-operative' attitude to the expansion of Common-wealth constitutional power was open to the Court is demonstrated by the early decisions in federal disputes made by the original bench. The Court certainly did not commence its work in a fashion which we might describe as terribly accommodating of the powers of the newly created Commonwealth – aiming as it did to reserve as much of the States' pre-existing colonial powers, even when this generated rather artificial results.[8] How sustainable a pro-States stance was likely to prove as the twentieth century unfolded is debatable, but its demise began in earnest when the involvement of Australia in World War I saw the Commonwealth aggressively pursue an expansion of its powers.[9]

Second, and to approach the issue from a deeper perspective, the course set by the High Court in *Engineers* for the interpretation of the Constitution was bound to place it in the role of assisting Commonwealth powers to run free of judicial interference generally – not simply when they collided with State interests. The effect of *Engineers* was to settle upon an approach to the Constitution favouring the 'natural' or 'ordinary' meaning' of its text, and to reject the making of implications 'arrived at by the Court on the opinions of

---

7   (1920) 28 CLR 129.

8   The early Court's efforts to shield the States from Commonwealth power was through the two implied doctrines of reserved state powers and the reciprocal immunity of instrumentalities.

9   See generally, Michael Coper and George Williams, *How Many Cheers for* Engineers? (Sydney: Federation Press, 1997).

Judges as to hopes and expectations respecting vague external conditions'.[10] In particular, it was seen as illegitimate to impose limits on those grants of power borne of distrust of government and its possible abuse of those powers. In a passage which reads rather remarkably to those in jurisdictions where judicial power is regularly applied for the protection of individual liberty, the majority judgment declared:

> When the people of Australia, to use the words of the Constitution itself, "united in a Federal Commonwealth," they took power to control by ordinary constitutional means any attempt on the part of the national Parliament to misuse its powers. If it be conceivable that the representatives of the people of Australia as a whole would ever proceed to use their national powers to injure the people of Australia considered sectionally, it is certainly within the power of the people themselves to resent and reverse what may be done. No protection of this Court in such a case is necessary or proper.[11]

While the Court did not prohibit the drawing of implications,[12] it committed itself to dong so only when these necessarily arose from the 'text and structure of the Constitution'.[13] As Justice McHugh affirmed many years later, the significance of the *Engineers' Case* was that the Court 'held that it is not legitimate to construe the Constitution by reference to political principles or theories that find no support in the text of the Constitution'.[14] Indeed the only vaguely overarching principle which might be said to have been used consistently by the Court as a gloss upon its interpretation of the text is to prefer a liberal or generous reading of the powers given their location in a constitution rather than an ordinary statute.[15]

It is hardly surprising that the adoption of this approach would be to the benefit of the political organs of the national government. The Constitution is primarily focused on the powers and operations of the Commonwealth which it is designed to create. A cursory look at the document reveals that the bulk of its provisions are directed towards the establishment and capacities of the new Commonwealth government, with issues regarding the States coming to the fore only towards the end in Chapter V. By committing to resolve constitutional

---

10 (1920) 28 CLR 129, 145.

11 (1920) 28 CLR 129, 151–52.

12 *Australian Capital Television Pty Ltd v Commonwealth* (1992) 177 CLR 106, 133–36 (Mason CJ).

13 *Theophanous v Herald & Weekly Times Ltd* (1994) 182 CLR 104, 197 (McHugh J).

14 Ibid, 198.

15 *Jumbunna Coal Mine NL v Victorian Coal Miners' Association* (1908) 6 CLR 309, 367–68. Justice Heydon has recently argued that not enough attention is given to the caveat accompanying this principle that a narrower interpretation may, in some instances, be justified by a contextual understanding of the Constitution, in which his Honour included federal considerations: *Pape v Commissioner of Taxation* [2009] HCA 23 (7 July 2009) [411]–[425].

issues almost exclusively through the 'natural' meaning of the document's text, the Court inevitably privileged the political institutions of the Commonwealth with which its provisions are overwhelmingly concerned.

The *Engineers* methodology has proven remarkably resilient and remains the orthodoxy of Australian constitutional interpretation. But to briefly acknowledge the major milestones of its impact on federal power, one would highlight the effect of such reasoning upon the ability of the Commonwealth, initially under cover of war-time emergency[16] but later confirmed in peace,[17] to use a combination of its taxing and spending powers so as to effectively destroy the financial independence of the States. Far from this being an unexpected product of the decisions, it was an expressly acknowledged result of the guiding interpretative methodology:

> The amount of the [federal] grants could be determined in fact by the satisfaction of the Commonwealth with the policies, legislative or other, of the respective States, no reference being made to such matters in any Commonwealth statute. Thus, if the Commonwealth Parliament were prepared to pass such legislation, all State powers would be controlled by the Commonwealth – a result which would mean the end of the political independence of the States. Such a result cannot be prevented by any legal decision. The determination of the propriety of any such policy must rest with the Commonwealth Parliament and ultimately with the people. The remedy for alleged abuse of power or for the use of power to promote what are thought to be improper objects is to be found in the political arena and not in the Courts.[18]

By the early 1980s the emergence of a vast reservoir of Commonwealth legislative power in the areas of external affairs[19] and corporations[20] – both confirmed in the landmark *Commonwealth v Tasmania (Tasmanian Dams Case)*[21] led many to think the other express powers had been rendered superfluous to requirements.[22] Any doubt over just how accommodating the Court viewed the power of the national parliament to make laws with respect to corporations was obliterated by the 2006 case of *New South Wales v Commonwealth (Work Choices Case)*[23] – a result which despite being entirely predictable, made the abundant capacity of that particular legislative power so apparent as to prompt a dissenting judge to complain that 'there is nothing in the text or the structure of the *Constitution* to suggest that the Commonwealth's

---

16   *South Australia v Commonwealth* (1942) 65 CLR 373.
17   *Victoria v Commonwealth* (1957) 99 CLR 575.
18   (1942) 65 CLR 373, 429 (Latham CJ) cf. 443 (Starke J).
19   *Commonwealth Constitution*, s 51(xxix).
20   *Commonwealth Constitution*, s 51(xx).
21   (1983) 158 CLR 1.
22   Sir Daryl Dawson, 'The Constitution – Major Overhaul or Simple Tune-up?' (1984) 14 *Melbourne University Law Review* 353, 358.
23   (2006) 229 CLR 1.

powers should be enlarged, by successive decisions of this Court, so that the Parliament of each State is progressively reduced until it becomes no more than an impotent debating society'.[24]

Even aside from federal battles with the States, the High Court has shown a remarkable disinclination to make life difficult for the Commonwealth government. An excellent example of this in the crucial area of expenditure of public money, is provided by the 2005 case of *Combet v Commonwealth*.[25] The case involved a challenge by the Australian Council of Trade Unions to government spending of $22 million so as to promote its planned changes to industrial relations laws through an advertising campaign. The advertisements preceded the introduction of the relevant legislation to the Parliament by four whole months and could hardly be described as explaining the effect or operation of the scheme the government was devising. Instead, they asserted the political case made by the government for changes to Australian working conditions – one hotly contested by the union movement and the federal opposition.

The legal basis of the challenge was that the expenditure on the advertising campaign through a general appropriation from consolidated revenue was unauthorised because the promotion of a general policy of changing the industrial relations laws could not be linked to the stipulated outcome on which the Parliament had agreed to allow the monies to be appropriated by the executive. From amongst the three possible outcomes identified by the Appropriation Act covering the relevant period, the government sought to justify its $22 million campaign as meeting that of 'higher productivity, higher pay workplaces'. The outcomes found in appropriation Acts are, unsurprisingly, stated very broadly, but the Union's case was that executive expenditure on advertising legislative changes to the country's industrial conditions which were yet to even appear before the Parliament as a bill could hardly be said to have a sufficient relationship to those stated outcomes.

The Union lost the case with five of the seven Justices of the Court upholding the expenditure as authorised by the Act. The two dissenters were not satisfied that the expenditure could be connected to the outcomes identified in the Act, with one of them, Justice McHugh, declaring that he could find 'no rational connection' whatsoever.[26] The Chief Justice was among the majority of five, but he was careful to reason his way to a connection between the advertisements and

---

24   Ibid, 322 (Callinan J). For further analysis, see Andrew Stewart and George Williams, *Work Choices – What the High Court Said* (The Federation Press: Annandale, 2006).

25   (2005) 224 CLR 494.

26   Ibid, 532.

the purpose for which the appropriation had been allowed. His Honour proceeded on the basis that 'if Parliament formulates the purposes of appropriation in broad, general terms, then those terms must be applied with the breadth and generality they bear'.[27]

While his Honour might be said to have been rather too easily satisfied of the connection between the advertisements and the terms upon which public money had been released to the government, his approach still accords with sound constitutional principle. By contrast, the joint opinion of his fellow Judges in the majority interpreted the Appropriations Act in such as way as to make it unnecessary that the expenditure be conducive to achieving either of the outcomes identified by the Act – higher productivity or higher pay.[28] In effect, the majority view was that not every appropriation and expenditure of money by the executive must be for a purpose stated, even very generally, in the enabling legislation. The dissenting Justices pointed out that earlier recognition by members of the Court that s 81 of the Constitution requires appropriations from Consolidated Revenue to be for the 'purposes' of the Commonwealth – and thus cannot be 'in blank' or made with no reference to purpose, meant that the majority's generous construction of the statute risked its constitutional invalidity.[29] They also complained that the majority had determined the case in the Commonwealth's favour via a construction which not only had neither party adequately addressed but which was actually counter to the arguments advanced by the Commonwealth in its defence of the expenditure.[30] In short, *Combet* demonstrates co-operation from a majority of the Court above and beyond that sought by the government!

Combet is clearly an extreme example of the genre, but it is just one among many cases where the court defers to the political process to resolve issues which in other jurisdictions appear to receive more direct judicial involvement. But it is necessary to also provide some balance to the picture established so far – and consider those cases where the Court has severely frustrated the Commonwealth government. The fact that the decisions discussed in this regard are regarded as classics in the High Court's constitutional canon indicates how rare such occasions have generally been – and, as a result, how dramatic an upset they seem when they occur.

---

27   Ibid, 530.
28   Ibid, 566 (Gummow, Hayne, Callinan and Heydon JJ).
29   Ibid, 553–54 (McHugh J); 597 (Kirby J) cf. 568 (Gummow, Hayne, Callinan and Heydon JJ).
30   Ibid, 550 (McHugh J); 615–16 (Kirby J).

Cases of Conflict

In considering the notable decisions where the Court has been manifestly unco-operative to the Commonwealth Parliament, it is important to recognise the very extreme nature of the laws in question. In two cases, not very far apart in the mid-years of the 20th century, the High Court decided matters against the Commonwealth which were of huge interest and importance to the governments concerned and the broader community. The first of these is the *Bank of NSW v Commonwealth (Bank Nationalisation Case)*[31] of 1948, the loss of which by the Commonwealth, Peter Johnston reports, provoked 'rejoicing in the streets of Australia's capital cities'.[32] The case concerned the Chifley Labor government's attempt through the *Banking Act 1947* to end private banking in Australia by transferring the assets and business of private financial institutions to the government's own Commonwealth Bank.

The Act at the heart of the case was the latest in a string of moves made against the private banking sector by the Labor government in the 1940s. While increased regulatory requirements during the war period were endured, as just part of the many adjustments necessitated by the conflict, in 1945 the government had attempted to force States and their statutory authorities to move their custom to the Commonwealth Bank.[33] That law was successfully challenged in the High Court, which significantly recognised an implied limitation upon the Commonwealth's constitutional powers preventing it from enacting a law destructive of the independence and autonomy of the States.[34]

Having failed through one means, the Commonwealth government devised and enacted the *Banking Act* of 1947. The law attempted nationalisation of the country's private banks through the compulsory acquisition of their management, their assets and liabilities, plus a prohibition on the carrying on of a private banking business. The Commonwealth Attorney-General, HV Evatt, who had been a Justice of the High Court in the 1930s felt confident as to the

---

31   (1948) 76 CLR 1. The case was further appealed to the Judicial Committee of the Privy Council in the United Kingdom (*Commonwealth v Bank of NSW* [1950] AC 235) which endorsed the result in the High Court. The possibility of appeal to the Privy Council from the High Court on a matter of federal law was terminated in 1968 and utterly in 1975. Since 1986, the High Court of Australia is the final court of appeal for all litigation.

32   Peter Johnston, 'The *Bank Nationalisation* Cases: The Defeat of Labor's Most Controversial Economic Initiative' in HP Lee & George Winterton, *Australian Constitutional Landmarks* (CUP: Cambridge, 2003) 85.

33   *Banking Act 1945* (Cth).

34   *Melbourne Corporation v Commonwealth* (1947) 74 CLR 31.

law's constitutionality. But some have argued that he failed to take into account jurisprudential developments on the Court since his departure in 1940.[35]

Certainly the case is most famous for the clear emergence of a broadly-couched 'individual right' theory underpinning the express guarantee in s 92 of the Constitution that interstate trade and commerce is to be 'absolutely free'.[36] The provision of the Act that sealed the Commonwealth's defeat as a breach of s 92 was the prohibition in section 46 on private banks carrying on any business. This was found to be an impermissible interference with interstate trade and commerce – of both the banks themselves and also their trading customers.[37] The other ground upon which the Act fell down was the failure of the legislation to provide adequate compensation for the acquisition of the banks – their shares, management and assets. This amounted to a breach of one of the other few express guarantees in the Australian Constitution – that a compulsory acquisition of property should be on 'just terms'.[38]

The absence of suitable means of determining and providing compensation would have been easily remediable in a relaunched Act. Further, Sawer has argued that s 46, which was instrumental in causing the law to fall foul of s 92 was not even necessary to the achievement of the Act's objects.[39] Presumably a new Bill attempting nationalisation and managing to avoid the constitutional potholes identified by the court in the *Bank Nationalisation Case* might have been attempted by the Chifley government. However, rather than resort to yet another legislative attempt, the government took the matter on appeal to the Privy Council in London, still a possibility in those days, where it also met defeat. By then any possibility of revisiting the issue through new legislation had well and truly passed the Chifley government by and it was voted out of office the year after.[40]

Its successor was the conservative Liberal-Country Party coalition which had won power largely through its strident opposition to the supposed socialist agenda of the Chifley government. Additionally, the new government had

---

35   Michael Coper, *Freedom of Interstate Trade under the Australian Constitution* (Butterworths: Sydney, 1983) 93 and 100–01.

36   Ibid, 106; Peter Johnston, 'The *Bank Nationalisation* Cases: The Defeat of Labor's Most Controversial Economic Initiative' in HP Lee & George Winterton, *Australian Constitutional Landmarks* (CUP: Cambridge, 2003) 97.

37   (1948) 76 CLR 1, 258–59 (Rich and Williams JJ); 324–35 (Starke J); and 380–81 (Dixon J).

38   *Commonwealth Constitution*, s 51(xxxi).

39   Geoffrey Sawer, *Australian Federalism in the Courts* (MUP: Melbourne, 1967) 185.

40   See generally Peter Johnston, 'The *Bank Nationalisation* Cases: The Defeat of Labor's Most Controversial Economic Initiative' in HP Lee & George Winterton, *Australian Constitutional Landmarks* (CUP: Cambridge, 2003) 98–100.

campaigned on a promise of banning the Communist Party in Australia. There were certainly antecedents for this – the conservative Commonwealth administration of the 1930s had attempted to ban the Friends of the Soviet Union organisation and in the early years of the War the Communist party itself had been banned as a 'subversive association'.[41] A further attraction, beyond pure ideology, for the new Menzies government in moving against the Communist Party again in 1950 was undoubtedly the political damage and division it would inflict upon the Labor opposition.

The *Communist Party Dissolution Act* of 1950 was by any measure an extreme piece of legislation. Its rejection by the High Court, operating without regard to any express or implied freedoms, was described by Winterton as one of the 'greatest triumphs' of Australian constitutionalism.[42] The Act not only abolished the CPA and confiscated its property without compensation, it also empowered the Governor-General, acting on advice of the government, to declare other organisations to be affiliated with communism and, if satisfied that they were prejudicial to national security, abolish them also. It was an offence attracting 5 years jail for a person to be a member of either the CPA or other 'declared' organisations. Additionally, the Governor-General was able to declare that an individual held communist sympathies and was engaged or likely to be engaged in activities prejudicial to security. Restrictions then applied to such persons' ability to work for government, the union movement or in an industry related to defence. As the identification of a 'communist' hinged loosely on support for the objectives or teachings of Marx and Lenin, the Australian Labor Party, while attempting to run a responsible line on the danger of politically subversive activities recognised that it was itself potentially vulnerable to the operation of the Act.[43]

When the CPA challenged the Act in the High Court immediately after it was enacted, they employed the services of HV Evatt, now shadow Attorney-General. This time Evatt was on the winning side. While the entire court agreed that the Commonwealth had the power to defend itself from subversive activities, the law's validity depended on whether it actually met this description. But crucially the Court found that this was a determination for it to make rather than for the legislature or executive to assert. The reason a majority found the

---

41 See Roger Douglas, 'Keeping the Revolution at Bay: The Unlawful Associations Provisions of the Commonwealth Crimes Act' (2001) 22 *Adelaide Law Review* 259.

42 George Winterton, 'The Significance of the *Communist Party* Case' (1992) 18 *Melbourne University Law Review* 630, 630. This is the classic treatment of the case and forms the basis for much of the description offered in this chapter.

43 See Jenny Hocking, *Gough Whitlam – A Moment in History* (MUP: Melbourne, 2008) 144–145.

Act invalid was due to the way it purported to itself establish the crucial fact upon which its connection to constitutional power depended.[44] By asserting the dangers of the CPA and abolishing it and also allowing the executive to 'declare' other subversive associations *without also providing the means for judicial review of the facts behind any of these assessments*, the law attempted to provide its own connection to the power of defence. In so doing it usurped the power of the High Court to determine the validity of legislative and executive action under the Commonwealth Constitution. While the court acknowledged its earlier decisions that in times of 'hot war' the validity of executive determinations of which organisations and individuals constituted a threat to national security absent judicial review might be excused,[45] those circumstances did not presently pertain.[46] Exceptional cases of emergency aside, Parliament cannot validate legislation on its own assertion, or that of members of the executive, that relevant constitutional facts exist which unlock the necessary power.

The Menzies government, thwarted by the Court's decision and apparently unwilling to amend its Act by allowing judicial review – which the opposition had urged in parliamentary debate on the bill, decided to take the question to the people. A referendum was held in 1951 on the possibility of conferring the Commonwealth with sufficient power to ban the CPA, but despite public fears over 'reds under the beds' the government motion was lost.

Both the *Bank Nationalisation* and *Communist Party* cases enjoy an iconic status in Australian constitutional law. In the case of the latter this is certainly due to the lasting significance of its legal principle, but that is most definitely not so with respect to the former decision which might very well be decided differently today given radical changes to the understanding of the freedom of interstate trade and commerce.[47] What both decisions share is the magnitude of the blow delivered to the plans of the Commonwealth government in each. In the post-*Engineers* era, when the Commonwealth had become steadily accustomed to emerging from the court victorious, defeat over issues so central to the policy position of both governments was a notable assertion by the Court of its latent power – confirmed by the failure of the respective administrations to overcome the Court's decision through appeals to, respectively, the Privy Council or the people. But that inability to secure support for the measures elsewhere must be

---

44   *Australian Communist Party v Commonwealth* (1951) 83 CLR 1, 199 (Dixon J); 266 (Fullagar J).

45   *Lloyd v Wallach* (1915) 20 CLR 299; *Ex parte Walsh* [1942] ALR 359.

46   *Australian Communist Party v Commonwealth* (1951) 83 CLR 1, 266 (Fullagar J).

47   The dominant 'individual rights' theory of the guarantee in section 92 which underpinned this aspect of the Court's decision in the case was steadily undermined in the years following and did not survive the establishment of a new orthodoxy in *Cole v Whitfield* (1988) CLR 360.

seen as saying something in itself about the Court's willingness to defy rather than co-operate with the Commonwealth in each case. The legislation at the heart of both decisions was extreme. It has been said of the *Banking Act* that it offered an 'unnecessarily large target',[48] but this comment may be applied to the *Communist Party Dissolution Act* as well. Through these cases the Court made it clear that while it generally had a restrained view of its place in the polity, its compliance could not simply be assumed.

These high profile upsets aside, in the normal course of things the Commonwealth continued to benefit from the expansion of its legislative powers which the *Engineers* methodology fuelled. As its grasp of the purse strings strengthened, so too did its willingness to foray into areas once considered the preserve of the States. The absence of many significant constitutional constraints upon Commonwealth power ensured that inconvenience by judicial decisions, while not wholly avoided in areas such as national regulation of and engagement in acts of intra-state trade and commerce[49] or the ability of the federal judiciary to exercise jurisdiction over all aspects of custodial matters in family law matters,[50] was very much the exception to the norm.

The Mason era

It was this history which made the far less predictable decisions of the Court in the late 80s and early 90s under the Chief Justiceship of Sir Anthony Mason produce such a nervous time for the federal government. All of a sudden it seemed as though the rules of the game were changing.

The Attorney-General for much of the relevant period, Michael Lavarch, admitted in retrospect that 'the Mason Court's approach to interpreting the Constitution and developing the common law brought the relationship between the Court, the Parliament and the Executive into focus'.[51] He was keen to play down portrayal of that relationship as one marked by 'tension' by emphasising the complementary aspects of the different roles which each arm of government played in the period. The example Lavarch gave of this interplay between the institutions was in their respective roles in the recognition of the native title

---

48   Geoffrey Lindell quoted in Peter Johnston, 'The *Bank Nationalisation* Cases: The Defeat of Labor's Most Controversial Economic Initiative' in HP Lee & George Winterton, *Australian Constitutional Landmarks* (CUP: Cambridge, 2003) 90.

49   *Attorney-General (WA) v Australian national Airlines Commission* (1976) 138 CLR 492

50   *In Marriage of Cormick* (1984) 156 CLR 170.

51   Michael Lavarch, 'The Court, the Parliament and the Executive' in Cheryl Saunders (ed), *Courts of Final Jurisdiction* (Sydney: Federation Press, 1996) 15, 18.

interests of indigenous Australians to land. He described that sequence of events as comprising:

A. Parliament's acceptance of international human rights obligations leading to the passage of the *Racial Discrimination Act* 1975;
B. Over time that Act 'significantly influenced the Court's thinking on the issues of equality, discrimination and indigenous rights'[52] so as to lead to the 1992 decision of *Mabo v Queensland [No 2]*[53] recognising the survival of native title after European settlement;
C. *Mabo* in turn provided both the occasion and the doctrinal basis for the *Native Title Act* of 1993.

I do not demur from that account but would add that thinking of the Court's contribution in this way says much about the distinctly non-passive role which the High Court played at this time. The decision of *Mabo* was of seismic significance. Although Lavarch was able to position it positively amongst several political developments for indigenous people, it would be quite a false reading of those events to describe the judicial decision in *Mabo* as in any way an instance of simple 'co-operation'. That the Court's foray into the hitherto unrecognised property rights of Aboriginal Australians had serious potential to fuel conflict was made very clear five years later when the High Court decided the case of *The Wik Peoples v Queensland*[54] concerning the effect of these developments on pastoral lease holdings. The different political mindset of the conservative government which greeted that later decision saw the Court embroiled in probably the fiercest conflict it has ever experienced. It was at this time that the political class of Australia felt it perfectly acceptable not simply to criticise its decisions, but to publicly denigrate the Court and its members to an extraordinary degree.[55] No better indication of the ferocity of these attacks on the judiciary can be found than the need felt to publicly respond to them by Mason's successor, Chief Justice Brenan and by the Chief Justices of all States and Territories through a jointly issued Declaration of Judicial Independence.[56]

A consideration of just some of the other jurisprudential developments of the Mason era illustrates that its 'innovative' approach tended to present a challenge to government power rather than accede to it:

---

52   Ibid, 19.
53   (1992) 175 CLR 1.
54   (1996) 187 CLR 1.
55   See Patapan, above n 6, 144 and 166; Jason L Pierce, *Inside the Mason Court Revolution – The High Court of Australia Transformed* (2006) (Durham: Carolina Academic Press, 2006) 263–67.
56   Ibid, 265.

- In *Dietrich v The Queen*[57] the Court held that where an accused charged with a serious offence is unable to obtain legal representation through no fault of his or her own, the Court may order a stay if to continue would amount to an unfair trial. This case effectively overruled the earlier decision in *McInnis v The Queen*[58] that an accused had no right to be provided with legal counsel;
- In *Minister for Immigration and Ethnic Affairs v Teoh*[59] the Court found that individuals may hold 'legitimate expectations' that administrative decisions will comply with Australia's international obligations under ratified treaties, giving rise to procedural requirements on the part of the decision-maker; and
- In *Australian Capital Television v Commonwealth*[60] the government's attempts to regulate political advertising, and so reduce the necessity for raising campaign funds, was invalidated by the Court as in breach of a previously unrecognised constitutionally-implied freedom of political expression.

Why and why then?

That these and other decisions might be seen as part of the Mason Court's tendency to 'conflict' with the legislature and executive has been said to owe something to the lack of any significant public debate in Australia up to that point on the role of the judiciary. It is intriguing that the attention of political scientists to the judiciary just happened to be enlivened, with the publication of Brian Galligan's seminal *The Politics of the High Court*,[61] in the first year of Sir Anthony Mason's tenure as Chief Justice. The Court proceeded to conduct itself in such a way as to ensure sustained attention from outside the narrow interest of the legal profession[62] – and this may have more readily enhanced the perception of it as being in 'conflict' with the other arms of government.

Several convergent factors have been used to explain the phenomenon of the Mason High Court and why it happened when it did.[63] But to take just one of particular relevance to the question at the heart of this chapter, some members of the Court gave express indications that their role was affected by the recognition

---

57   (1992) 163 CLR 344.
58   (1979) 143 CLR 575.
59   (1995) 183 CLR 273.
60   (1992) 177 CLR 106.
61   Brian Galligan, *The Politics of the High Court* (St Lucia: UQP, 1987).
62   See also David Solomon, *The Political Impact of the High Court* (Sydney: Allen & Unwin, 1992).
63   Pierce, above n 55; Saunders, above n 51.

that, having finally severed legal ties with Britain through the *Australia Acts* of 1986, the sole legitimating force for the Commonwealth Constitution was the popular sovereignty of the Australian people.[64] This move away from a legalistic, toward a more overtly political, conception of Australia's constitutional underpinnings unsurprisingly altered the judiciary's positioning of itself relative to both government and the broader community.[65]

Former High Court Justice, Michael Kirby has observed that the various developments which contributed to the High Court's sense of itself as existing in a new national and judicial environment[66] had the effect of liberating constitutional interpretation from the straitjacket of traditional principles and techniques of statutory construction which had held sway since the time of *Engineers*. The domination of those principles had severely crabbed the Court's constitutional methodology. By contrast, in the Mason era the Court's traditional view that the operation of the Westminster doctrine responsible government was generally a cure-all for the political abuse of powers appeared to admit a new willingness from the courts to provide a legal intervention on occasion.

Writing at the end of the Mason era, Lavarch said it was up to the Court to more fully articulate its new role as against that of the directly elected representatives of the people.[67] That has not come to pass. Instead, after the brief tenure of Sir Gerard Brennan as Chief Justice, his replacement Murray Gleeson chose not to consolidate or continue the Court's redeveloped role. Rather, he very consciously employed the language of legalism to retreat those judicial advances. 'Conflict' gave way to the far more usual 'co-operation'. There are always exceptions however, such as when the raw appeal of high technique got the better of the Court in the case of *Re Wakim; Ex parte McNally*[68] leading it to strike down the cross-vesting of judicial power between Commonwealth, State and Territory courts – thus frustrating the legislatures and executives of all nine jurisdictions in one hit. But as Gelber points out elsewhere in this collection, the Court has always guarded the independence and purity of federal judicial power with great zeal – even if it is desultory about then applying it to hamstring the executive in its endeavours.

---

64   *Australian Capital Television v Commonwealth* (1992) 177 CLR 106, 138 (Mason CJ); *Theophanous v Herald & Weekly Times Ltd* (1994) 182 CLR 104, 171 (Deane J).

65   This point has been commented on in many of the political treatments of this era of the High Court referred to in this chapter.

66   Michael Kirby, 'Sir Anthony Mason Lecture 1996: AF Mason – From *Trigwell* to *Teoh*' (1996) 20 *Melbourne University Law Review* 1087.

67   Lavarch, above n 51, 19.

68   (1999) 198 CLR 511.

Conclusion

In conclusion, it appears that there is no simple answer to the question posed by the title of this chapter. The characterisation of the High Court of Australia as essentially co-operative to the political arms of government is probably sound, but as so often in the law, the true picture emerges only upon an examination of the exceptions. This chapter has focused substantially on those cases demonstrating conflict not simply because they are much more interesting than the many which evidence co-operation, but because they help convey where the balance must be said to truly lie.

The High Court has not been afraid of conflict with the executive or legislature – regardless of how it viewed itself or to what methodology it ascribed at any particular point in time. It will not hesitate to strike at government initiatives which are, by any standard, extreme, particularly when it perceives they contain a weakening of the judicial power conferred upon it under the Constitution. However, it must be recognised that such occasions tend to be rare and within the normal run of things the Commonwealth government benefits from a method of constitutional interpretation which accords it power with few robust restrictions.

While the intellectual repositioning of the Court in the Mason era rendered such an outcome rather less predictable, it remains to be seen whether the Court will again place itself more directly in the frame of political and social controversies. Certainly if a Human Rights Act is the eventual product of the current consultation process into that possibility, such a development would seem inevitable. We would need to wait and see whether that produces 'conflict' or simply the desired 'dialogue' between the courts and the political arms. That would, of course, open up a whole new context in which the nuances of terminology describing judicial relations with government would need to be very carefully unpacked.

Dieter Dörr

The Basic Law´s Concept of the Communication Freedoms and their Significance for a Modern "Multicultural" and Democratic Society

Introduction

On May 23rd 1949 at the stroke of midnight it became effective – the 'Grundgesetz' (Basic Law) for the Federal Republic of Germany. A written constitution. Konrad Adenauer induced the signing of the Grundgesetz in the parliamentary council with the words: "A new chapter in the changeful history of our people begins". And the Grundgesetz is sure enough a great success story. The constitution that was originally planned as a temporary solution for a separated country became a stable and permanent foundation of the democratic constitutional state. The deliberate scope of interpretation offers freedom for political actions and legal appraisements. The Bundesverfassungsgericht (Federal Constitutional Court, BVerfG) as an independent supreme federal body and keeper of the basic rights has shaped the constitutional interpretation and reality essentially. With my lecture I want to give you an understanding of the German media constitution. As you will see the extensive guidelines that are deduced from Article 5 cannot always be taken directly from the written law. But the judicature of the Bundesverfassungsgericht (Federal Constitutional Court) has developed extensive conclusions from the short text. In probably no other European state has the broadcasting freedom been developed so deliberately and intensely by case law as Germany.[1]

The purpose of Art. 5 GG as initial point

The media law of the Federal Republic of Germany primarily assures the communicating infrastructure, establishes equal opportunities for media producers respectively prevents shielding of the markets, secures the diversity of opinions and cultural diversity (pluralism), recipient protection as well as

---

1   *Hoffmann-Riem*, Stadien des Rundfunk-Richterrechts, in: Jarren (Ed.), Medienwandel – Gesellschaftswandel?, 1994, P. 17.

personal rights and the protection of minors as well as the protection of intellectual property.

The most important source of law for the enforcement of these goals is the Grundgesetz. Regarding this it contains especially in Art. 5 the most important vertices of our media constitution and in Art. 70 following GG the competence assignations in the media law. Competence assignation means that either the federal state or one of the states is authorized to set illustrative regulations. Generally you can keep in mind that the competences for the media law, in particular for the press and broadcasting, are held by the individual states, so the media law of the states, especially the freedom of the press and broadcasting law, is an important source of law for the media law.

But before I go into detail on the individual areas of media law, I want to point out the surprisingly short wording of Art. 5:

Article 5
[Freedom of expression, arts and sciences]
(1) Every person shall have the right freely to express and disseminate his opinions in speech, writing and pictures, and to inform himself without hindrance from generally accessible sources. Freedom of the press and freedom of reporting by means of broadcasts and films shall be guaranteed. There shall be no censorship.
(2) These rights shall find their limits in the provisions of general laws, in provisions for the protection of young persons, and in the right to personal honour.
(3) Arts and sciences, research and teaching shall be free. The freedom of teaching shall not release any person from allegiance to the constitution.

The Structure of Art. 5 GG

Art. 5 GG unites five different communication freedoms: freedom of speech, freedom of information, freedom of the press, broadcasting and film freedom.

Based on the wording of Art. 5 you can distinguish between individual and institutional media law.

A. The individual media law contains the rights of the ones involved in the making process as well as the rights of the recipients and users.
B. The institutional media law provides the standards for establishing different media products and purports the role of the state within media law.

One the one hand media law creates the space that is needed for a free development of media and so fulfils its constitutional obligation. In doing so the degree of control intensity varies depending on particularities concerning the medium in question and the particular media technology. On the other hand media law also includes all the regulations, which restrict media enterprises but are supposed to prevent freedom restricting effects of the media, such as a dominant influence over the expression of opinion or the breach of personal rights.[2]

The freedom of broadcasting

Preface

Now I want to give you an impression on how the jurisdiction of the Bundesverfassungsgericht understands and has shaped the broadcasting freedom. I begin with the wording of Art. 5 paragraph 1 sentence 2 GG. The phrasing implies that only the reporting through broadcasting is included in the protection. But the Bundesverfassungsgericht has from the very beginning seen the whole broadcasting freedom as protected, not only the coverage. In doing so it understands broadcasting freedom as a "serving freedom".[3] This form of understanding is based on the thought that the basic rights usually include freedoms, which shall secure individual fulfilment and therefore constitute acting rights, which serve subjectively legal interests. But in addition there are also guaranties of rights, which shall stay free from compulsion and interference by the state to secure third parties' interests. These basic rights are considered as serving freedoms.

As one of these the broadcasting freedom is primarily a serving freedom. It serves free, individual and public forming of opinion and is also a basic requirement for democracy. In all of the newer decisions the Bundesverfassungsgericht assumes that Art. 5 paragraph 1 sentence 2 GG not only implies the repelling of state influence. In fact the broadcasting freedom rather demands the generation of a system, which guarantees a diversity of opinions and ensures that broadcast is not at the mercy of the state or particular private groups much less one singular private group. So it would go against the dictate of constitutional law to on the one hand guarantee the freedom of broadcasting if broadcast on the other hand was left as fair game to the different forces.

So this jurisdiction obligates the legislator to create a system that ensures the normative intentions of Art. 5 I 2 GG. It shall guarantee the freedom of information for the citizens and therefore the balance and diversity of the whole

---

2   Cf. with different emphases *Beater*, JZ 2005, 822 ff., "Medienrecht als eigenständiges Rechtsgebiet".

3   Cf. BVerfGE 87, 181, 197; 83, 238, 295; 57, 295, 319.

broadcast programme. So the legal regulations have to be made in a way that the complete programme of all native broadcasting stations equates to the diversity of opinion, that broadcast is not at the mercy of particular private groups and that all forces in question are heard in the complete programme.

The most important broadcasting decisions of the Bundesverfassungsgericht

Broadcasting freedom is characterized by the decisions of the BVerfG like hardly any other basic right. The constitution assumes the meaning of broadcasting without giving a definition. Therefore the broadcasting freedom is not clearly specified, so the jurisdiction of the BVerfG has provided the substance of Art. 5.[4] It has – as the interpreter of the Grundgesetz – developed sophisticated and extensive requirements for the broadcasting system of the Federal Republic of Germany. How the broadcasting freedom is interpreted can be seen especially in ten important decisions.[5] Of these I want to give you a short impression.

The famous first "Television-Decision" from the 28.02.1961[6], also called the Magna Charta of the broadcasting law, was about the outlines of administrative and legislative competences on the subject of broadcasting between the federal government and the individual states. The court clearly confirmed that the states are responsible for the broadcasting sector. It also purported the freedom from state interference for broadcasting, which it derived from broadcasting freedom. Because of this demand, it is forbidden for the state to conduct broadcasting, even in a private way. So the broadcasting stations under public law have to remain distant from the state as well.

The second broadcasting decision[7] entered into the question whether broadcasting was liable to sales tax. Here the broadcasting stations under public law were categorised as distant from the state and as institutions of the public law that are protected by the fundamental rights.

In the decision about the licence for the FRAG (Freie Rundfunk-AG – Free Broadcasting-Corporation)[8] the BVerfG had to decide about the legitimacy of

---

4   *Ipsen*, Rundfunk im Europäischen Gemeinschaftsrecht, 1983, P. 24.
5   BVerfG, decision from 28.2.1961, BVerfGE 12, 205 ff.; decision from 27.7.1971, BVerfGE 31, 314 ff.; decision from 16.6.1981, BVerfGE 57, 295 ff.; decision from 4.11.1986, BVerfGE 73, 118 ff.; enactment from 24.3.1987, BVerfGE 74, 297 ff.; decision from 5.2.1991, BVerfGE 83, 238 ff.; enactment from 6.10.1992, BVerfGE 87, 181 ff.; decision from 22.2.1994, BVerfGE 90, 60 ff.; decision from 11.09.2007, BVerfGE 119, 181; decision from 12.03.2008, NVwZ 2008, 658 ff.
6   BVerfGE 12, 205 ff.
7   BVerfGE 31, 314 ff.
8   BVerfGE 57, 295 ff.

private broadcast. It considered private forms of broadcasting to be allowed but demanded some form of legal authorisation, which had to fulfil certain requirements. So through this decision the base for the so called "Dual-Broadcasting-System", where private broadcasting stations and those under public law are able to coexist, was built. But therefore certain conditions have to be kept such as strict legal guidelines for private broadcasting, that are similar to those required of broadcasting under public law, mostly to secure pluralism.

Resulting from this decision the individual states enacted their first state media laws. In the so called "Niedersachsen-Decision"[9] the BVerfG had to decide whether the requirements addressed to the private broadcasting stations in the Niedersachsen state media law were sufficed, especially concerning the protection of pluralism. The court reduced the strict guidelines for private broadcasting companies, which it had developed in the previous decision. In regard to the financing through advertisement deficits in program diversity have to be accepted or else private broadcasting could not exist. In return public broadcasters has to ensure comprehensive information for the population to the full extend, also called the 'basic supply' (Grundversorgung) of broadcasting. Only then are lower standards for private broadcasting acceptable. So private broadcasting is dependent on public broadcasting. This was an advancement compared to the third broadcasting decision. As a reaction the states passed the "Inter State Treaty for the rearrangement of the broadcasting system" – (Rundfunkstaatsvertrag), which came into effect on the first of December 1987.

The fifth broadcasting decision[10] was about the state media law of Baden-Württemberg. The BVerfG clarified that the so called basic supply (Grundversorgung) was not to be fractional but overall and included extensive information for all people and a fundamental supply of all different types of broadcasting, which had to be offered in a way that everybody could technically accesses them. Furthermore procedural assurances have to guarantee a balanced and diverse service, which also reflects the different flows in society.

In the so called "WDR-Decision" from 1991[11] the BVerfG had to decide about the constitutionality of the WDR law, in particular the definition of the basic supply. The court understands the basic supply to be dynamic and therefore sees a necessity for an existence and development guarantee in favour of public broadcasting.

---

9   BVerfGE 73, 118 ff.
10   BVerfGE 74, 297 ff.
11   BVerfGE 83, 238 ff.

In the seventh broadcasting decision[12] the BVerfG granted the public broadcasting companies an adequate financing derived from the broadcasting freedom, which was already hinted in the previous decision. The court confirmed emphatically that public broadcasting was not only presently but above all prospectively essential to fulfil constitutional standards and moreover ensure pluralism in the dual broadcasting system. Therefore, according to its true judgement, public broadcasting has to be able to compete with private providers. So from that results the title of guaranteed financing, which obligates the state to finance broadcasting under state law in an adequate way. That way public broadcasting can meet its upcoming challenges in the dual system. But how this title should be realised in the process of fixing the licence fee was not clarified.

This subject was broached in the first licence fee decision of 1994[13]. The court revoked previous way of fixing the licence fee because of a breech of the policy of freedom from state interference. Based on this fact it set a three-step proceeding, which in its opinion balances the interests of the taxpayers and the broadcasting stations and ensures the public broadcasting stations' financing, that is necessary for the fulfilment of their obligations. The first step is the application of the requirements. The demands then have to be checked by an expert committee, which consists of members free from broadcasting as well as politics. The committee's suggestion is binding for the states, which have to fix the licence fee on the third step in an interstate treaty or in a different way. Variations are only accepted if they can validate themselves in front of the broadcasting freedom. This decision shows the detailed guidelines the BVerfG derives from the broadcasting freedom. It dictates a strict proceeding, in which the states have only little room for own decisions.

As a result of this decision the three-step system was constituted in the third Broadcasting Modification Interstate Treaty. The public broadcasters now have to declare their demands based on their assignments, which first will be checked by a committee of authorized experts – (Kommission zur Überprüfung und Ermittlung des Finanzbedarfs der Rundfunkanstalten (KEF), the Committee for the Survey and Calculation of Broadcasting stations' Financial Requirements (CCS)). Based on these requirements the committee makes a concrete recommendation every four years, which is used as a foundation for the fixing of the licence fee in an Interstate Treaty, which has to pass in the state parliaments.

The second licence fee decision[14] dealt with the question whether and under which circumstances the states were allowed to modify the suggestions of the

---

12   BVerfGE 87, 181 ff.
13   BVerfGE 90, 60 ff.
14   BVerfGE 119, 181 ff.

Committee. The states had not completely realised the guidelines of the CCS during the previous process of fixing the licence fee. The court took this as an opportunity to deal with the definition of the dual broadcasting system against the background of digitalization and convergence in principal. In unison the judges emphasised that despite of the now ceased exceptional situation, which had been created by a shortage of frequencies, a legitimate arrangement was still needed. Especially because of its broad effect, topicality and suggestive influence broadcasting had such an important relevance, that legal regulations were needed. On private broadcasting stations an increasing amount of trivialization and scandalisation could be detected and a future concentration in this area had to be expected. For the protection of pluralism as well as for the quality of the programmes public broadcasting is still very important also in times of digitalization. But therefore public broadcasting really has to fulfil its obligation. The court confirmed that the broadcasting fee had to be free from political influence and emphasized financing according to the needs of public broadcasters. For this reason it is forbidden for the legislator to use broadcasting financing as an instrument of political power and influence. Therefore divergences have to be based on adequate facts, that have to be explained thoroughly, and the whole process has to be public. Because the states had not considered this, the deviation from the suggestions of the CCS was considered unconstitutional. Furthermore the court commented on whether or not other financing besides the licence fee are allowed for public broadcasting. Accordingly other financing sources (sponsoring and advertisement) were not excluded but were not allowed to take over priority. In addition the benefits of sponsoring and advertisement always had to outbalance the visible drawbacks for the programme.

In the tenth broadcasting decision[15] the BVerfG had to decide whether an absolute prohibition for political parties to take a holding on private broadcasting stations was in accordance with the constitution. Again the court explained that broadcasting freedom needed legal regulations. The court also confirmed that Art. 5 I 2 GG calls for the repelling of state influence. This principal also fully applies to the political parties, which may not directly belong to the state but are close to the state nevertheless. On the other hand the court states that the political parties are entitled to broadcasting freedom because through broadcasting they can be part of the public decision-making process. To exclude them completely from all involvement in private broadcasting stations would be inappropriate. But the legislator is free to deny the party access to private broadcasting stations if they thereby exert substantial influence on programming.

---

15 VerfG NVwZ 2008, 658 ff.

The Freedom of Speech

Besides the broadcasting freedom Art. 5 Paragraph 1 GG contains the individual freedom of speech as a subjective right, which also belongs to the communication freedoms.[16] As a political basic right, it ensures the mental debate between the people. Regulations, which try to influence or hinder the expression or spreading of opinions, are considered an intervention into the freedom of speech. As well, the expression of one's opinion may not depend on any requirements.[17] The expression of opinion also does not have to be rational or justified to subsist; it can be emotional, unfounded or even useless.

The meaning of this basic right was clarified and emphasised by the BVerfG. In the famous Lüth-Decision from 1958 for example it stated that "the freedom of speech as a direct expression of one's personality generally was one of the grandest human rights. It is plainly constitutive for a liberal democratic state system."[18] In this decision the BVerfG also had to decide whether the basic rights applied to citizens among each other as well or if they simply were defensive rights against the state. The BVerfG denied direct effects between the citizens but allowed indirect third-party effect. Due to my limited amount of time I cannot explain what this means in detail. But in any case like all state authority, civil jurisdiction is bound to the basic rights. In disputes between civilians the basic rights especially have to be minded when interpreting vague legal terms. If the civil decision does not factor the constitutional requirements, the BVerfG can check whether it has violated the appellant's basic rights. The Lüth-decision was about Erich Lüth, who had called for (a) boycott of a, in terms of content uninteresting, film made by Veit Harlan. In the Third Reich Veit Harlan was responsible for the Nazi propaganda film Jud Süß. So Lüth asked all Germans not to visit Harlan's film. Lüth lost the civil suit because a call for boycott is always considered an immoral injury in the sense of § 826 BGB. So the BVerfG had to decide, if the civil court had factored the freedom of speech in an adequate way, also in regard to other conflicting constitutionally protected interests, when interpreting the concept of immoral injury. The judges emphasised that the freedom of speech is the foundation of any other freedom and has to be granted high protection. Especially when the freedom of speech is used as a contribution to a problem concerning essential public interests, it takes priority over Harlan's personal rights or those of the film distributers. This has been affirmed in Lüth's case. Therefore the BVerfG reversed the civil court's

---

16   *Dörr/Schwartmann*, Medienrecht, marginal number 55.

17   *Fechner*, Medienrecht, 3. Kapitel, marginal number 48.

18   BVerfGE 7, 198, 208.

verdict because of a violation of Art. 5 paragraph 1 GG. Ever since then the consideration rule "in case of doubt, pro freedom of speech" applies. But this rule only applies when intellectual instruments and no economic pressure are used.[19]

The limitations for the publication of photos

The consideration between the freedom of speech respectively freedom of the press and personal rights is a current and very important problem as well when applying to the publishing of celebrity's pictures – also across the German border.

Particularly pictures of paparazzis lead time and again to disputes, not only in German courts. Especially Princess Caroline von Hannover has defended herself against publications of images of her and her family in a variety of cases. The freedom of the press and the individual rights of the person concerned have to be balanced in court when concerning the publishing of celebrity's pictures. The general right to be left alone or right of personality give every person the right to decide if and to which extent he or she wants to allow public access to his or her life. You can decide how you want to be pictured in public; particularly nobody shall be forced to appear in public against their will. The general right of personality is an instrument according to civil law that constitutes a right of defence. According to the jurisdiction of the BVerfG this is also a constitutional right that is deduced from two articles of the GG namely the general freedom of action of Art. 2 I connected with the human dignity of Art. 1 I GG. So it has a constitutional status alike the freedom of speech and the freedom of the press.

Until the year 2004 the BVerfG accepted the jurisdiction of the highest civil court in Germany (BGH). The BGH separated between private persons and relative as well as absolute persons of contemporary history when judging the legitimacy of publishing photos. According to this separation pictures of absolute persons of contemporary history were allowed to be published nearly at all times without the consent of the person concerned. This even applied when the pictures were about everyday life. Exceptions were only made for special areas.

Caroline von Hannover, who was always classified as an absolute person of contemporary history, defended herself against this jurisdiction. She sued at the European Court of Human Rights, who pronounced a startling judgement in 2004. The ECHR claimed that the German jurisdiction violated the Right to

---

19   BVerfGE 25, 256, 266.

Respect of Private and Family Life of Art. 8 ECHR (European Convention on Human Rights).[20] Especially the separation between relative and absolute persons of contemporary history was criticized. Publication of photos could only be allowed if it contributed to a discussion of general concerns.[21]

To which extent the German jurisdiction is bound by the decisions of the ECHR[22] is highly controversial in jurisdiction as well as in literature and cannot be explained in this presentation. Along with this problem comes the question of how much influence the European Convention of Human Rights and the jurisdiction of the ECHR have on the basic rights in the constitution. In any case the ECHR and the jurisdiction have to be minded when interpreting the basic rights.

Newer decisions of the BGH and the BVerfG show that the opinions of the ECHR concerning the general personal rights slowly but continuously take effect on the German jurisdiction.[23]

Now the major consideration is the public interest of the photos. The more it contributes to the shaping of public opinion, the more important the freedom of the press gets. Under reference to the ECHR the BGH decided in a fundamental judgement that it is decisive if the picture is of private nature or not. In contrast the BVerfG also considers the text belonging to the photo. Thus the freedom of the press can have priority if the report with the corresponding pictures concerning the prominent person is important for socially critical considerations of the readers.[24] The BVerfG affirmed this for one report with a photo, which had been the subject of the fundamental judgement of the BGH. However the freedom of the press does not have priority when the illustrated report about the prominent person is not of public interest. Until today the discussion about the publishing of photos is not yet completed and, after the last decision of the BVerfG, may again employ the ECHR.

Conclusion

I hope my presentation could give you an impression of how important the communication freedoms of Art. 5 GG are. Primarily this is also due to the judicature of the BVerfG, which has ensured that the past 60 years of the Grundgesetz have been a success story. The BVerfG has significantly influenced

---

20   EGMR NJW 2004, 2647, 2651.
21   EGMR NJW 2004, 2647, 2651.
22   *Dörr* JuS 2008, 1107.
23   Cf. *Stender-Vorwachs* NJW 2009, 334 ff.
24   BVerfG NJW 2008, 1793.

through its jurisdiction the media law. Given the short wording of Art. 5 GG it is surprising but also a little problematic to see the complex guidelines, which the BVerfG has derived from this clause. At least the limits of an acceptable constitutional interpretation are reached or even crossed – freely adapted from later Chief Justice of the US Supreme Court Charles Evans Hughes' legendary sentence: "We are under a constitution, but a constitution is what the judges say it is." But resulting: The contribution of the Karlsruher Justices to the preservation and advancement of a democratic, pluralistic and cultural vivid broadcasting cannot be valued enough.[25]

Thank you for your attention.

---

25   *Dörr*, Unabhängig und gemeinnützig, Ein Modell von gestern? in: ARD (Ed.), 50 Jahre ARD, 2000, S. 12 ff., S. 15 f.

Craig Collins

The Concept of the Communication Freedoms and their Significance for a Modern 'Multicultural' and 'Democratic' Society in Australia

As part of a conference marking the 60th anniversary of the German Constitution, and for the purpose of enabling comparisons to be made and contrasts to be drawn with the German Basic Law's concept of the 'Communication Freedoms', this paper seeks to sketch the concept of 'Communication Freedoms' as perceived 'through the eyes of Australia'.

Introduction

In talking about 'the concept of the communication freedoms', Professor Dörr has a distinct advantage. Article 5 of the German Basic Law says just what that concept is. As we have just heard, this concept contains five different communication freedoms: freedom of speech, freedom of information, freedom of the press, broadcasting freedom and film freedom. By a process of deductive reasoning, the Federal Constitutional Court 'has developed extensive conclusions from the short text' of Article 5. While Professor Dorr paid particular attention to the broadcasting freedom and freedom of speech, it seems clear that there are many further layers of analysis, and questions about how the 'concept of the communications freedoms' might weigh in the balance with competing rights, or be applied in practice, and so on.

From the Australian perspective, free speech pervades our law, our culture and our traditions. I am here using 'free speech' in the widest possible sense. Yet, it is no simple task for me to identify an original, all-encompassing concept of free speech in Australian law. While Professor Dörr had a simple starting point in Article 5, I have quite a bit of explaining to do.

The quest to find a concept of communication freedoms in Australian law is something like searching for a black cat ... inside a dark room ... at night ... while wearing a blindfold. The cat is virtually invisible. Yet, one can always sense its presence. And, occasionally, one is reminded of the cat by stepping on its tail.

Into the Void

Having scanned the Australian constitutions, our statutory laws and our common law rights of action for this elusive concept, I am left to conclude that it must reside somewhere *other* than in each of those things. In other words, if there is an original, all-encompassing concept of free speech in Australian law, then it must inhabit the void left unregulated by the things that pass for Australian law.

Lifting one's gaze beyond the common law rights of action to a more general notion of the common law as customary rights and liberties – incorporating the idea of an unwritten English constitution – gives confirmation to this perception. With due allowance for a medieval mentality and shaky translations, article 29 of the Magna Carta seems to capture this thought, albeit as a then already long-established custom, in the following words:

> No freeman shall be arrested or imprisoned or disseised or outlawed or exiled or in any other way harmed. Nor will we [the king] proceed against him, or send others to do so, except according to the lawful sentence of his peers and according to the Common Law.[1]

This is the English Magna Carta of the year 1215, not to be confused with 'the Magna Carta of the broadcasting law' of 1961, as mentioned by Professor Dörr.[2] Of course, it may be the case that the cultural traditions of those illustrious Germanic tribes, the Angles and the Saxons, had some sort of cultural influence upon both versions.

While Professor Dörr can point to a precise moment in time for the enactment of the Article 5 communication freedoms – the stroke of midnight on 23 May 1949 – I am left to rely upon a lawyer's option of last resort: something traceable to 'time immemorial'. Nevertheless, the central idea in the common law tradition is that law – of the enforceable kind – marks the boundaries of, but does not itself generate, freedom.

Further confirmation, that our elusive concept is to be defined by what it is not, comes from the High Court of Australia in the 1997 landmark case, *Lange v Australian Broadcasting Corporation*:

> Under a legal system based on the common law, 'everyone is free to do anything, subject only to the provisions of the law', so that one proceeds 'upon an assumption of freedom of speech' and turns to the law 'to discover the established exceptions to it'.[3]

So, as a starting point, this seems to be the best we can do. By contrast with the German Basic Law, in Australia we start with an ill-defined assumption, not a

---

1   The 1215 Magna Carta http://www.magnacartaplus.org/magnacarta/ at 22 May 2009.

2   'otherwise known as the 'famous first "Television Decision"'.

3   *Lange v Australian Broadcasting Corporation* (1997) CLR 520, 564 quoting *Attorney-General v Guardian Newspapers [No 2]* [1990] 1 AC 109, 283.

concept – the anniversary of which is lost in the mists of time, somewhere on the far side of the world.

Before turning back to the law more specifically, the topic invites a wider exploration of freedom of speech, democracy and multiculturalism. It is significant that, while the German Basic Law is the product of the mid-twentieth century, Australian habits of mind and language about each these things were largely forged in the nineteenth century.

Nineteenth Century Influences

If law marks the boundaries of freedom, then one might expect there to be very little space left for the convicts who sailed with the First Fleet, in 1788, on its mission to colonise New South Wales. And it is true to say that Governor Phillip carried on board a written commission vesting in him the full power of the British state. Read literally, the words certainly suggested the prospect of a military tyranny. But also on board was an invisible cargo – the laws of England, including the 'unwritten common law' derived by judges from English custom and tradition. As Alan Atkinson notes, '[t]he common law's most basic value was liberty' and, '[t]alking and the freedom of speech were the essence of the English idea of liberty'.[4] Referring to this as an oral culture, Atkinson further says that:

> The convicts and the class from which they came in Britain took their ideas about society and government from a culture shaped by the living voice, and in England and its colonies the living voice was privileged far beyond any other country in the world. The idea of freedom of speech had very deep roots in English life.[5]

This tension – between an all-powerful authority and the heart-felt liberty of free settlers and emancipated convicts – is the story of early Australia. Remarkably, these tensions were largely contained. Despite the Governors' all-powerful authority – said to stretch across half the continent, and from the top to the bottom, no less – the practical limits of time, attention and resources told another story. In our country, space and distance worked in favour of freedom.[6] On top of this, the British authorities were more sensitive to public opinion here, mindful, as they were, of the loss of their American colonies. In essence, the colonisation of Australia was an experiment. And how best to accommodate the

---

4   Alan Atkinson, *The Europeans in Australia: A history,* vol. 1 (1998) 4.
5   Ibid x.
6   Alan Atkinson, 'Conquest' in Deryck Schreuder and Stuart Ward (eds), *Australia's Empire* (2008) 36–9.

tensions between authority and freedom was something which was 'made up' along the way, rather than set in place by any preconceived, Grand Design.[7]

Now, while today marks a special anniversary for the German Basic Law, we are also just 12 days away from the 185th anniversary of the birth of the free press in the Australian colonies. This time, I can match Professor Dörr's capacity for horoscopic precision. The birth of the free press occurred in Hobart Town on Friday, the 4th of June 1824, at about 20 minutes before two o'clock in the afternoon.[8] It was at this moment that the printer of the *Hobart Town Gazette*, Andrew Bent, effectively sacked his Government-appointed editor and censor, asserting full ownership and independence of the only printing press in the colony.[9] My interest in promoting this little known event has nothing whatsoever to do with the fact that Andrew Bent is my great, great, great, great grandfather. But it was an extraordinary thing – a free press established in the middle of a penal colony conceived by some as little more than 'One Big Gaol'.[10]

Six months later, two lawyers, William Charles Wentworth and Robert Wardell, commenced *The Australian* newspaper in Sydney as an independent concern.[11] In both cases, the freedom of the press was assumed – and asserted – without prior permission from the authorities. Bent, Wentworth and Wardell all gave effect to the idea that 'everyone is free to do anything' – unless and until a valid law might be enforced to stop them. The authorities acquiesced, with Governor Brisbane justifying these events to London as 'the experiment of the full latitude of the freedom of the press'.[12] The common law idea of free speech developed, and found room to express itself, not only in a pre-democratic age, but also in a penal setting.

Democracy, too, was achieved in the Australian colonies in the 1850s to a degree that was only matched in Britain some 60 years later, in 1918.[13] The campaign for responsible and representative government in New South Wales was framed around the British idea of liberty – and the strength of this idea, as Peter Cochrane describes it, was its lack of any precise definition:

---

7   See generally, Alan Atkinson, 'The First Plans for Governing New South Wales, 1786–87' (1990) 94 *Australian Historical Studies* 22.

8   Craig Collins, 'Andrew Bent and the Birth of the Free Press in the Australian Colonies' (Paper to Australian Media Traditions conference, Canberra, 24 November 2005).

9   Ibid.

10   Alan Atkinson, 'Writing About Convicts: Our Escape From The One Big Gaol' (1999) 6(2) *Tasmanian Historical Studies*, 17–28.

11   Collins, above n 8.

12   Robin Walker, *The Newspaper Press in New South Wales, 1803–1920* (1976) 6.

13   John Hirst, 'Empire, State, Nation' in Deryck Schreuder and Stuart Ward (eds), *Australia's Empire* (2008) 144

Liberty ... was more than an abstract ideal. It was an active principle in the empire ... Liberty was a powerful, chameleon thing, ravaged by contestation, misuse and overuse, destined to drive change through the British colonies of settlement. It was a marvellous mix of delusion and promise.[14]

This idea of liberty was asserted from below, rather than dispensed from above. Here is Robert Lowe, a political candidate, addressing a Sydney public meeting of more than 2000 people in 1848:

That [British] Constitution was not founded by closet politicians, scheming experimentalists, speculative empirics, or crack-brained philosophers, nor was it forced upon unwilling millions by the hand of the arbitrary power. It has ripened with time – is coextensive with the wants of the people – has been, from time to time, adapted to circumstances as they arose – and is not founded in abstract theory – but has sprung from the practical experience and wisdom of ages. It has grown with our growth, strengthened with our strength – and has expanded with the expanding wants of society...[15]

The idea of British liberty was sufficiently vague to see diverse groups and interests combining together in the face any specific threat, marshalling the force of public opinion, and winning compromise from the authorities.[16] In this way, we became acculturated to the idea of a workable freedom under authority.

Speaking of diversity, the range of languages, accents and voices which featured in the Australian landscape in the nineteenth century might be wider than you might think. There was, of course, a pre-existing, rich and diverse range of indigenous cultures. And Britain's own multi-racial origins have been described as a 'dog's breakfast' which, when projected over a global empire, comprised a menagerie of distinct living cultures and diverse peoples, who intermingled. Sydney, as well, was a seaport, with busy human traffic passing to and from such places as China, India, the Americas, Asia, the Pacific Islands and the Cape of Good Hope, and beyond. Writing in 1828, Peter Cunningham observed in Sydney the many:

... gentleman foreigners, tempted by the fineness of our country and climate to take up permanent abode among us. Frenchmen, Spaniards, Germans ... Americans ... all add to the variety of language current among us.[17]

---

14   Peter Cochrane, *Colonial Ambition: Foundations of Australian democracy* (2006) 11. Further, '[Liberty] was not a privilege; it was a right ... an entitlement that British citizens held dear, perhaps the more dear the further they were from home. And with entitlement came indignation when rights were withheld'.

15   Ibid 165.

16   Ibid, see especially the account of the public response to Earl Grey's draft constitution at 162–6.

17   David Malouf, *A Spirit of Play; the Making of Australian Consciousness* (2000) 87.

Noteworthy for this conference is that, over the entire colonial period and up until the first world war, German people formed the largest non-British group of immigrants to Australia.[18] And, when the colony of Queensland was formed out of New South Wales in 1859, one in ten Queenslanders was German speaking.[19]

The final point of context I wish to make concerns the combined voices which, together, formed the Australian form of the English language. Language, of course, is not only the vehicle by which free speech is expressed, 'but [also] for most of us it is also a machine for thinking, [and] for feeling'.[20] Significantly, '[w]hile other languages move by logic, English [moves by association]'.[21] We see this in common law reasoning by analogy and precedent, rather than by strict logic. David Malouf observes that:

> Shakespeare made metaphor the form through which English illuminates the world and its connexions, uncovers meaning, makes those imaginative sideways leaps that constitute our peculiar way of thinking ... but also of 'touching' the objects that comprise our world by making them immediate and real.[22]

Before our time, the Americans inherited a form of English that was '[p]assionately evangelical and utopian, deeply imbued with the religious fanaticism and radical violence' of the seventeenth century and the later Jacobean rhetoric of liberty and dissent, and 'emotional appeals to great abstractions'.[23] By contrast, the Australian colonies inherited the more moderate language of the late English and Scottish Enlightenment. This tendency towards understatement, pragmatism and restraint was laced with the colour of a strong sense of humour, especially irony, and a larrikin sense of play – said to derive from our cockney and convict origins.[24] To similar effect, '[t]he business of politics became negotiation, and of conflict compromise'.[25]

The Australian Constitution was written – within this already established context of common law, free speech and freedom of the press; of colonial democracies and multiculturalism; of language and habits of mind; of negotiation and compromise – as Stephen Gageler says, 'with a British heart and

---

18   Ibid 89.
19   Ibid.
20   David Malouf, 'Made in England: Australia's British Inheritance' 12 *Quarterly Essay* (2003) 44.
21   Ibid.
22   Ibid.
23   Ibid 46–8.
24   Ibid 46–9. '[Our form of language] created that peculiar mildness of social interaction here that has for more than two centuries now kept all kinds of extremism beyond the possibilities of acceptable public discourse'.
25   Ibid 48.

an American federal body'[26]. The 'prevailing sentiment' of the time was that 'the citizen's rights were best left to the protection of the common law in association with the doctrine of parliamentary supremacy'.[27] The Australian nation was born into this milieu, in 1901.

Free Speech and the Right to Reputation

I would now like to turn back to the law in more detail. Recall our starting point. The common law proceeds 'upon an assumption of freedom of speech' and turns to the law 'to discover the established exceptions to it'.[28] What boundaries mark the open space within which society freely expresses itself?

The extent to which laws may impinge upon the assumption of free speech is not sharply defined in advance. This is because the common law adopts bottom-up – or inductive – reasoning. A court will only venture so far towards limiting 'the assumption of freedom' as is necessary to resolve the particular dispute before it, consistently with precedent.[29]

Courts incrementally creep towards and probe the boundaries of free speech rather than apply pre-conceived, theoretical lines, as might occur with a process of top-down – or deductive – reasoning. In this way, common law method maximises the assumption of freedom.

So what are the 'established exceptions' to the assumption of free speech? At common law, these include laws against 'defamation, incitement to a crime or to violence ... obscenity, blasphemy, ... [in]decency and ... contempt of court'.[30] Statutory intervention has also proliferated over the decades, with parliaments generating constraints upon free speech in fields such as: broadcasting and telecommunications; anti-discrimination; anti-terrorism; privacy; intellectual property, and so on.

---

26   Stephen Gageler, 'Foundations of Australian Federalism and the Role of Judicial Review' (1987) 17 *Federal Law Review* 162, 172.

27   *Australian Capital Television Pty Ltd v Commonwealth* [1992] 177 CLR 106, 136.

28   *Lange v Australian Broadcasting Corporation* (1997) CLR 520, 564 quoting *Attorney-General v Guardian Newspapers [No 2]* [1990] 1 AC 109, 283.

29   For a discussion of top-down and bottom-up reasoning in this context, see Adrienne Stone, 'Freedom of Political Communication, the Constitution and the Common Law' (1998) 26 *Federal Law Review* 219, 238 'A hallmark of common law reasoning is that law is made through the adjudication of individual disputes. The proposition for which a case is taken to stand is determined by a later court which then applies, distinguishes, develops or (if the later court is a superior court) overrules it'.

30   Peter Bailey, *The Human Rights Enterprise in Australia and Internationally* (2009) 653.

For now, I would like to focus upon the largest and most litigated of the common law-based 'established exceptions' – defamation law. This law offers a right of action, with a remedy in damages, for harm to reputation.

Writing in 1832, Thomas Starkie, referred to the 'comparative imperfection' of the laws relating to injuries which are 'intellectual, where the wrong is completed by the mere communication of certain ideas', compared with injuries more forcible in nature.[31] One of the reasons for this, he said, was the 'intrinsic difficulty of the subject', which 'is more subtle and refined, and does not admit of the broad and plain limits and distinctions which may be established in respect of forcible injuries'.[32] He continued:

> To determine, therefore, with precision, the limits of verbal and written communication, is a problem easy of enunciation, but exceedingly complicated in its solution: it involves the consideration of the habits, manners, and even fancies and prejudices of the people for whose government it is intended, and may require alterations corresponding with the changes effected in the state of society.[33]

One of the great, historic battles for free speech in our tradition has concerned the question of who gets to decide the meaning and defamatory effect of a communication. In England, this was won in 1792 for the jury which, in the common imagination, links back to the Magna Carta rights. Historically, the jury was 'considered to be the touchstone of the community and the constitutional safeguard against injustice'.[34] Indeed, as Atkinson says, '[t]rial by jury was highly prized as a classic method of giving power to common voices'.[35] Civil juries were adopted in the Australian colonies at an early stage. As it happens, Andrew Bent was the defendant in the first civil case tried by a civil jury in the Supreme Court of Van Diemens Land, in 1830.[36]

For this reason, the common law treats the meaning and defamatory effect of a communication as a question of fact, not law. In the English language, at least, deciding meaning and effect is not amenable to any rigorous, intricate or precise analysis. Rather, the fact of defamatory meaning is judged by the standard of an ordinary reasonable person, of average intelligence, forming a general

---

31   Thomas Starkie, *The Law of Slander* (1832, 1997 ed) xxv.

32   Ibid xxv and xxvi.

33   Ibid xxxiii

34   *Fox's Libel Act 1792*; See generally, Patrick George, *Defamation Law in Australia* (2006) 226.

35   Atkinson, above n 4, x.

36   *Butler v Bent* (Supreme Court of Van Diemens Land, Pedder CJ, 10 May 1830). See generally, David Neal, 'The Campaign for Trial by Jury' in *The Rule of Law in a Penal Colony: Law and power in early New South Wales* (2002) 167–88.

impression of the material.[37] Further, '[t]he jury are taken to share a moral or social standard by which to judge the defamatory character of the meaning, being a standard common to society in general, and which necessarily changes over time'.[38]

While defamation law might be seen as an 'established exception' to the assumption of free speech, it is, within itself, a two-sided thing. Defences may be raised which, over time, have crystallised into some very specific, finely crafted legal concepts supporting free speech. The defence of fair comment is one such example, whereby an opinion, no matter how 'wrong, grossly exaggerated or based on prejudice or bias', may still defeat the right to reputation.[39] Further, from at least 1689, parliaments and courts attained a kind of sacred status as arenas of absolute freedom of speech. Speech occurring within these places is free and protected, without legal qualification, by the doctrine of absolute privilege.[40]

The Implied Constitutional Freedom of Government and Political Discussion

I would now like to say something more about the Australian Constitution. Our starting point is that no express, positive or personal rights to any communication freedoms can be found in its terms.

However, in 1992, the High Court recognised in the Constitution an *implied* freedom of government and political discussion. So, whereas common law free speech preceded, and helped to create our democracies, the constitutional concept was implied as a necessary feature, or consequence, of the system of representative government established by the Australian Constitution.

One of the original 1992 cases, *Australian Capital Television v Common-wealth*, concerned a broadcasting law. The Federal Act was designed to restrict political advertising on broadcast media during election campaigns.[41] The public policy purpose was to reduce reliance upon political donations and fundraising and, so it was said, reduce the risk of corruption attached to those activities.

---

37 George, above n 34, 130–1.
38 Ibid 159.
39 Ibid 345.
40 Article 9 of the Bill of Rights 1689 states, 'That the freedom of speech and debates or proceedings in Parliament ought not to be impeached or questioned in any court or place out of Parliament'. Note that the common law also provided a defence of absolute privilege for a petition made to parliament: *Lake v King* (1680) 85 ER 137.
41 *Australian Capital Television v Commonwealth* (1992) 177 CLR 106.

Under the regime, broadcasters were also required to supply free advertising time to political candidates proportionately with their share of the vote at the previous election. The High Court then implied the freedom of political discussion from the Constitution and used this to strike down the Act.

While, between 1992 and 1997, there was much uncertainty about the reach and scope of the implied freedom – with speculation that it might open up a general communications freedom of the type found in a Bill of Rights – the High Court's 7-nil, unanimous judgment in *Lange v Australian Broadcasting Corporation* modified, clarified and circumscribed this concept. Here, the implied freedom was more narrowly and concretely attached to the constitutional provisions prescribing free elections.[42] A constitutional standard was also set "according to which a law that burdens the freedom of communication must be 'reasonably appropriate and adapted to serve a legitimate end'".[43] In applying this test to both statutory and common law, the High Court held that some adjustment to the defamation defence of qualified privilege was required. In effect, the Court did two things. It widened the concept of qualified privilege (and thereby free speech of the relevant kind), but it also added a constraint – requiring 'reasonableness' on the part of the publisher.[44] Since 1997, there has been a mixed response from media organisations as to whether this adjustment has made any practical difference to the overall scope of free speech, from their point of view.[45] What is significant, though, is that the High Court has constitutionalised free speech in this kind of way, with room for further developing the implied freedom into the future.

The Force of Public Opinion

In talking about free speech, there is also an important, non-Constitutional restraint upon law-making and governmental powers. This is the force of public opinion. Putting to one side its merely transitory or ephemeral aspects, public opinion is at its core a manifestation of entrenched habits of mind. It seems to me that the force of public opinion is usually the line of last defence when it comes to preserving free speech.

We see this in Andrew Bent's newspaper, the *Hobart Town Gazette*, when the realities of running a free press under an autocratic government were being felt,

---

42   *Lange v Australian Broadcasting Corporation* (1997) CLR 520.
43   Stone, above n 29, 254.
44   *Lange v Australian Broadcasting Corporation* (1997) CLR 520, 570–1.
45   Russell Weaver and others, *The Right to Speak Ill: Defamation, Reputation and Free Speech* (2006), 201–14.

at some personal cost. Surveying the battlefield, the editorial in the *Gazette* edition of 8 July 1825 said:

> It is a fearful struggle in which we are now to contend, opposed to the whole weight of a powerful Government ... the more strenuous are the efforts of our enemies to stifle our humble exertions; the more we hope to receive the generous protection of our countrymen.[46]

In the contest between freedom and authority, the force of public opinion is a powerful ally. And, to the extent that the forces of technology and globalisation may diminish or manipulate the diverse voices that, taken together, make up public opinion, our assumed and accepted freedoms are put at serious risk. Professor Dörr has also mentioned the significance of public opinion in his discussion about the German broadcasting freedom. We can learn from this jurisprudence – whether to inform our public policy and parliamentary debates about media regulation, to explore creatively the reach of the implied constitutional freedom of political communication, or to further the recently launched experiment of statutory charters of rights in this country.

Conclusion

To conclude. In Australia, then, whatever may be the letter of the law as it applies from time to time, in the manner of a stepped-upon cat, free speech has a long tradition of asserting and protecting itself. And for our cultural tradition, it makes more sense to imagine the abstract notion of free speech through the use of such things as black-cat metaphors – rather than by attempts at precise definition, such as Article 5 of the German Basic Law.

David Malouf is one of Australia's most celebrated writers. In 1998, he delivered the Boyer Lectures, entitled, *A Spirit of Play: The making of Australian consciousness.*[47] And, in 2003, Malouf published a Quarterly Essay entitled, *Made in England: Australia's British Inheritance.*[48] Towards the end of his essay, Malouf meditates upon the implications of our British inheritance:

> We may treat Britain itself in any way we please... What we cannot remove is the language we speak, and all that is inherent in it: a way of laying out our experience, of seeing, that comes with the syntax, a body of half-forgotten customs, and events, fables, insights, jokes, that make up its idioms...
>
> We may modify and 'naturalise' the institutions we brought here, the Westminster system, the Common Law, so that they make a better fit with what we now are, but they have provided

---

46   *Hobart Town Gazette (Bent)*, 8 July 1825.

47   Malouf, above n 17.

48   Malouf, above n 20.

so much of the context of what we have created here, and value and would want to preserve, that to abandon them, or allow them to decay, would be an act of national suicide. And there, for the moment, we stand.[49]

But Malouf does not stop there. Consistently with the worth and value of a conference such as this, of openness to human rights and constitutional discourses about communication freedoms, of hearing about other ways for expressing our freedom of expression, Malouf points to the on-going and adaptable nature of 'the Australian experiment'. He concludes:

> This venture we call "Australia" was always an experiment... It ought to make us sceptical of conclusions, of any belief that where we are now is more than a moment along the way. An experiment is open, all conclusions provisional. Even the conclusiveness of a full stop is no more, so long as there is breath, than a conventional gesture towards pause in a continuing argument.[50]

---

49   Ibid 65.
50   Ibid 65–6.

Thomas John/Cornelia Koch*

The Genesis of the German Constitution – From Total Devastation to the Dawn of a New Era

A. Introduction

The German Constitution originated under extraordinary circumstances. Unlike some other constitutions, it was not the product of an evolutionary process, a popular revolution or a war of independence.[1] Instead, it was the result of the most terrible war the world had ever seen, the Second World War. For Germany, the war ended in unconditional surrender and led to its occupation by foreign military forces. At that time, much of the country lay in ruins, millions had died and the institutions of government were completely destroyed.

However, only four years later two German states emerged from the devastation of the war, both founded by new constitutions.[2] The western state, the Federal Republic of Germany, came into being with the entry into force of the 'Basic Law' (*Grundgesetz*).[3] On the solemn occasion of its promulgation, Konrad Adenauer declared:

---

*   Thomas John is a legal practitioner working for the Commonwealth Attorney-General's Department. Any views expressed in this chapter are his own and should not be attributed to the Commonwealth of Australia or the Department.
    Cornelia Koch is a Senior Lecturer in the Adelaide Law School at the University of Adelaide.
1   Like, for example, the Constitutions of the Commonwealth of Australia, the French Republic and The United States of America respectively.
2   Because the West German constitution ultimately became the constitution for the reunited Germany in 1990, this paper will only consider its history and not deal in detail with the constitutional developments in East Germany from 1945 to 1990. The eastern part of Germany was under Soviet occupation in the immediate aftermath of the war. The German Democratic Republic was founded on 7 October 1949. Its first constitution, the Constitution of the German Democratic Republic (*Verfassung der Deutschen Demokratischen Republik*) of 7 October 1949, was replaced by the Constitution of the German Democratic Republic of 6 April 1968, in force until reunification in 1990.
3   '*Grundgesetz*' is commonly translated into English with the phrase 'Basic Law'. The authors follow this convention in this article. On the accuracy of the translation of '*Grundgesetz*' into 'Basic Law' see the remarks in fn 67 below.

Today ... marks the beginning of a new chapter in the changeful history of our people. Today ... the Federal Republic of Germany will enter the stage of history. ... [The Basic Law shall] be a sacred treasure for us, which we wish to safeguard, care for and develop.[4]

The proclamation of the Basic Law marked the beginning of an unprecedented era of constitutionalism in Germany. In this sense, Germans have indeed treasured their constitution, thus fulfilling the wish expressed by Adenauer.

Because the Basic Law is a direct product of the post-war period, its coming into being must be considered in the wider context of the circumstances in Germany at the time. Accordingly, the first part of this article portrays the situation in the occupied country in the years following the war. Starting from the unconditional surrender, it describes the major events leading to the birth of the new state. This discussion encompasses the division of the country into four zones of occupation, the gradual return to political life within the zones via intra-zonal institutions and the establishment of supra-zonal institutions. It also canvasses the gradual drifting apart of the western and the eastern parts of Germany, caused by a continuous deterioration of the relationship between the three western Allies[5] on one hand and the Soviet Union on the other. This development culminated in the founding of two separate states – the Federal Republic of Germany and the German Democratic Republic.

Part two focuses more directly on the path towards the Basic Law. After explaining the important role of the reestablished federal States (*Länder*) in this regard, it examines the work of the bodies which framed the new constitution, the Constitutional Convention and the Parliamentary Council. This is followed by an outline of the major features of the Basic Law. The article concludes in the final part with a recognition of the unprecedented longevity and success which the Basic Law has had as a German constitution.[6]

---

4   'Heute ... beginnt ein neuer Abschnitt in der wechselvollen Geschichte unseres Volkes. Heute wird ... die Bundesrepublik Deutschland in die Geschichte eintreten. ... [Das Grundgesetz soll] uns ... ein heiliger Besitz sein, den wir wahren, den wir pflegen und den wir ausbauen wollen.' (translation by the authors). Konrad Adenauer was the President of the Parliamentary Council, the body which framed the Basic Law. Later he was elected to be the first Chancellor (head of government) of the Federal Republic of Germany, a position which he held for fourteen years. The quotation is from a speech which he gave in the final session of the Parliamentary Council on 23 May 1949, at which the Basic Law was ceremonially promulgated.
      A recording of the whole speech can be found at <http://www.mitmischen.de/index.php/ Informativ/Zeitleiste/pos/0/infobox/22330> (21/11/09).

5   The United States of America, The United Kingdom and France.

6   For information on German post-war history from 1945 to 1949 in the English language see, for example, Mary Fulbrook, *A Concise History of Germany*, Cambridge University Press (2nd ed, 2004) at 205–12; Lothar Kettenacker, *Germany since 1945*, Oxford University Press

B. From the Capitulation to the Establishment of Supra-Zonal Institutions

1. Capitulation and Occupation

Long before the end of the Second World War, the allied powers[7] developed a plan for the future of a defeated Germany. The Allies believed that Germany's aggressive role as the initiator of both World Wars was evidence of this country's inherently aggressive nature. Thus, their post-war aim was to eliminate permanently the threat of Germany starting another war in the future, *inter alia*, by fundamentally changing its internal order. To achieve this, the Allies agreed only to end the war if their enemy's military forces and the civilian government surrendered unconditionally.[8] In other words, there would be no armistice or deal of any kind with Hitler. After Germany's capitulation, the victorious powers would seize all authority in the country and then reshape it as they saw fit.[9]

The Allies reached their goal on 7 and 8 May 1945, when Germany declared its unconditional surrender.[10] With this declaration, the war in Europe came to an end.[11] Notably, contrary to the Allies' original plan, only the German armed

---

(1997) at 5–52, 281–85; Mark Allinson et al, *Contemporary Germany*, Pearson Education Limited (2000) at 3–16; Henry Ashby Turner, *The Two Germanies Since 1945*, Yale University Press (1987) at 1–53; Martin Kitchen, *A History of Modern Germany 1800–2000*, Blackwell Publishing (2006) at 316–28; Elmar M Hucko, 'Introduction' in Elmar M Hucko, *The Democratic Tradition – Four German Constitutions*, Berg Publishers Limited (1987) at 62–76; Peter H Merkl, *The Origin of the West German Republic*, Oxford University Press (1963); John Ford Golay, *The Founding of the Federal Republic of Germany*, The University of Chicago Press (1958).

7   The United States of America, The United Kingdom, The Soviet Union and France.

8   This aim was first proclaimed by Franklin D Roosevelt and Winston Churchill in the Declaration of Casablanca, 21 January 1943, and reinforced at the Yalta Conference between The United States of America, Great Britain and the Soviet Union, which took place from 4 to 11 February 1945.

9   Dietmar Willoweit, *Deutsche Verfassungsgeschichte*, 2nd ed, CH Beck, 1992 at 323–4.

10   The surrender occurred in two steps. On 6 May 1945, Great Admiral Karl Dönitz, President of the *German Reich's* last government since Hitler's suicide on 30 April 1945, authorised Colonel General Alfred Jodl to agree to the unconditional surrender of 'all forces at land, sea, and in the air'. Jodl signed this surrender on 7 May 1945 at Rheims in France. Subsequently, Dönitz authorised the commanders in chief of the German army, navy and air force, General Field Marshal Wilhelm Keitel, General Admiral Hans-Georg von Friedeburg and Colonel General Hans-Jürgen Stumpff, to ratify this surrender. The ratification took place on 8 May 1945 in Berlin.

11   The war in the pacific continued until the unconditional surrender of Japan on 2 September 1945, which marked the end of the Second World War.

forces surrendered, not the civilian government. As a consequence, the *Deutsches Reich* continued to exist as a state in a legal sense.[12] In a practical sense, however, all civilian state authority had ceased to exist when Adolf Hitler committed suicide and Berlin fell, if not earlier. Therefore, all German state power passed factually to the victorious Allies,[13] who recognised this *status quo* on 5 June 1945 in Berlin, declaring that they assumed 'supreme authority with respect to Germany, including all the powers possessed by the German Government, the High Command and any state, municipal, or local government or authority.'[14]

In accordance with agreements entered into before the end of the war,[15] the Allies divided Germany into four zones of occupation, controlled by The United States of America, The Soviet Union, The United Kingdom and France respectively. In these zones, the will of the occupying forces reigned supreme. Zone Commanders (*Zonenbefehlshaber*) were at the apex of authority.

2. The Emergence of Intra-Zonal Institutions

Whilst the Allies possessed the ultimate power in the zones, they were not capable of governing them without the assistance of an administrative apparatus made up of German nationals. Each Zone Commander was responsible for a large number of Germans whom the war had left with very little.[16] Providing enough clean drinking water, food and shelter presented enormous problems. The impending winter of 1945 created an additional challenge as there were real

---

12   BVerfGE 5, 85 at 326. Note that Germany was not annexed by the Allies, see the Declaration Regarding the Defeat of Germany and the Assumption of Supreme Authority by the Allied Powers, signed at Berlin, 5 June 1945, full text available at <http://www.ena.lu/allied-declaration-regarding-defeat-germany-june-1945-020004326.html> (20/11/09). Because allied authority was derived from the fact of occupation, rather than from a transfer of power by the capitulating government, the first post-war government of the Federal Republic of Germany, the successor state of the *Reich*, was able to exercise the 'original' German state authority. No re-transfer of this authority by the Allies was needed; BVerfGE 36, 1 at 15–7.

13   Dietmar Willoweit, *Deutsche Verfassungsgeschichte*, 2nd ed, CH Beck, 1992 at 324.

14   Declaration Regarding the Defeat of Germany and the Assumption of Supreme Authority by the Allied Powers, signed at Berlin, 5 June 1945. Full text available at <http://www.ena.lu/allied-declaration-regarding-defeat-germany-june-1945-020004326.html> (20/11/09).

15   See the conferences of Teheran (from 28 November to 1 December 1943) and Yalta (from 4 to 11 February 1945) and the Protocol on Zones of Occupation in Germany and Administration of the 'Greater Berlin Area', London, 12 September 1944, as amended by agreement of 14 November 1944.

16   The British zone, for example, had 22.3 million inhabitants and the American zone 17.2 million; see Lothar Kettenacker, *Germany since 1945*, Oxford University Press (1997) at 22.

prospects that large numbers of people would freeze or starve to death.[17] In order to cope with these and other problems, the occupying forces had to reestablish administrative structures in their zones as quickly as possible.

At the conference of Potsdam, the Allies had agreed that Germany was to be reconstructed from the bottom up.[18] In the western zones this approach was indeed taken. The Zone Commanders commenced their rebuilding efforts by appointing German office bearers at local and communal level, particularly local councillors and mayors. Initially these officials had no independent political power. They could be removed from office at the whim of the Zone Commander.[19] Their appointment was nevertheless significant because it constituted the first, fledgling step on the long road back to German national sovereignty.[20]

A milestone in the reemergence of Germany's political structures, particularly in the western zones, was the reestablishment of the federal States (*Länder*). Under Hitler's centralist regime, State parliaments had been abolished and the States brought under the direct control of the central government.[21] By reconstituting the States as regional administrative entities within their zones,[22] the western Allies laid the foundation for a federal system of government. This process commenced shortly after the beginning of the occupation.[23] Initially, the

---

17 For a brief description of the rather desperate situation of the German population at that time see Mary Fulbrook, *A Concise History of Germany*, Cambridge University Press (2nd ed, 2004) at 209–10; Martin Kitchen, *A History of Modern Germany 1800–2000*, Blackwell Publishing (2006) at 316.

18 Potsdam Agreement of 2 August 1945.

19 For example Konrad Adenauer, who became the Mayor of Cologne in May 1945 and was later elected to be the first Chancellor of the Federal Republic of Germany, was sacked in October 1945 for lack of initiative and incompetence. It appears that Adenauer's dismissal was triggered by a dispute with the British Brigadier Barraclough. The United Kingdom had prohibited the distribution of coal and other flammable materials to the people of Cologne, despite the impending winter. Adenauer strongly disagreed with this policy; see <http://www.konrad-adenauer.de/index.php?key=&menu_sel=29&menu_sel2=&menu_ sel3=&menu_sel4=> (17/11/09).

20 Germany only achieved full sovereignty forty-six years later, with the entry into force of the *Treaty on the Final Settlement with Respect to Germany* on 15 March 1991.

21 Dietmar Willoweit, *Deutsche Verfassungsgeschichte*, 2nd ed, CH Beck, 1992 at 311–2.

22 Note that most of these States did not have the same name and were not covering the same geographical area as they had during the Weimar Republic.

23 For example, in the American zone the States of Bavaria (*Bayern*), Württemberg-Baden and Hesse (*Hessen*) were created on 19 September 1945 by Proclamation Number 2 of the Military Government.

State governments, lead by Minister Presidents (*Ministerpräsidenten*),[24] were appointed by the Allies, but subsequently democratic elections to State Parliaments were conducted. By late 1946, elections to the Parliaments of the States (*Landtage*) (and also to local councils) had been held in all zones and each State had a government of German politicians. While this was a significant achievement, it must be stressed that these governments were ultimately responsible to their respective Zone Commander, rather than to the elected State Parliaments.[25] But despite the office bearers' strong dependence on the Allies, the appointment and election of Germans to political and administrative positions constituted one of the steps towards a retransfer of power to the German people.

The reemergence of the States in the West was also important from a constitutional perspective because, as discussed below, the western Minister Presidents and Parliaments were to play a pivotal role in the developments that brought the Basic Law into existence.

In contrast to the western Allies, the Soviet Union did not approach the rebuilding of its zone from the bottom up. While it reestablished the States early, on 9 July 1945, it also conferred powers upon one central administration that operated across all eastern States.[26] This preempted the emergence of any strong federal notions as were developing in the West.[27]

The Soviet Union was also early in licensing political parties in its zone.[28] Keen to create a state based on Marxist-Leninist ideas, it coerced the fusion of the Social-Democratic Party (SPD) and the Communist Party (KPD) into the Socialist Unity Party (SED) in April 1946.[29] The local, communal and State elections following this merger in October of the same year were dominated by the SED. They resulted in SED-led State Parliaments and governments.[30]

---

24   The head of government of a German State (*Land*), equivalent to a Premier in the Australian States.

25   Mark Allinson et al, *Contemporary Germany*, Pearson Education Limited (2000) at 7. For more detail on the reestablishment of the States in the different zones see Peter H Merkl, *The Origin of the West German Republic*, Oxford University Press (1963) at 8–13, 14–7.

26   Peter H Merkl, *The Origin of the West German Republic*, Oxford University Press (1963) at 15–6.

27   With the coming into being of the German Democratic Republic in 1949, the eastern States lost most of their functions. In 1952 they were abolished; Peter H Merkl, *The Origin of the West German Republic*, Oxford University Press (1963) at 17.

28   10 June 1945.

29   Mark Allinson et al, *Contemporary Germany*, Pearson Education Limited (2000) at 8–11.

30   Although apparently the SED did not achieve absolute power in all States and local and communal districts; see Stefan Creuzberger, 'The Soviet Military Administration and East

214

Apparently, these elections were strongly manipulated by the Soviet Military Administration in order to achieve this result.[31]

3. The Emergence of Supra-Zonal Institutions

While the Allies had agreed before the war that Germany would be divided into several zones of occupation, each governed independently by one of the occupying powers, they had also recognised the need for some form of central administration. Therefore, the Allied Control Council (*Alliierter Kontrollrat*) was created to coordinate the four military governments and deal with matters which concerned the whole of Germany.[32] Its members were the four supreme military commanders of the occupying forces. Decision-making was by consensus. The Council was intended to be the pivotal executive and legislative institution for Germany. Its laws, regulations and orders were binding on all Germans. Among its major functions were the denazification (*Entnazifizierung*) of German society[33] and the country's disarmament and demilitarisation. The Council was also charged with creating a unified economic area across all four zones.

However, the Council was not able to fulfil all of these ambitious goals because shortly after the end of the war the relationship between the three western Allies on one hand and the Soviet Union on the other began to deteriorate. A rift could already be detected at the Potsdam Conference in July and August 1945. While the Allies were able to agree on denazification and disarmament, they did not have a common vision for the future of Germany. They broadly agreed that the country should be developed in a uniform way across the four zones and there was also basic agreement that German political life should be reconstructed 'on a democratic basis'.[34] However, their views on how this was to occur in detail differed greatly: the western powers favoured a

---

German Elections, Autumn 1946' (1999) 45 *Australian Journal of Politics and History* 89 at 96.

31   See for a detailed discussion of these events Stefan Creuzberger, 'The Soviet Military Administration and East German Elections, Autumn 1946' (1999) 45 *Australian Journal of Politics and History* 89.

32   The Allied Control Council was established on 5 June 1945. Its role was defined in more detail in the Potsdam Agreement of 2 August 1945.

33   Denazification was an allied initiative to remove any remnants of the Nazi regime from German society, including culture, press, economy, judiciary and politics, agreed upon by The United States of America, The United Kingdom and The Soviet Union in the Potsdam Agreement of 2 August 1945.

34   Potsdam Agreement of 2 August 1945.

system of liberal democracy with a capitalist market economy, while the Soviet Union aimed at establishing a system of government based on Marxist-Leninist principles. From this point onwards, developments in Germany were inextricably linked with the unfolding of the Cold War. As a result, the Allied Control Council was increasingly unable to make consensual decisions. It ceased most of its activities in March 1948,[35] when the Soviet Representative walked out during a Council meeting, never to return.[36]

Notably, the Potsdam Agreement had envisaged the participation of German nationals in supra-zonal institutions. As pointed out above, the Agreement had charged the Allied Control Council with establishing a unified economic area across all four zones of occupation. To assist the Council in this endeavour, central administrative bodies for the whole of Germany, headed by state secretaries (*Staatssekretäre*) of German nationality, were to be created. This would have constituted the first involvement of German citizens in a central, supra-zonal administration since the end of the war, albeit under the direction of the Control Council. However, because the Allies were unable to agree on vital details, any attempt to develop these institutions had failed by mid-1946.[37]

Despite this failure, attempts to create a larger economic area in Germany did not come to an end. Early 1947 saw the establishment of 'Bizonia', the economic entity comprising the American and British zones.[38] The administration of this area was carried out by newly formed institutions, run by German nationals, to assist the allied commanders. The establishment of these Administrative Councils (*Verwaltungsräte*) marked the beginning of the reestablishment of German institutions across more than one occupation zone, which ultimately lead to the formation of a West German state.

In the early part of Bizonia's existence, its system of governance was restructured a number of times,[39] but by March 1948 it featured the following

---

35 Except in relation to the administration of the Spandau Prison, which held the prisoners convicted at the Nurnberg War Crimes Trials. The Allied Control Council ceased to exist with the entry into force of the *Treaty on the Final Settlement With Respect to Germany* on 15 March 1991.

36 This occurred in response to the fact that the Soviet Union had not been invited to the Six-Powers Conference in London in early 1948 (discussed below, see text accompanying fns 59–65); Mark Allinson et al, *Contemporary Germany*, Pearson Education Limited (2000) at 7.

37 Particularly the French government was opposed to the creation of these central German administrative bodies. Dietmar Willoweit, *Deutsche Verfassungsgeschichte*, 2nd ed, CH Beck, 1992 at 327.

38 This arrangement entered into operation on 1 January 1947.

39 The original institutions of Bizonia were Administrative Councils covering the following portfolios: economy, road infrastructure, food and agriculture, post and telecommunication

institutions: (1) an Administrative Council, carrying out mainly executive functions;[40] (2) an Economic Council that resembled a parliament with limited legislative competencies and whose members were elected from the Parliaments of the States located in Bizonia; (3) a States' Council (*Länderrat*) that was comprised of one full-time delegate from each State, charged with representing the interests of the States;[41] (4) a High Court and (5) a Central Bank.[42] Like all governmental institutions at that time, these supra-zonal bodies were ultimately responsible to the military governours.

France did not initially take part in this process of economic unification, but it acceded to the unified zone in August 1948, thus creating 'Trizonia'.[43]

Due to the deteriorating relationship between the western powers and the Soviet Union, the eastern zone never joined the common economic area. The resulting division of Germany into two discrete economic zones constitutes one of the milestones on the way towards two separate German states.

In this context, a remark in the *Neue Zeitung*, an American-sponsored newspaper, is telling. Following the last restructuring of the system of governance of Bizonia in February 1948, the paper introduced the new system to its readership as 'a preliminary government to serve as a basis for the making of a constitution for West Germany.'[44] Apparently, by early 1948, the western Allies were already preparing the population in their zones for the establishment of a West German state. The chances for German unification had grown very slim, at least in the short term.

In summary, whilst immediately after the war the Allies seemed to display the common desire to create an at least economically unified Germany, very soon the ideas of the western powers and the Soviet Union about the future of the country diverged. The rift and final split into two independent states was pre-programmed.

---

services and finance. They were located in several cities, in order to avoid any perception that they constituted a central administration for the two zones.

40   Compared to the original Administrative Councils, this Council was also in charge of the additional portfolios of industrial relations, social welfare and justice.

41   The three Councils were located in Frankfurt, Cologne and Wiesbaden.

42   Peter H Merkl, *The Origin of the West German Republic*, Oxford University Press (1963) at 13–4.

43   Bruno Schmidt-Bleibtreu and Axel Hopfauf, 'Einleitung zum Grundgesetz', in B Schmidt-Bleibtreu/F Klein (eds), *GG – Kommentar zum Grundgesetz*, Luchterhand (10th ed, 2004) at 66.

44   Peter H Merkl, *The Origin of the West German Republic*, Oxford University Press (1963), Chapter 1, note 50.

C. The Genesis of the Basic Law

Having examined the broader circumstances in Germany in the post-war years, we now turn to a consideration of the events which led more immediately to the adoption of the Basic Law. This part begins with an explanation of the role of the reestablished federal States and their constitutions in this process. Subsequently, it discusses the work of the bodies which framed the new constitution, the Constitutional Convention and the Parliamentary Council. Finally, an outline of the major features of the Basic Law is provided.

1. The Role of the States and Their Constitutions

As explained above, the reestablishment of the States in the western zones was a milestone in the reemergence of Germany's political structures. After initially appointing the members of the governments of the States, including the Minister Presidents, the Allies conducted democratic elections to State Parliaments.[45] Gradually, the States were also given new constitutions. The way in which the state constitutions came into being differed in the four zones of allied occupation. The most democratic approach was taken in the American zone,[46] where the people elected constituent state assemblies which developed and passed the State constitutions under allied supervision. These constitutions were subsequently approved by the people in referenda and by The United States. The process in the French zone[47] was similar, but less democratic. The constituent State assemblies were not elected by the people but consisted of representatives from local and communal administrative bodies. Otherwise, a similar system as in the US sector was employed. In contrast, the development of State constitutions in the UK zone[48] lagged behind compared to the other western Allies. Before 1949 only preliminary constitutional arrangements had been made. State constitutions were only finalised after the founding of the Federal Republic of Germany and entry into force of the Basic Law in 1949. The constitutions were adopted by elected State Parliaments and subsequently ratified by the people by way of popular referendum.[49]

---

45 See text accompanying fns 22–6.
46 Bayern, Württemberg-Baden, Hessen, Bremen.
47 Baden, Württemberg-Hohenzollern, Rheinland-Pfalz, Saarland.
48 Niedersachsen, Nordrhein-Westfalen, Schleswig-Holstein, Hamburg.
49 Dietmar Willoweit, *Deutsche Verfassungsgeschichte*, 2nd ed, CH Beck, 1992 at 326.

The western State constitutions and the way in which they came into being are relevant for the framing and adoption of the Basic Law because they were examples of successful constitution making in occupied Germany. As such, they provided inspiration for the procedures used to prepare and enact the federal constitution.[50] In addition, the western States played a significant role in the creation of the Basic Law in the following ways: first, the States' Minister Presidents were the representatives of the German people with whom the Allies negotiated about the development of a new constitution for West Germany; secondly, Minister Presidents set up the Constitutional Convention, a body which carried out the preparatory work for the main assembly charged with framing the Basic Law, the Parliamentary Council; thirdly, State Parliaments elected State MPs as delegates to the Parliamentary Council; and finally, the Basic Law needed the approval of the State Parliaments before it could enter into force.

Compared to the western zones, the making of State constitutions in the East occurred in a different manner, adhering to the dictate of the dominant political party and lacking an element of popular democracy. As indicated above, the States in this area were created shortly after the end of the war.[51] Elections conducted in October 1946 were dominated by the Social Unity Party (SED), which resulted in SED-led State Parliaments.[52] Subsequently, the party presented these Parliaments with uniform draft State constitutions, which were duly adopted by way of parliamentary majority.[53]

2. The Movement Towards a West German State

The divergence in the systems of government established in the western and eastern zones and the worsening relationship between the western Allies and the Soviet Union created a climate in which the division of Germany into two separate states became more and more likely. To combat this trend, the Bavarian government convened a conference of all German Minister Presidents in June 1947. This was the only time in German post-war history until unification that all heads of government of the States met in one place. At the conference, the representatives of the eastern States wanted to debate general political issues relating to the creation of a central German government, while their West

---

50   John Ford Golay, *The Founding of the Federal Republic of Germany*, The University of Chicago Press (1958) at 18.
51   Brandenburg, Mecklenburg, Sachsen, Sachsen-Anhalt, Thüringen, all founded on 9 July 1945.
52   See text accompanying fns 28–31.
53   Dietmar Willoweit, *Deutsche Verfassungsgeschichte*, 2nd ed, CH Beck, 1992 at 326–7.

German counterparts rejected this approach. This was due to a number of reasons. For example, France had not permitted delegates from its zone to discuss issues going beyond economic matters. Furthermore, the West German Minister Presidents did not regard their eastern colleagues as having sufficient democratic legitimacy because they were part of the SED or supported by it. Additionally, all Minister Presidents were completely dependent on the will of their zone's occupying power. In these circumstances it was impossible to develop any constitutional policy for the whole of Germany. The gathering failed before it had really started, when the Eastern Minister Presidents walked out after their proposed items for discussions were not added to the conference's agenda.[54]

The year 1947 also saw a series of unsuccessful meetings between the Allies' foreign ministers, in which they failed to reach agreement on the question of Germany's future. The series culminated in the London conference in late 1947[55] which, according to Kettenacker, constituted the 'definite breakup of the wartime alliance' and led to an 'intensification of the Cold War.'[56] The failures of finding a unified stance on Germany also resulted in the creation of Bizonia, discussed above,[57] and, possibly most importantly, the currency reform in the western zones which led to the Berlin Blockade.[58]

Arguably the decisive step towards the ultimate division of Germany was the Six-Powers Conference in London in the first half of 1948, to which The Soviet

---

54   Willoweit, *Deutsche Verfassungsgeschichte*, 2nd ed, CH Beck, 1992 at 328; Mark Allinson et al, *Contemporary Germany*, Pearson Education Limited (2000) at 7.

55   Fifth Conference of Foreign Ministers, London, held from 25 November to 15 December 1947.

56   Lothar Kettenacker, *Germany since 1945*, Oxford University Press (1997) at 282; see also at 30.

57   See text accompanying fns 38–42.

58   Geographically, Berlin was within The Soviet Union's zone of occupation. Administratively, however, it was not part of that zone because immediately after the end of the Second World War Berlin had been granted a 'special status'. Unlike the rest of Germany, it did not belong to one zone of occupation but was jointly administered by the four allied powers. Each power controlled one sector of the city. Following the currency reform in the western zones on 20 June 1948, The Soviet Union blocked all land access from the western zones to the three western sectors of Berlin on 24 June 1948. The blockade lasted for almost one year, until 12 May 1949. During this time an Anglo-American airlift (*die Luftbrücke*) provided the city with essential supplies; see Mark Allinson et al, *Contemporary Germany*, Pearson Education Limited (2000) at 7–8; Lothar Kettenacker, *Germany since 1945*, Oxford University Press (1997) at 30–3.

Union was not invited.[59] This conference paved the way for the constitutional future of the Federal Republic of Germany.[60] Its key outcome in that regard was the decision to found a West German state with a federal system of government, integrated into an organisation for the rebuilding of (western) Europe.[61]

To commence this process, the conference created the Frankfurt Documents, often referred to as the 'birth certificate' of the Federal Republic.[62] The Documents were delivered to the eleven western State Minister Presidents in Frankfurt on 1 July 1948.[63] The first instructed the Minister Presidents to convene a national constituent assembly, charged with framing a constitution for a sovereign West German state.[64] This assembly should commence its work within two months, by 1 September 1948.

In addition to setting out the procedure by which the constitution should be drafted, the first Frankfurt Document also established the framework for its substance. Federal and democratic in character, the constitution should protect the rights of the States, create appropriate federal institutions, guarantee rights and freedoms of the individual and be so designed as to facilitate the eventual restoration of German unity. Ratification should occur through popular referenda in each of the states and the document should enter into force in all States once two-thirds of the States had ratified it.[65]

On receipt of the Document, the western State Minister Presidents faced the following dilemma: whilst generally agreeing with the recommendations, they realised that their implementation would deepen the rift between the western and eastern parts of Germany. Consequently, the Minister Presidents gave their in

---

59   The six powers were Great Britain, France, The United States, Luxemburg, The Netherlands and Belgium. The conference met from 23 February to 6 March and 20 April to 2 June; see Lothar Kettenacker, *Germany since 1945*, Oxford University Press (1997) at 282.

60   Edmund Spevack, *Allied Control and German Freedom*, LIT Verlag (2001) at 113; Michael Sachs, 'Einführung zum Grundgesetz', in Michael Sachs (ed), *Grundgesetz Kommentar*, Verlag C. H. Beck (3rd ed, 2003) at 9.

61   The Organisation for European Economic Co-Operation (OEEC), which emerged from the Marshall Plan. The western zones of Germany acceded to the OEEC on the date when it was established, 16 April 1948; <http://www.oecd.org/document/48/0,3343,en_2649_201185_1876912_1_1_1_1,00.html> (03/12/2009). Eastern European countries were also invited to join the OEEC, but their pro-Soviet governments refused the invitation.

62   Lothar Kettenacker, *Germany since 1945*, Oxford University Press (1997) at 37.

63   Because they were a product of the London conference, some sources refer to them as the 'London Documents.'

64   The other two Frankfurt Documents related to State boundaries and the occupation statute. English language versions of all three Documents can be found at <http://germanhistory docs.ghi-dc.org/sub_document.cfm?document_id=2850> (18/11/09).

65   See Document I: Constituent Assembly at <http://germanhistorydocs.ghi-dc.org/sub_document.cfm?document_id=2850> (18/11/09).

principle support, but suggested to modify the proposal so that initially only a provisional solution for West Germany would be sought. The adoption of a constitution should be delayed until reunification had been achieved. Therefore, the Minister Presidents disagreed with the ideas of convening a constituent assembly comprised of directly elected delegates and of ratifying the final document by way of referenda. Both procedures would symbolise the creation of a permanent West German state, rather than the entry into a provisional arrangement pending reunification.[66] Instead of a directly elected 'constituent assembly' the Minister Presidents suggested to convene a 'Parliamentary Council', consisting of delegates who were members of State Parliaments. The Council would not be charged with the drafting of a 'constitution', but with the framing of a provisional administrative statute (*Verwaltungsstatut*) for West Germany, called the 'Basic Law' (*Grundgesetz*).[67] The Basic Law would not be ratified by the citizens of the States but only by State Parliaments.[68]

After initial resistance, the Allies accepted these procedural modifications. This acceptance in itself is remarkable because it was the first time since 1945 that the Allies had negotiated with German officials, instead of simply dictating their terms. The significance of this change in attitude was recognised by the Minister President of Hesse, Christian Stock, at the opening ceremony of the Parliamentary Council when he said:

---

66   In addition, the Minister Presidents were concerned that political campaigns conducted as part of the referendum could be dominated by extremist forces on the left and the right, thus threatening the success of the new order; see US Delegation Minutes of Meeting Between the Western Military Governors and the German Minister Presidents Regarding the German Reply to the Frankfurt Documents, 26 July 1948, <http://germanhistorydocs.ghi-dc.org/sub_document.cfm?document_id=2852> (24/11/2009).

67   '*Grundgesetz*' is commonly translated into English with the phrase 'Basic Law'. However, this translation does not fully capture the meaning of the term in the context of the time. The use of '*Grundgesetz*' can be traced back to the early 19th century, when it was derived from the Latin phrase '*lex fundamentalis*'. The Minister Presidents' choice of the term '*Grundgesetz*' therefore was not only intended to signal the provisional nature of the new document, but also to emphasise the fundamentality of the principles promulgated by it. Therefore, the Minister Presidents agreed that the term should be translated as 'Basic Constitutional Law'; see Bruno Schmidt-Bleibtreu and Axel Hopfauf, 'Einleitung zum Grundgesetz', in B Schmidt-Bleibtreu/F Klein (eds), *GG – Kommentar zum Grundgesetz*, Luchterhand (10th ed, 2004) at 88. While agreeing that 'Basic Constitutional Law' would capture the meaning of '*Grundgesetz*' better, the authors have chosen to adhere to the accepted convention of using the term 'Basic Law' in order to avoid confusion.

68   The Minister Presidents agreed on their response to the Frankfurt Documents at a conference in Koblenz on 8 – 10 July 1948. The text of their response can be found at <http://germanhistorydocs.ghi-dc.org/sub_document.cfm?document_id=2851> (24/11/2009).

Today, for the first time in the recent history of Germany since the capitulation, we act not under a dictate but in accordance with agreements which have been entered into by the military governours and the Minister Presidents.[69]

Unfortunately, the precautions taken by the Minister Presidents were in vain. Their worst fears were realised in the following year when two separate German states were founded. It would take forty-one years until both parts were reunified.

3. The Constitutional Convention

To prepare for the deliberations of the Parliamentary Council, the Minister Presidents organised a Constitutional Convention (*Verfassungskonvent*), a conference of mostly constitutional law experts, which met from 10 to 23 August at Herrenchiemsee.[70] Each western State was represented by two delegates. Initially, the Convention identified the major shortcomings of the Constitution of the Weimar Republic[71] which had allowed the democratic system to be dismantled from within by extremist forces.

In its later years, the Weimar Republic had suffered from a power struggle between the President and the Parliament. Both were elected by popular vote, which had created a form of double legitimacy. With the benefit of hindsight, the Herrenchiemsee Convention perceived the strength of the Weimar *Reichspräsident* as a major problem. The President had had the power to pass emergency legislation and appoint certain types of presidential cabinets (*Präsidialkabinette*) without the involvement of the democratically elected Parliament. He or she had also had the almost unfettered ability to dissolve the Parliament.[72]

Another flaw of the Weimar Constitution was Parliament's ability to topple governments and individual ministers through a vote of no confidence without

---

69 'Wir handeln heute zum ersten Male in der neuen deutschen Geschichte seit der Kapitulation nicht nach einem Diktat, sondern nach Vereinbarungen, die zwischen den Herren Militärgouverneuren und den Ministerpräsidenten zustandegekommen sind.' (translation by the authors); see <http://www.parlamentarischerrat.de/festakt_892_festakt=56_seitentiefe= 2.html> (29/11/2009).

70 On the work of the Convention see Peter H Merkl, *The Origin of the West German Republic*, Oxford University Press (1963) at 55–8.

71 *Verfassung des Deutschen Reichs*, ('*Weimarer Reichsverfassung*'), 11 August 1919, see <http://www.documentarchiv.de/brd.html> (20/11/09).

72 Dietmar Willoweit, *Deutsche Verfassungsgeschichte*, 2nd ed, CH Beck, 1992 at 299–300.

the need to agree on and appoint a successor. This had led to political instability in the Republic.

The third problem were certain elements of direct democracy, in particular referenda, peoples' laws and plebiscites. Hitler had been able to use these methods to legitimise his rule[73] and the Herrenchiemsee delegates thus regarded them with suspicion.

A further shortcoming of the Weimar Constitution was the lack of a proper constitutional court to review compliance with the constitution. It therefore lacked a vital enforcement mechanism.

Finally, while guarantees of the fundamental rights of the individual were recognised in the Constitution, they were framed as mere aspirations of the state. Therefore, they were not adequately safeguarded against infringements.[74]

Mindful of the Weimar experience, the members of the Constitutional Convention attempted to create a better, more resilient constitutional system. The result of the deliberations of the Constitutional Convention was an outstanding achievement in the history of constitutional assemblies.[75] While only charged with preparing the work of the Parliamentary Council, the Convention's members managed in only two weeks to create a complete draft constitutional document coupled with a comprehensive report of the considerations governing the proposals put forward in the draft and a further commentary on individual articles. The document featured crucial elements which were later enshrined in the Basic Law, including a catalogue of unalterable human rights, a bicameral parliamentary system, a strong executive and a constitutional court.[76] The Parliamentary Council used the draft as the basis for its deliberations. Its influence on the Council's work was significant.[77]

---

73   Dietmar Willoweit, *Deutsche Verfassungsgeschichte*, 2nd ed, CH Beck, 1992 at 312; Mark Allinson et al, *Contemporary Germany*, Pearson Education Limited (2000) at 12.

74   See for a discussion of the flaws in the Weimar Constitution Bruno Schmidt-Bleibtreu and Axel Hopfauf, 'Einleitung zum Grundgesetz', in B Schmidt-Bleibtreu/F Klein (eds), *GG – Kommentar zum Grundgesetz*, Luchterhand (10th ed, 2004) at 70–2.

75   Lothar Kettenacker, *Germany since 1945*, Oxford University Press (1997) at 39; John Ford Golay, *The Founding of the Federal Republic of Germany*, The University of Chicago Press (1958) at 18.

76   Bruno Schmidt-Bleibtreu and Axel Hopfauf, 'Einleitung zum Grundgesetz', in B Schmidt-Bleibtreu/F Klein (eds), *GG – Kommentar zum Grundgesetz*, Luchterhand (10th ed, 2004) at 70; Lothar Kettenacker, *Germany since 1945*, Oxford University Press (1997) at 39.

77   Michael Sachs, 'Einführung zum Grundgesetz', in Michael Sachs (ed), *Grundgesetz Kommentar*, Verlag C. H. Beck (3rd ed, 2003) at 9; Martin Kitchen, *A History of Modern Germany 1800–2000*, Blackwell Publishing (2006) at 323.

4. The Parliamentary Council

The Parliamentary Council commenced its work on 1 September 1948 in Bonn. Its deliberations lasted for nine months. The Council was comprised of sixty-five members of the Parliaments of the States, who had been elected by their peers.[78] Due to its special status, Berlin was prohibited from exercising a vote, but sent five advisory members.[79] The collective political experience and expertise in constitutional law of the delegates was impressive. Almost half of them had belonged to high profile political institutions before Hitler's takeover of power in 1933, including the Parliament of the Weimar Republic (*Reichstag*), State Parliaments and Parliaments of Prussian Provinces. Some had even been members of the national assembly (*Nationalversammlung*) of 1919 which framed the Weimar Constitution.[80]

The Council was exclusively composed of representatives of the German people and the Allies were thus not directly involved in its deliberations. Nevertheless, their influence was clearly felt. As explained above, the Allies had provided the framework for the new constitutional arrangement in the Frankfurt Documents.[81] Furthermore, they communicated with the Council by way of explanations and submissions. For example in an *Aide Memoire* of 22 November 1948, the western powers set, *inter alia*, the following minimum requirements for the Basic Law: a strong federal structure; financial limitations on the federal level; the reservation of certain areas of legislative power to the States;[82] a bicameral parliament with a strong state chamber; an independent judiciary with strong adjudicative powers;[83] a non-political civil service and the independence of members of the federal parliament.[84]

Of course, there were differences of opinion within the Council. Largely, they related to the structure of the federation and, in particular, how much power the

---

78   The election of the delegates occurred in accordance with specific, uniform electoral laws, laying down the rules for this election, which each State Parliament had passed; Dietmar Willoweit, *Deutsche Verfassungsgeschichte*, 2nd ed, CH Beck, 1992 at 330.

79   On the special status of Berlin see note 58 above. The city retained this status until reunification in 1990.

80   Dietmar Willoweit, *Deutsche Verfassungsgeschichte*, 2nd ed, CH Beck, 1992 at 330.

81   See text accompanying fns 62–65.

82   The areas of education, cultural and religious affairs, local government and public health were specifically listed.

83   The judiciary should be empowered to review federal legislation and the exercise of federal executive power, to adjudicate conflicts between federal and State authorities or between State authorities and to protect the fundamental rights of individuals.

84   The text of the *Aide Memoire* can be found in John Ford Golay, *The Founding of the Federal Republic of Germany*, The University of Chicago Press (1958) at 263–4.

federal authorities should have as opposed to the States. Therefore, most disagreements centered on the form and powers of the second parliamentary chamber, the division of legislative powers between the federal Parliament and the States and the financial powers of each level of government.[85] Tension arose not only within the Council but also between it and the Allies.[86] However, a closer analysis of these disagreements goes beyond the scope of this article.

On 8 May 1949, exactly four years after the capitulation, the Parliamentary Council adopted the draft Basic Law with 53:12 votes.[87] Four days later, the Allies authorised the new constitution with some caveats concerning Berlin and the creation of a federal police.[88] Subsequently, ten of the eleven State Parliaments ratified the Basic Law. Only Bavaria rejected the document because, according to the Bavarian Parliament, it did not allocate enough power to the States.[89] On 23 May 1949 the Parliamentary Council promulgated the Basic Law in a ceremonial public session. This marked the beginning of a new era of constitutionalism in Germany.

5. The Major Features of the Basic Law

The result of the Council's work was a document which provided a new order for a new nation.[90] It was a product of the deliberations of the Council in the light of the lessons learned from the demise of the Weimar Constitution and

---

85 John Ford Golay, *The Founding of the Federal Republic of Germany*, The University of Chicago Press (1958) at 18 and 27–137; Peter H Merkl, *The Origin of the West German Republic*, Oxford University Press (1963) at 57–8 and 66–79, 90–103.

86 See for a number of examples Peter H Merkl, *The Origin of the West German Republic*, Oxford University Press (1963) at 114–27.

87 Against the votes of two delegates of the *Deutsche Partei*, two delegates of the *Zentrum* party, two delegates of the Communist Party (KPD) and six delegates of the Christian Socialist Party (CSU).

88 This did not require a change to the wording of the document. Instead, the Allies produced a statement stipulating, *inter alia*, that they reserved for themselves the right to intervene, should there be an excessive concentration of power in the federal authorities. An English language version of the letter is available at <http://germanhistorydocs.ghi-dc.org/sub_document.cfm?document_id=2854> (20/11/09); see also Peter H Merkl, *The Origin of the West German Republic*, Oxford University Press (1963) at 125–6.

89 However, the Bavarian Parliament did so in the knowledge that its refusal to pass the Basic Law would not prevent its entry into force in all States (including Bavaria) because under Article 144(1) Basic Law adoption by only two-thirds of the States was required.

90 The original version of the Basic Law can be found at <http://www.documentarchiv.de/brd.html> (20/11/09). Please note that all references to articles of the Basic Law in the following part relate to this original version.

within the parameters set by the Allies. The following part will briefly outline its major features.[91]

Central to the Basic Law is the catalogue of fundamental and human rights of the individual, which has been placed in prime position, occupying the first nineteen articles of the document. Prominent among them, the protection of human dignity is enshrined in article 1(1). All three arms of government, the executive, legislature and judiciary are bound by these basic rights.[92] In contrast to the situation under the Weimar Constitution, individuals can defend themselves against infringements of their rights in the courts.[93]

The Basic Law creates a federal system of government, in which the States have a strong position. In part this is due to pressure from the Allies. France in particular pushed for a federal structure with a weak central state. This sentiment was shared by The United States and, to a lesser degree, by The United Kingdom.[94] In addition, the strong position of the States can be explained by the fact that the new federal compact needed the approval of the Parliaments of two-thirds of the States for its ratification.[95] Particularly the southern States exerted considerable pressure on the Parliamentary Council in order to ensure that they would play a powerful role in the new federation.[96]

One of the features that characterises the Basic Law as a federal compact is a bicameral federal Parliament, with one house, the *Bundesrat*, representing the States' interests. The *Bundesrat* has full legislative power in relation to laws which affect the States.[97] Another feature is the division of legislative competences between the federal and State level. While some subject matters are exclusively within the power of either the federal Parliament or the States, others

---

91   A more detailed discussion of the main features of the Basic Law, as a reaction to the experiences made during the Weimar Republic and the Third Reich can be found in Mark Allinson et al, *Contemporary Germany*, Pearson Education Limited (2000) at 11–15.

92   Article 1(3) Basic Law.

93   A special legal avenue for individuals to the Federal Constitutional Court, the constitutional complaint (*Verfassungsbeschwerde*), was not contained in the original draft of the Basic Law. It was introduced into federal law on 12 March 1951 (*Gesetz über das Bundes-verfassungsgericht*) and enshrined in article 93(1),(4a) Basic Law on 29 January 1969.

94   H Hofmann, 'Article 20', in B Schmidt-Bleibtreu/F Klein (eds), *GG – Kommentar zum Grundgesetz*, Luchterhand (10th ed, 2004) at 653; Bruno Schmidt-Bleibtreu and Axel Hopfauf, 'Einleitung zum Grundgesetz', in B Schmidt-Bleibtreu/F Klein (eds), *GG – Kommentar zum Grundgesetz*, Luchterhand (10th ed, 2004) at 71.

95   Article 144(1) Basic Law.

96   Bruno Schmidt-Bleibtreu and Axel Hopfauf, 'Einleitung zum Grundgesetz', in B Schmidt-Bleibtreu/F Klein (eds), *GG – Kommentar zum Grundgesetz*, Luchterhand (10th ed, 2004) at 71.

97   Article 29(7) Basic Law.

fall within an area of concurrent power, where the States can legislate unless the federal Parliament does. In these areas, conflicts between State and federal laws are resolved in favour of the latter.[98]

The Basic Law also contains comprehensive and complex provisions dealing with the financial arrangements within the federation.[99] Broadly, these provisions were designed to stipulate the optimal interaction between political (and legal) competencies, the ability to raise revenue, the distribution of political and financial burdens and the allocation of revenue between the federal and the State levels of government. As Brockmeyer observes, under the influence of the Allies, the financial system was initially intended to weaken the fiscal position of the central administration. Despite several reforms since 1949, the fiscal arrangements within the federation remain a topic for robust discussions.[100]

Another major feature of the Basic Law is a 'weakened parliamentary system'.[101] The Federal Republic of Germany's Parliament is weaker than its Weimar counterpart because, under the Basic Law, Parliament cannot dismiss individual ministers from office. If confidence in the government is lost, it has to dismiss the Chancellor[102] and all ministers by way of a 'constructive vote of no confidence'. Under this procedure, a successor government has to be determined and installed immediately, which guarantees the continuity of government and thus greater political stability in comparison to the Weimar Republic.[103]

When compared with the situation under the Weimar Constitution, the Basic Law also weakens the position of the German President significantly, while strengthening that of the Chancellor. Unlike the Weimar *Reichspräsident*, the *Bundespräsident* is not directly elected by the people[104] and he or she is less powerful. While the *Reichspräsident* could wield real political power, the *Bundespräsident* fulfils a largely formalistic and ceremonial role. He or she usually acts on the advice of the government when giving assent to legislation, appointing and dismissing federal office bearers, including the Chancellor, and representing the nation on the international scene as its head of state.[105] The

---

98 Articles 31, 70–5, Basic Law.

99 See 'The Financial System' (*Das Finanzwesen*) in Part X. (articles 105–115) of the Basic Law.

100 H-B Brockmeyer, 'Vorbemerkungen zur Finanzverfassung', in B Schmidt-Bleibtreu/F Klein (eds), *GG – Kommentar zum Grundgesetz*, Luchterhand (10th ed, 2004) at 1846–9.

101 Ekkehart Stein, *Staatsrecht*, J C B Mohr (Paul Siebeck) Tübingen (10th ed, 1986) at 35.

102 The Chancellor is the head of government and thus the most powerful politician in Germany.

103 Article 67 Basic Law.

104 The President is elected by a special institution (*Bundesversammlung*), which comprises an equal number of members of the lower house of the federal Parliament (*Bundestag*) and representatives elected by State Parliaments, article 54 Basic Law.

105 Articles 58–60 Basic Law.

indirect election of the president avoids a form of double legitimacy for Parliament on the one hand and the President on the other and seeks to prevent a power struggle between the two. The weakened position of the *Bundespräsident* was thus devised to prevent the development of a presidential dictatorship capable of sidelining the federal Parliament as had occurred in the final years of the Weimar Republic.[106]

The framers of the Basic Law made it one of the most rigid constitutions in the world in order to safeguard its most fundamental features for as long as it is in force. Therefore, the principles of respect for human rights, the rule of law and the federal, democratic and social nature of the German state cannot be removed by way of constitutional amendment.[107]

In response to the rise of the Nazi party during the Weimar Republic, the Basic Law also creates a 'belligerent democracy' (*wehrhafte Demokratie*) by demanding that the internal organisational structures of all political parties must comply with democratic principles. It stipulates that a party which aims at reducing or abolishing the liberal and democratic system of government or threatens the existence of the Federal Republic is unconstitutional and can be banned by the Constitutional Court.[108]

In order to protect the new constitutional order, the framers of the Basic Law created the Federal Constitutional Court, a specialised court charged with safeguarding the Constitution.[109]

Finally, as explained above, the Basic Law was intended to be only temporary.[110] This characteristic manifested itself in the provisions relating to its applicability. Article 146 stipulated that the Basic Law would 'cease to be in force on the day of entry into force of a constitution which has been adopted by a free decision of the German people,' foreshadowing that the provisional document would one day be superseded by a 'proper' constitution. The ultimate aim of the Basic Law was the reunification of East and West Germany, as expressed in its preamble. Article 23(2) stipulated that other parts of the country could unilaterally declare their entry in or accession to western Germany. This provision was intended to facilitate an accession of the German Democratic Republic or some of its territory.

---

106   Jörn Ipsen, *Staatsrect I: Staatsorganisationsrecht*, Alfred Metzner Verlag (4th ed, 1992) at 139.
107   Article 79(3).
108   Article 21(2) Basic Law. So far only two political parties have been banned by the Federal Constitutional Court, the Socialist Party of the Realm (SRP) in 1952 (BVerfGE 2, 1) and the Communist Party (KPD) in 1956 (BVerfGE 5, 85).
109   Articles 93–4, 99, 100 Basic Law.
110   Text accompanying fns 66–68.

As is well known, it took forty-one years until the West and the East reunited. When East Germany acceded to the Federal Republic, the Basic Law became the constitution for the whole nation. Although originally intended to be provisional, the Basic Law had been a great success. It had established an economically prosperous and politically stable society in West Germany, where people lived freely, in democratic self-determination under the rule of law. Honouring this successful legacy, the first all-German parliament of the unified nation decided in 1990 to retain the Basic Law as the constitution for Germany, instead of replacing it with a new one.

D. Conclusion – Happy 60th Anniversary!

Driven by the will to regain independence and national sovereignty, a nation slowly emerged from the devastation of the war. West German post-war history is a success story. Little by little, the Federal Republic of Germany re-entered the world stage, gaining membership in the community of nations and the European Communities. Its economy grew to one of the strongest in the world. It overcame its past and is today widely respected. On 3 October 1990 Germans fulfilled peacefully their destiny, when the eastern and western parts of the country were reunited. Through all of Germany's ups and downs after the Second World War, one document endured; a document which was originally intended to be only provisional. Forged in the years after the most terrible war the world had ever seen, the Basic Law became the longest-lasting and most successful German constitution,[111] celebrating its 60th anniversary in 2009.

---

111   Lothar Kettenacker, *Germany since 1945*, Oxford University Press (1997) at 38.

Öffentliches und Internationales Recht

Herausgegeben von Udo Fink, Dieter Dörr und Rolf Schwartmann

www.peterlang.de